# FERRIES
## OF THE
# UPPER THAMES

# FERRIES
## OF THE
# UPPER THAMES

*Joan Tucker*

AMBERLEY

The illustrations in this book are the property of the author unless otherwise stated.

The map references in this book are to Ordnance Survey Explorer series at 1:20 000 scale (2$\frac{1}{2}$ inches to 1 mile). The modern spellings of place names are taken from these maps.

First published 2012

Amberley Publishing
The Hill, Stroud
Gloucestershire, GL5 4EP

www.amberley-books.com

British Library Cataloguing in Publication Data.
A catalogue record for this book is available from the British Library.

ISBN 978 1 84868 967 1

Typeset in 10pt on 12pt Sabon.
Typesetting and Origination by Amberley Publishing.
Printed in the UK.

# Contents

# Acknowledgements

While researching this book I have spent many happy hours in the following repositories. My thanks are due to the staff who made this possible.

Berkshire Record Office
British Library
Buckinghamshire Record Office
The Crown Estate
English Heritage – NMR and Library
Environment Agency
Gloucestershire Archives
Hertfordshire Archives & Local Studies
Oxford Local Studies Centre
Oxfordshire Record Office

My thanks go also to numerous friends and relatives and particularly to these listed below.

Iain Bain
John & Tina Farr
Arnold Grayson
Dawn Greening-Steer
Heatons of Tisbury
David Hanks
Ian Leith
Tracey Ponting
Ken & Doreen Townsend
Nigel Wilkins
Keith & Sheila Wright

# Preface

In *Sweet Thames Run Softly* Robert Gibbings describes how in 1939 he saw a window of Blackwell's Bookshop in Broad Street, Oxford full of books on the Thames. He was daunted by this as he had just engaged in writing and illustrating his own lovely book. There were histories of the river and of the villages beside it. Bridges spanning the river were the subject of several books and also the natural history of it, as well as how to fish and row. Accounts of journeys and explorations were profuse, as were maps, charts and guidebooks. But there were no books on crossing the Thames by ford and ferry before the advent of bridges. Gibbings himself does not mention them, nor have any been written since.

The present volume aims to provide a history of the fords and ferries on the Upper Thames, how they came about and by whom and how they were used. Some information can be gleaned from old documents but ancient passages like these are seldom acknowledged. Commonly, antiquarian historians concerned themselves with the manors and churches, although as most ferries were set up originally by monastic establishments situated on the banks, records would have been lost or destroyed. Unlike the previous volume, *Ferries of the Lower Thames*, there are no Acts of Parliament, legal actions or newspaper reports of disasters to be consulted. Instead, information has been taken from evidence on the ground, journals of local history, a few websites, and some books, usually nostalgic, which mention ferries in passing as well as three major sources noted below.

At the height of the 'picturesque' movement the *History of the River Thames* was published in 1794 in two volumes by John and Joseph Boydell. It was illustrated with hand-coloured etchings by Joseph Farington RA, there being forty-three full-page plates in the first volume which ends at Windsor, having begun at the source at Thames Head in Gloucestershire. Although not indicated on the title page, the writer of the preface and text was William Coombe. The book, known by the book world as 'Boydell's Thames' was the first in a projected series to be called *An History of the Principal Rivers of Great Britain*. However, it was not a success and no further volumes were published. Critics thought the text was too flowery and the illustrations too blue[1]. However, despite the heavy cost of production (Farington made nothing out of it although he was a partner in the enterprise), the work was instrumental in publicising the Thames as a place of picturesque intrinsic beauty. As trade on the river declined it became a place for tourism and leisure and a favourite location for 'desirable residences'. Coombe wrote 'The river historian must sometimes throw upon the same page historical relation and antiquarian research, the criticism of modern taste and the sketch of landscape beauty'.

This is a difficult task but was accomplished to some extent by Fred S. Thacker (Frederick Samuel Thacker) of Isleworth, Middlesex. As a labour of love he spent twelve years exploring the Thames, from the source to Kew, both on foot and sculling. In Reading he researched the records of the Thames Commission and the Thames Conservators, particularly the papers of the Treacher family who for three generations were surveyors to both those bodies. In a letter to an acquaintance, A. E. Preston of Abingdon, written in 1925 he confessed, 'I still paddle about in the Public Record Office (Chancery Lane, London) but usually go into the legal room, it is so much more free and easy there, and facilities are not so limited'.[2] Thacker drew his own maps – one accompanies each section – and took his own photographs along the river. It proved to be a scholarly, well-researched work, although unfortunately it was produced before notes and references became *de rigueur*. Nevertheless, publishers were not interested; they considered there was no market in it. The public had more serious problems on their minds. Thacker published *The Thames Highway Volume I General History* himself from 3 Dyers' Buildings, Holborn, at 5s in 1914.

Again, Thacker published *The Thames Highway Volume II A History of the Locks and Weirs* himself from 105 Mortlake Road, Kew, Surrey at 12/6d by subscription in 1920. The book gives a detailed account of the structures of the river from the source to Kew and covers not just locks and weirs but bridges, some islands or eyots and most, but not all, of the ferries and ferrymen. Nothing can be found yet about Thacker – the man, his background, occupation or even his dates. From the three letters he wrote to his correspondent, Mr Preston, of further discoveries about Shillingford Bridge, it is evident that he was a quiet, unassuming man who liked to be independent, although willing to share his knowledge. On the other hand, Arthur Edwin Preston FSA (1852–1942) was a well-known figure in Abingdon. He practised as a chartered accountant, with an office in Cornmarket, Oxford, and was elected Mayor of Abingdon although unusually he was not on the council. His historical researches extended round Abingdon and some were issued. Although Preston spent thirty years on a history of his native town it was not published.

Henry William Taunt (1842–1922) was born in Oxford, the son of a plumber/glazier. On leaving school he worked in various shops in the High Street, Oxford, until at sixteen he joined Edward Bracher, an early Oxford photographer. Aged twenty-one he married and five years later set up as photographer on his own account.[3] His main business was in portrait photography but his interest in painting led him to the landscape, particularly the Thames Valley. In 1859 Taunt took a solitary trip on the river from Oxford to Lechlade.[4] Despite having an almost disastrous accident at Hart's Weir, he was now a confirmed devotee of the Thames and continued to photograph it for the rest of his life, often returning to take the same view for several years. Taunt decided to produce a book on the Thames illustrated with his own photographs. The fifth edition has the title *A New Map of the River Thames from Thames Head to London* (on a scale of 2 inches to 1 mile) 'From Entirely New Surveys Finished During the Summer of 1878 and Corrected to the Present Time'. For this edition Taunt checked on improvements and changes that had taken place, most notably above Oxford. Each section of the river is described and illustrated with a simple map with the river clearly marked in blue. Loose thumbnail photographs are pasted around the maps. Details of hostelries, distances, camping grounds, boat hirers etc. are given, but ferries are merely noted. Taunt was justly proud of his book and declared his efforts were 'carried out at our own cost, without the slightest help from the Commissioners or Conservators of the river in any way'. He went on to produce other books and maps of the Thames.

H. W. Taunt was a commercial photographer and perhaps the first to use the Thames as a subject in a commercial way. Therefore the places he chose to photograph were those which had a good chance of selling to the public. There are no images of ferries on the river, except Bablockhythe, which was a favourite place for excursions by Oxford undergraduates. Ferries were still not considered as anything special. However, many other images are used in this book because they give a sense of place set in time and are beautiful.

For those who wish to seek out the landing places of fords and ferries it is a most rewarding experience but requires patience, perseverance and persistence. Most of them are interesting, out-of-the-way and very lovely. To get to them has been made fairly easy by following the designated Thames Path using the published guidebooks. The idea for the long-distance walk was first mooted in the 1930s by some local authorities who thought to make use of the Thames towing path which still existed. After the war the proposal was taken up again and a report by the Countryside Commission was published in 1987.[5] They realised that most ferries were no longer running and it would not be feasible to recommence them. Alternative ways and means of crossings were worked out and a National Trail was declared in 1989.[6] The lack of ferries was a major obstacle and was overcome by the path being diverted along different paths or sometimes footbridges being built and crossings made over some locks. All in all it is a miracle it happened. Certainly it could not be done in the present climate.

The public does not have a right of access to the River Thames. Nor does it have a right to be on the water. It is not, as previously thought, a Royal River, but is owned for the large part by riparian owners who own not only the bank on their land but halfway across the river itself, including the bed. At present the Environment Agency has jurisdiction over the water, including issuing licences for use by boats, canoes and for fishing. The ferries had rights of way leading to them. These are marked on the large-scale Ordnance Survey Explorer maps. Set up by the Thames Conservancy for towing horses at about fifteen feet wide, they are now being eroded gradually. Of course, the paths now terminate at the water's edge, but at least they still give access to the river legitimately. Neighbouring properties have appropriated land on either side of paths, thus reducing the width to about 18 inches in some cases. This has been seen when the erection of new fences is in operation. The nearer the walker gets to London, the more notices like 'Private Keep Out' are encountered.

This is not a new phenomenon. Writing in *Thames Valley Villages Volume 1* published in 1910, Charles G. Harper said about the neighbourhood of Goring, 'Every piece of land and every access are jealously guarded' – including rights of way which are hidden by notices, "Private Road", "Trespasses Prosecuted" etc. The stranger who desires to wander at will is well-advised to disregard all such.'[7] A Thames Preservation League was set up in around 1900 with the object of preserving the existing rights and privileges in the Thames for the national enjoyment.[8] It became defunct and the only body with similar aspirations now is Support the Rivers Access Campaign, which is concerned mainly with the right of navigation along rivers for canoes.[9]

# CHAPTER ONE
# Crossing the River

There are no ferries operating now on the Upper Thames. In recent times it was calculated there was an average of one per mile between Kew and Lechlade. Many of the crossings were very old, dating back even to prehistoric times and predated the church which often was situated alongside the landing place on the river bank. A small chapel would provide shelter and afford a chance to pray for a safe crossing. These chapels were then replaced by churches; Lechlade, Abingdon, Sonning, Streatley, Wallingford and Whitchurch-on-Thames are examples of this development.

'Aren't fords one of the minor pleasures of existence?' wrote Geoffrey Grigson.[1] He went on to describe them as an epitome of the English landscape, reached down a leafy lane with the water rippling and shining as one got nearer. A ford is defined as a place in a watercourse shallow enough to be crossed on horseback or in a wheeled vehicle. Often they would become impassable after heavy rain or in times of flood. They are not found on major roads but in earliest times they would be the normal way of crossing a river. The Upper Thames Valley had many fords; generally they served minor roads like Kempsford, and Shillingford. Only two with the suffix 'ford' – Wallingford and Oxford – grew into major towns. Duxford near Hinton Waldrist is the only one that can still function as a ford when the water levels are right. Few places in the bed of the river afforded a natural firm-enough base of stone slabs or gravel to support the traffic of a ford, and then perhaps only in summer. Most of them are in the higher reaches. Clifton Hampden where the river bed was hard greensand rock was replaced by a ferry and at a much later date by a bridge. At the head of navigation, Lechlade and Cricklade are derived from *gelād*, meaning a 'river passage'. Wallingford was the lowest point on the Thames where the ford was dependable to afford a reliable crossing all year round.

The simplest means of propulsion over a river from bank to bank was by pick-a-back. A strong ferryman would pick up a passenger, man or woman, and carry them over the water. St Christopher is thus depicted in many churches as a mural or in stained-glass windows, although the legend is not written in the Bible. He carried the Christ child over a shallow stream or ford, and as he went the child grew heavier and heavier until, when they reached the further bank, the child revealed himself as Christ the Saviour. In living memory a ferryman would lift a passenger in this way over the mudflats of the Severn to his rowboat when the river was low.

Not many fords were paved artificially; the Romans after colonisation did pave some with stones held by mortar and piles, with slopes down to the water for horses, and occasionally with steps for foot passengers. Dorothy Hartley in *Water in England* describes how bridges, fords and weirs were constructed; an art she claims is lost.[2] When a tree or boulder fell into running water, sand, gravel and stones pile up in front of it, whilst behind the obstruction the drag of water scooped out a hollow. So a line of loosely woven hurdles was made across the stream for water to pass through. Then the debris from cutting rushes and clearing banks would float down and pile up against the barrier until it collapsed and fell, leaving a slight ridge across the river bed. Stones were added until there was a substantial barrier underwater. A cut was made in the middle of it, which the river flowed through – deepening the centre of the bed – and earth would build up at the sides. This was because it was necessary for the back of the obstruction to be strengthened as a matter of principle. Some constructions involved the use of willow baskets filled with stones, in the same manner as gabions are used today. Mortar was added to make the structure firm. It is thought quicklime was the agent for drying out the mortar, thus giving a stone hard finish. The width of the fords was the same as the width of a wagon and was marked at each side by staves or stakes. Over small streams the ford would have a wooden footbridge with a rail alongside for foot passengers. These were called 'water splashes'. By the end of the nineteenth century fords were almost obsolete and were replaced by timber bridges.

As the need for more reliable crossings became necessary for better communications, fords were replaced by ferries with improved access to them from land. At first foot passengers would be taken over the river by boat, leaving horses carts and carriages to use the ford as before. For the very beginnings of river crossings we look to the method of military operations.

Ferries are defined as the passage of a boat carrying passengers, and on occasion vehicles and livestock, from a fixed point on the bank of a river to another point on the opposite bank, either straight or diagonally across. Ideally there should be a scheduled service or on demand from the public. In law it is only a public ferry if a public right of way exists to it on both banks. A rowing boat propelled by one ferryman with two oars was the traditional way of crossing, but on the Upper Thames a punt with a punt pole was the norm. The well-known legend of Charon, who ferried the dead across the River Styx, is depicted with a sort of punt pole. Archaeologists have found Roman burials where the skeleton was holding a coin in the mouth to pay Charon.[3]

Stepping stones offered a useful method of crossing a young river. Woodcut from Thomas Bewick, *A General History of Quadrupeds.*

Another legend concerns St Julian the Hospitaller. His story is depicted in thirty panels of a stained-glass window in Rouen Cathedral, France. When he was a child it was predicted that he would kill both his parents. To avoid this he left home and made his own way in the world and found a wife. The parents came to find him but the Devil tricked him into murdering them as strangers. When St Julian discovered what had happened he fled in despair and settled by a river where he founded a hospital and ran a ferry as penance. One stormy night someone called his name from the opposite bank. He rowed across and found the passenger was a leper. St Julian took him into the hospital, gave him food, clothes and a bed for the night. The next morning the leper revealed himself to be Jesus Christ, and announced that Julian was redeemed. In the year 160 Julian was martyred at Alexandria and became the patron saint of travellers. Gustav Flaubert, a native of Rouen, used the window as inspiration to write his own much-embroidered version of the story, published as one of his *Three Tales*.

Of course there were other simple ways of crossing a river, especially when in its infancy. Some were engraved on wood by Thomas Bewick and used as tail-pieces in *A General History of Quadrupeds*, published in 1790. They range from activities including riding a horse, walking over a frozen river, wading and poling across. Stepping stones provided an aid for crossing, as did a plank resting on either bank. One delightful image is of a man crossing a river on stilts. It is likely to be Bewick's son Robert Elliot Bewick who, in a letter to his sister Jane who was staying at the house of Mr Robson, boat builder in South Shields, tells of his recent exploits while on a visit to the old family home at Cherryburn.[4] Nearby at Eltringham was 'Where I met with the finest fun that Ever I had in my life I have learned to walk upon stilts and can almost cross the Tyne upon them I expect a pair at the Forth soon Where I expect plenty of plodging with them when wet weather comes'. The letter was sent from Newcastle on 9 July 1799. A companion volume, *A History of British Birds*, has a not-to-be-recommended method of crossing: that of climbing along the branch of a tree which extended over the river, 'a tricky way to cross a river'. Bewick sketched these incidents on rivers in the hilly countryside of his native Northumberland.

Walking over a frozen river. Bewick vignette .

Pedlar wading across a river. Bewick.

Poling over a river. Bewick.

A primitive plank bridge. Bewick.

Man on stilts 'plodging' over a river. Bewick.

As the importance of communication increased, particularly after the industrial and agricultural revolutions, it became necessary for the ferries to be large and more regulated. Whilst many remained as one-man operated establishments, either privately owned or held by the manor, others became larger and mechanised. This happened when the towing paths were adapted to take horses and special boats; large flat punts were needed when the paths changed from one side to the other. Bewick depicted one in an engraving of a horse-ferry where two men are punting with poles from the back. Haulage was usually by a rope hung overhead and relied on the muscle power of the ferryman to pull hand over hand, sometimes helped by passengers. This was a process dangerous to people rowing on the river as the rope was at the level of their neck. If a chain was employed it would lie on the bottom and be hauled up by a spiked wheel operated on the boat.[5] When there was a powerful current, as on the Thames, the big boat would be attached to a windlass worked by hand on both banks. This required strong manpower. An example of a windlass is still to be seen at Bablockhythe.

Rafts were the most primitive form of craft on inland shallow waters and were invariably handled with poles. Punts developed from rafts and at first were used for fishing. The catch would be kept in a well made waterproof in the bottom. Fishing was a major industry on the Thames, particularly in the Oxford stretch of the river. There, fishermen would double-up as ferrymen.[6] Punts were built as if like a ladder, that is two sides about eighteen inches high with cross-bands linking them one foot apart, called treads. The craft were flat-bottomed, square-ended and particularly suited to the Thames, which was shallower than it is now.[7] They were 'more manoeuvrable and more capacious than boats with oars in shallow waters' and cheaper to build than conventional rowing boats with stems and keels. Traditionally, ferry punts would be 24 feet long by 3 feet wide. The sides, ends and till at the stern were made of hardwood, particularly oak; the treads of teak and the bottom were probably of elm. As the gravelly bed of the river would wear the bottom of the punt regularly, so it was made easy to replace, of long narrow planks placed fore and aft with a small space between to allow for swelling when wet. It was then caulked. Although usually punted from the stern when the ferryman would stand on the till, the punt could be worked from both ends to avoid turning. The verb 'punting' was used for the leisure activity which started on the Thames after 1860. In daily parlance it was called 'shoving'.

If a punt was heavy with passengers it required a shove and a walk along the boat to establish and then maintain momentum for a distance. Some expert ferrymen could manage this in just two or three shoves to the opposite bank. A very heavy barge-like punt could be walked by two men, one on each side, alternately shoving and walking back to keep a steady and even movement. A regular-sized punt with twenty passengers could be 'pricked' by one man if necessary. This meant he would shove from a standing position. If there were as many as fifty passengers, two men would be needed. But a large punt taking a coach and horses could be managed with only one man. Punt poles suitable for heavy working punts were made from straight stems of small larch trees, called 'natural' poles. Best white pine stems were used for better poles called 'made' poles. The thicker end of the poles was the bottom and this was shod with a metal tip called an 'iron' or a 'shoe'. In case of some difficulty two poles were carried, one shorter than the other.

Who used the ferries? The River Thames has always served as a frontier, it was a formidable barrier to invaders and there was very little interactivity both political and economic between the left and right banks.[8] In the Iron Age the territory of three tribes met at the area extending from the confluence of the River Cherwell below Oxford downstream to Wallingford. The Dobunni were to the west, the Catullvellauni to the east and the Atrebates to the south. Archaeological remains for the Late Bronze Age

*Above:* A horse ferry was needed when the towing path changed sides. A Thames punt is shallower than this one. Bewick.

*Below:* Rough sketch plan of a horse punt to take three horses. Made of timber 1½ inches thick at the sides, 2½ inches at the gunnels and 2¼ inches at the bottom.

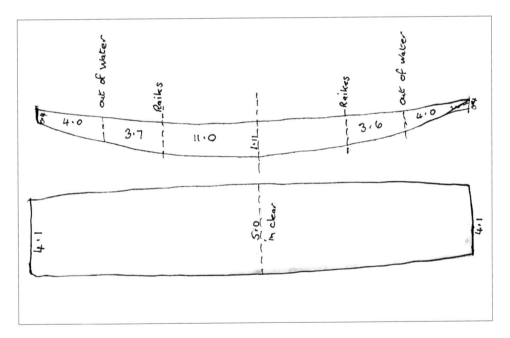

and Iron Age are abundant. Weaponry has been recovered from the river, some of it 'killed' by bending, others of such magnificence that they were never used in combat, but probably thrown in the water as a sacrifice to the gods. A bronze shield found near Dorchester-on-Thames had been punctured by a socketed spearhead. Also found there was a human pelvis with a Bronze Age spearhead embedded in it.

The Upper Thames Valley was one of the first regions to be settled by the Anglo-Saxons. In the year 571, the West Saxons defeated the Britons at Bedford and took the places that became Bensington and Eynsham, and thus they commanded the middle Thames.[9] The river was kept as the boundary when the shires were established, with Mercia to the north and Wessex to the south, until Mercian expansion in around AD 630. The Anglo-Saxon Chronicle records that in 1015 the Danish Cnut crossed the Thames at Cricklade and 'ravaged and burnt and killed all they came across' on their way through Gloucestershire into Warwickshire.[10] The following year he was accepted as King of England. It is significant that, although there was rivalry between peoples across its banks, the Thames remained a boundary after the invasions, including that of the Normans in 1066 when William took unto himself all the land in Britain and subsequently disposed of it to his friends who became riparian owners along the Thames. Rising in Gloucestershire on the north bank the Thames separated that county from Wiltshire. From Lechlade downstream, Oxfordshire was on the north and Berkshire on the south and after Maidenhead Buckinghamshire was on the north bank. The region of the Upper Thames changed to the Lower Thames at Staines. These boundaries were kept for a millennium until some changes were made in the local government reorganisations of 1974 when, for instance, Abingdon was transferred to Oxfordshire.

It was in Saxon times that ferries began to be set up along the river to service the growing number of monastic establishments on the banks. The Thames was much favoured by such bodies. Many grew to be very large and important and acquired lands near and far by purchase and bequest. This would necessitate much coming and going by land and water between the different estates held by each abbey or priory. Ferries on the Lower Thames were held by religious orders – Lambeth Horseferry was run for centuries by the Archbishop of Canterbury from Lambeth Palace. Therefore, it is safe to say that the case was likewise for the Upper Thames. Early charters exist for places in the Thames Valley and most involve the gift of land by a king to an abbey. Ferries are not mentioned specifically, but fords are and the places given are ones where it is known there was a ferry. The earliest charter recorded for Berkshire was in AD 687 when lands at Basildon ford and at Streatley were given to Abingdon Abbey.[11] The abbey had been founded twelve years previously by the West Saxons and survived destruction by the Danes in the reign of King Alfred. It also held lands in Hinksey, Wallingford and Swinford, as well as land in Abingdon itself where they owned the ferry which was subsequently replaced by the important bridge. Thomas Pentecost, the last abbot, surrendered the abbey in 1538 and Swinford was given to Charles, Duke of Suffolk.

Reading Abbey was reputed to be the greatest in the country; perhaps it grew rich because of the many religious mementoes it held to attract pilgrims.[12] They supposedly included a sliver from the Rod of Moses. The pilgrims would have crossed the Thames by the ford, which later became a ferry at Caversham to reach the Cluniac abbey, which was situated on the banks of the River Kennet to the south. It had been founded by Henry I in 1121 and was destroyed at the time of the Dissolution in 1538. Some ruins are now incorporated into a public park.

Not all gifts from kings mentioned in the charters (some of which may be fraudulent) are to religious bodies. Some were made to followers, friends and families. In Oxfordshire these included Shifford, Whitchurch, and Sandford, all of which had a ferry over the Thames at some time. In Berkshire, lands in Cookham, Cholsey, Moulsford and North and South Hinksey were listed.

Dorchester Abbey began as a church in AD 634 and became an Augustinian abbey in 1140.[13] The ferry at Little Wittenham led directly to it. Eynsham Abbey was founded in 1005, possibly on the site of an earlier seventh- or eighth-century foundation, and continued in the Benedictine order until 1538. It was fairly small but was given manors and churches by various kings and flourished in the Middle Ages. At the Dissolution the property was taken by the Earl of Derby. Remains can be seen surrounding the present church. The ferry was at Swinford, a few hundred yards away, and was the cause of a dispute before the bridge was built. Godstow was the next establishment just downstream near Wolvercote, 2 miles from Oxford. It was founded in about 1131–33 for Benedictine nuns. The few remains lie in a field, now owned by the university, on the edge of the Port Meadow where there were fords and then a ferry to Binsey. Henry VIII had granted the site to his physician, George Owen, who transformed the nunnery into a house. (The so-called Wytham Abbey close by was never monastic, just a house).

The town of Oxford developed rapidly once the university began to grow on its wet lands dissected by numerous waterways. Three monastic establishments were within its precincts. St Frideswide's nunnery, on the site of the college which became Christ Church, is supposed to have been at the very beginning of Oxford, when the ox-ford was first used. Oseney Abbey was founded as a priory in 1129 and later became an Augustinian Abbey. It surrendered in 1539 when its big bell, Great Tom, was awarded to Christ Church, along with all its property. It was situated near the present railway station. Rewley Abbey began as a monastery or studium for the White Monks but became a Cistercian abbey in 1281. Its site was plundered for building materials after it was dissolved in 1536. Before the site became St Frideswide Square in modern times, it was the station for the LMS railway.

Hurley Priory founded for the Benedictines in 1086 is up river from Great Marlow and still has its church in use today with other buildings close by, now used for residences. The grounds stretched down to the river where there was a ford, later a ferry. Now there is a lock cut and a lock. A short distance downriver is Bisham Abbey, now a national Sports Centre. It was founded in about 1260 as a community house for the Knights Templar. When they were suppressed in 1307, Edward II took over the manorial rights and granted them to his relatives. Henry VIII granted the manor to his divorced wife, Anne of Cleves, and it was later bought by the Hoby family, in whose hands it remained until 1768. Their monuments are in the Hoby chapel in Bisham Church, close by. The road to the former ferry skirts the churchyard.

Medmenham Abbey on the left bank below Marlow was founded in the twelfth century for the Cistercians, and came under the umbrella of Woburn Abbey in Bedfordshire. It was recognised by Royal Charter in the year 1200 and lasted until 1547 when it was given to the Moore family who then sold it to the Duffields. The subsequent history is well known. The road to the ferry skirts the walls of the abbey. Other minor monastic establishments were at Runnymede where a Benedictine Nunnery began in 1160, and a monastery at Cookham which had an important ford, then ferry. There was a priory at Goring. The Bishop of Salisbury had a palace at Sonning.

To provide food and shelter for their visitors, Dorothy Hartley suggests some abbeys set up ferry hostels on the river banks close to the ferry.[14] She does not provide examples to support her claim. They were purpose-built to accommodate pilgrims to the shrines and were barn-like in structure, with stabling on the ground floor and dormitories separated into cubicles above, lit by small windows. Usually there was at least one spring of fresh water on site. There were paddocks for horses, washing places

Bisham Abbey and church. Print from the *Copper Plate Magazine*, 1792

and perhaps a garden or small yard for poultry. If the weather was too bad to use the
ferry, travellers would need to stay for some time. Probably they resembled and were
run along the same lines as the early youth hostels. Following the Dissolution, these
ferry hostels were abolished but the buildings were put to other uses or demolished for
the materials. Some were turned into workhouses, barns or even almshouses. However,
most that survived had a new life as an inn, as travellers arriving at the ferry would
still need food and shelter while they waited. This must account for the tradition that
a public house is nearly always situated by a ferry. Indeed, some inns were the owners
of the ferry, although not as a matter of course on the Upper Thames.

The Thames, being the medieval boundary between the dioceses of Salisbury and
Lincoln and also a county boundary, meant that offenders could cross the river to
avoid prosecution. This is testified by court cases where witnesses from another
county over the river were cited.[15] Similarly, witnesses to wills were from 'foreign'
territory, perhaps to ensure secrecy for the testator. In cases of nonconformity, both
Protestant and Catholic, the river was a refuge. By travelling along the river or by
crossing it, protagonists could spread knowledge and gain support in secrecy. Roads
were few and difficult and kept to the higher ground; it was safer to take to the water,
especially by night.

Lollards presumably used this way of disseminating their heresy, the area between
the Berkshire Downs and the Chilterns in Buckinghamshire being one of their
strongholds in the fourteenth and fifteenth centuries, particularly Marlow, also the
lower Cherwell valley. They acquired this derogatory nickname from their habit
of murmuring. The name derived from the word 'lollard', the murmurings of pious
people. It came to mean 'heretic', first recorded in 1382 when it referred to the
followers of John Wyclif although the movement had begun some years earlier.[16]
Wyclif was a scholar, philosopher and theologian. Aided by John of Gaunt, he was
opposed to the supremacy of the Pope and maintained that Christian doctrine should
be based on what was written in the Bible. To make his point he translated the Bible
from Latin to vernacular English, thus attracting people other than academics to his

way of thinking. Wyclif spent most of his life in Oxford, and was Master of Balliol from 1360–61. He wrote many tracts against the Pope and was forced to retire to his parish of Lutterworth before his death in 1384. He had not been militant in his views but some followers were and they were regarded as heretics. The death penalty was imposed on heretics in 1401. Sir John Oldcastle became their leader and was persecuted and imprisoned in the Tower. A 'larger-than-life' character, Shakespeare based Sir John Falstaff on him in the Henry IV plays. He escaped from the Tower and died in 1417. Despite being severely suppressed, Lollardy continued to survive in the Thames Valley until well into the fifteenth century.

Following the death of the Catholic Queen Mary, recusancy was rife in the Upper Thames Valley. Many gentry families refused to attend services of the Church of England. From 1571 this was an offence punishable by fine which most families were prepared to pay. The Crown was not lenient about this because it swelled their coffers and the law was not rescinded until 1791. However, the Catholics persisted in breaking the law and therefore suffered even more indignities – imprisonment, land sequestered and even death.[17] In July 1586 a secret conference of Catholic families was held at Harleyford Manor, across the river from Hurley Priory, when it was decided that individual priests would be based in recusants' houses along the river and close to it. For this there was a death penalty. Priests' holes were constructed in some houses, including Ufton Court and Mapledurham where one is in the attic. The priest had to descend into it by rope.

Mapledurham in Oxfordshire was one of the most important centres for recusancy. Sir Michael Blount built the mansion, which was not completed until 1612, two years after his death. It has remained in the same Catholic family ever since. The Anglican church next door has a side aisle for Roman Catholic worship and burials which is kept locked, with no access from the main church. Although not far from Reading, the house is tucked away and the river would have been the easiest way to get to it. The Blounts built and owned the road from Caversham in about 1600. Other recusant houses in Oxfordshire were Shiplake Court owned by the Plowdens, Sandford near Oxford where the Powell family lived and Little Stoke one of the homes of the Hildesley or Ilesley family. The house is close by the ferry to Cholsey on the Berkshire bank. To this day the lane at its bottom end is Ferry Lane, but higher up it continues to Cholsey village by Papist Way.

The Catholic families intermarried and the Thames provided a link between them and a means of getting to London and Oxford, a hotbed of Catholicism, incognito. On the Berkshire side the Whiteknights estate near Reading was bought by Francis Englefield and became an important meeting place for recusants. The Stonor family owned several Thameside manor houses but the male line died out, as did many of the other Catholic families. However, yeoman other than gentry families had settled round the various manor houses and they flourished in the seventeenth century, especially in the area of South Oxfordshire and West Berkshire. The Prince family of Clifton Hampden were recusants from 1604 until 1720. Father Richard Prince of that family was one of the last Catholic clergy to die for his faith in England.

Another group of so-called recusants broke away from the Church of England in the sixteenth century.[18] Later to be known as Baptists, they could only believe that Christ was head of the church, not a king or queen. They were strongest in the same areas, particularly Berkshire, in which the Lollards had held sway. By the mid-seventeenth century, Baptists had become established with their own places of worship. On 8 October 1652, representatives from Henley, Reading and Abingdon met at Wormsley, the home of the Scrope family, to set up an association of Baptist chapels. The Scrope family, some of whom had been Roman Catholics, held the manor of Hambleden from the fourteenth century through to the seventeenth. The oldest Baptist chapels began in Abingdon, Faringdon and Newbury, all places where the Lollards had been strong, as well as Berkshire and Buckinghamshire. Once again the Thames was a lifeline to certain groups of people for transport and communications.

At Henley some Baptists were excommunicated, but in the reign of Charles II they obtained licences to worship. In 1649 the Act of Tolerance was passed. Robert Lovegrove, a solicitor of Wallingford, left the Anglican Church to join the Baptists. At that time they were meeting regularly at Roke, a hamlet near Benson, across the Thames. A footpath led beside the river from Wallingford to the landing place for the Benson ferry.

Apart from at Reading, there were no manufacturing industries sited on the Upper Thames. Some market towns had trades associated with agriculture. Therefore there was no great need for people to cross the river for work. The only roads that crossed the river by ferry were minor roads, as for Goring/Streatley, Shillingford, Whitchurch/Pangbourne, and Radley/Nuneham Courtney. In the late nineteenth and twentieth century, with better means of transport and people needing to commute to work, bridges became necessary. The bridges built to supply this need at Whitchurch, Clifton Hampden and particularly at Sonning, are single-lane bridges and now totally inadequate. The M4 motorway takes the long-distance traffic, but there is still considerable local traffic. There are surprisingly few bridges over the Upper Thames and more new ones are needed.

## CHAPTER TWO

# Crossing the Upper Reaches

Officially the Thames rises at Thames Head (Exp. 168 982 894) as a spring in Trewsbury Mead, but in fact the spring erupts only occasionally and as the water table has dropped, water is not marked on the latest map until a point below Thames Head Bridge on the Fosse Way (Exp.168 987 991), which is around 376 feet above sea level. It then flows generally in an easterly direction until it reaches the seawater of the estuary at The Nore off the coast of Kent, and only diverts northerly to skirt higher ground, as at Wytham Woods north of Oxford where it then returns to the original direction. Numerous tributaries contribute to the course of the river from high grounds to the north and south. The distance from Thames Head to the Nore in a straight line is around 125 miles, but if the bends and meanders are measured it is about 215 miles. Almost 6,160 square miles are drained by the Thames and its tributaries, which is about one-eighth the size of England.[1] Often called the Royal Thames, the name is derived from the former royal palaces along its route: Windsor, Richmond, Kew, Whitehall and Greenwich. The river is not owned by the Crown. Thacker refers to the Thames as a Royal River, but the Crown in his sense means Parliament, the people's government.

This book will trace the early crossing places, the fords, ferries and primitive bridges along the course of the Thames from its source at Thames Head to where it changes in character and administration at Staines, 120 miles downstream. The bridges that generally replaced the fords and ferries have been covered in several other books by other writers.

Around the headwaters of the Thames is a catchment area of high rainfall, with water coming off the Cotswolds and the Wiltshire Downs. The valley was fairly flat and sloped gently, thus making for a large marshy expanse of land. Recently, Win Scutt, an archaeologist, has published an online essay entitled 'An English Prehistory' in which he puts forward the theory that the whole area of the headwaters was covered by a huge lake or mere, or rather two: one to the west between South Cerney and Cricklade, and one to the east, smaller and to the west of Lechlade. He bases his premise on place names (not an infallible subject) pointing out the occurrence of village names containing the Old English element eg, meaning 'island'. He has picked out Oaksey, Eisey, Minety, South Cerney and Down Ampney as islands, being situated above the 85-metre contour, when he supposed the western mere had a depth of between 80 and 85 metres above sea level. Around the perimeter of the mere were places with 'water' names like Pool, Poulton, Pol, while to the east is Marston Meysey, indicating marsh.

Scutt suggests the meres would have stretched for some 23 kilometres (14 miles) and already drained when the Romans came and built a straight road from Silchester to

Trewsbury Mead, Gloucestershire. An early twentieth-century view of the spring that is the source of the Thames. The water table has now dropped and it is unusual to find surface water until about a mile further downstream. An ash tree used to mark the spot. The steep bank behind carries the Thames & Severn Canal. From a postcard.

Cirencester – the Ermin Way – with a crossing near Cricklade. Raised causeways were built over marshy ground leading to crossing places in the same manner as motorways are built today, by overcoming obstacles rather than avoiding them. Comments online indicate Scutt has some following for his theory, although some are sceptical about the Old English names. He dismisses this by pointing out that the Saxon elements had their origin in prehistoric times. A glance at the present-day Explorer Maps 168 and 169 shows that the area is once again two meres in the same places. Gravel extraction on a large scale in the last two decades has left a large area covered in water, and round it the footpaths and lanes deviate into strange lines on the map. One hundred and forty-seven lakes, large and small, now constitute the Cotswold Water Park.

> No bridge is there or boat to ferry o'er,
> But well-shod peasants step from stone to stone,
> Nor fail unsoused to reach the other shore.

This is the infant Thames as described by John Stapleton in *The Thames – A Poem*, published in 1878. Peasants today would not have need of stepping stones across the dry riverbed for the half mile to the first bridge at Thames Head, which carries the Fosse Way (A433), a Roman military road, between Exeter and Lincoln. There is a culvert beneath the bridge to carry any water. Close by, hidden in undergrowth, is the Hoar Stone – an ancient marker stone with steps cut out as if for a mounting block.[2] Saxon in origin, it is said to mark the lands of Malmesbury Abbey. By the time the Thames reaches the next bridge near Clayfurlong Farm (Exp. 168.980 979) it is a sizeable shallow stream. The bridge was constructed in stone about 1791 for the Cirencester–Malmesbury road (A429) and replaced Clay Ford.[3] The now disused branch railway line from Kemble to Cirencester also crosses at this point on an embankment.

The infant Thames at the bridge near Clayfurlong Farm. The embankment for the now-defunct Kemble to Cirencester railway line is in the background. Postcard by Dennis Moss, Cirencester.

The improved minor road between Kemble and Ewen crosses the Thames at Parker's Bridge, which had been part of a causeway constructed over marshy ground in the vicinity. It was of three low stone arches and was described as having no parapets by Mr and Mrs Hall. In their *Book of the Thames*, 1859, they relate a story concerning a rustic plank bridge hereabouts. While their artist was sketching the bridge, a small boy jumped out of a thicket and danced over the bridge, making the planks move up and down. At the same time he was calling to his sister, 'Come, Emmy, now don't be a fool Emmy', but she hesitated and would not cross the bridge without help. Asked what she was afraid of, if she looked over the rail she replied 'I see her face down there-down!' Assured by her brother and the artist that there was no face, she dried her tears and held their hands. When Emmy was safely on the other side, the boy came back to explain. The previous winter Emmy had been crossing the bridge with her grandmother on the way to school, but being a lively child she had been skipping and jumping. The planks were thick with snow and the river was iced up. With the movement, Granny slipped and fell through the ice, dragging Emmy after her. Those following rescued Emmy, but Granny was sucked under the ice and could not be saved. The boy said, 'I wish there was another road to school'. One of the many accounts of a ramble along the Thames, written at the end of the nineteenth century, describes one such plank bridge, which 'marks the first step in engineering advance from the tree-log of Somerford Mill'.[4] It was made of two tall trestles and three pairs of stout planks. The one from which Granny drowned must have been a much flimsier affair. At Somerford Keynes the river flows over a bed of gravel and there are several sites suitable to have been the ford which gave the village its name. Perhaps they were all used, but only in summer, to bring in the hay harvest from the lush meadows to the west. John Constable familiarises the scene in his oil painting *The Hay Wain*, which is crossing the mill pond at Flatford Mill in Suffolk.

THE RUSTIC BRIDGE.

The rustic plank bridge as described by Mr and Mrs S. C. Hall, showing Emmy who did not want to cross and her brother. From *Book of the Thames*.

Five old watermills, some medieval, are marked on Explorer Map 168 between Ewen and Ashton Keynes, but more are likely. All had a mill leat either diverted from the Thames or they used a smaller brook, and the water was returned to the river lower down. Most have rights of way leading to them which use footbridges over both the Thames and the mill leats. At Somerford Keynes, Kemble Mill (so named because it was in an enclave of Kemble), has a particularly complex system of waterways surrounding it. Close to the house, the river and mill leat form an island, now part of a beautiful large garden. A new channel with a deeper watercourse was cut some time ago to alleviate floods and now runs straight downstream to the ancient crossing place at Neigh Bridge, cutting out the many meanders of the river. Before wooden footbridges were made, fords utilised the gravel bed of the river, thus making it easier for the horses and carts to access the mills. Behind the mill buildings a footpath was formed and a new substantial timber footbridge was built to join up with the Thames Path which runs alongside the new cut to Neigh Bridge, where there was a bridge as early as 1327.[5]

From Neigh Bridge where the new Spine Road crosses the river from east to west, the Thames flows between hedges separating it from the adjoining lakes along a narrow, slightly raised bank. At Ashton Keynes, now seemingly marooned amid manmade lakes, the Thames with the attendant Thames Path enters the village by the moated manor house, next to the church, with the likelihood of a gravel ford at this point. It then divides into many different channels which practically serve as drains to the streets. Some channels are dry most of the time; others, once fords or water splashes, are now crossed by small bridges, giving access to the houses and farms. Occasionally the bridges retain the original stone slabs (resembling gravestones) with which they were built. The scene is very picturesque, but where is the Thames?

That is a difficult question to answer; so many changes to the landscape have taken place so quickly in this area. The Thames Path has not been allowed to run beside the river beyond Ashton Keynes so has been diverted from it by quite a long way and skirts eastwards around several lakes and meets up with the main stream again after Hailstone Hill when it turns southwards towards Cricklade. This circumstance is further illustrated by the Thames crossing at Cricklade. The suffix 'lade' is the same as 'lode' on the River Severn, meaning a passage or ferry. Cricklade is interpreted as 'a strong ford'. The town of Cricklade is situated just off the Roman Ermin Way and the original Thames course formed its eastern boundary. Excavations in the 1950s revealed that the present bed of the river where the road alignment crosses is not the original course. A section cut in the field north of that crossing showed the rubble foundation of the Roman road. The original course of the river over which the Roman crossing was made is now a small stream which the parish boundary still follows. Further excavations in a dry summer confirmed this finding and proved that the crossing is indicated by a double bend in the older course where the ramp of the ford or bridge was situated, with a causeway, or other means of dealing with the marshy ground.[6] This was obviously an important crossing but with so many watercourses nearby, fords in other places are likely. Those suggested are Oaklade at the confluence with the Swill Brook at Ashton Keynes; near High Bridge and below Hailstone Hill in the neighbourhood of Cricklade. Each of them was later replaced by a small bridge.

Cricklade, being an ancient borough, was surrounded by a town wall, the remains of which are still recorded on the map. Outside the wall in the parish of St Mary, a priory was founded before 1231 by Warin, a chaplain to King Henry III. A hospital dedicated to St John the Baptist catered for travellers with a xenodochium or separate guest house. The priory stood a few yards to the north of the Thames and close to the crossing.[7] The establishment continued until the Dissolution. From the town, Thames Lane runs eastwards to Hatchetts Ford which was used until the 1890s by the Particular Baptists for their baptismal ceremony.[8] A simple bridge replaced the ford, and in turn a concrete bridge was built to provide access to a sports field.

Eisey or Eysey (pronounced 'A-sey') is close to Cricklade, (as the crow flies) being just over the Ermin Way, (the dual carriageway A419), but to reach the place – now just a manor house and farm – is a long way round (Exp.169 112 941). The farmer explained that his quickest way to reach Cricklade on foot was along the bed of the Thames just at the bottom of the field to the south. The Thames Path follows the river to Cricklade along the bank. Normally the bed is dry, but in wet seasons the river floods quite badly. The land to the north of the Thames which forms the boundary here of the former ancient Forest of Braden is flat and was common land where the ridge-and-furrow system can be seen clearly. To the south is a patchwork of small fields, lacking habitations and rising to the Wiltshire Downs at Brunsdon and stretching to Highworth in the east.

Two public footpaths converge at the crossing point over the Thames. One begins at a stile from the track which runs alongside the Thames & Severn Canal close to the farm. It then crosses a field to another stile, and crosses a narrow meadow to the timber bridge. Eysey was never a settlement of any size but has certainly shrunk since several farmsteads occupied this area and two watermills were recorded in Domesday. From archaeological finds it is certain the area was occupied in the Bronze Age and Iron Age. There was a church on a knoll in the next field to the east. It was given with some land to the abbey at Cirencester and was in use by 1195. In 1844 it was replaced by another structure, and was demolished in 1953 when it had become obsolete, the parish being transferred to Latton. The churchyard was left but the site is now covered by a dense thicket.

A ford was shown on old maps at a place where a gravel bed would have given a firm crossing, perhaps near a mill. Over the river a footpath led to the Roman Road at Calcutt and on to Cricklade. This is now obliterated and a continuous line of hedges marks the way. A rustic bridge with a handrail 'for the safety of foot passengers' replaced the ford.[9] The Thames Conservators when they took over control of navigation and opened it up again to Cricklade built new bridges. They were not received with equanimity. Reginald Blunt, a tourist writing in August 1890 describes Eysey footbridge as 'one of the new, straight, substantial but unlovely spans with which the Conservators have replaced quaint old structures of the past'.[10]

Less than a mile downstream from Water Eaton, Wiltshire, was another church, a daughter to that at Eysey (Exp.169 124 930). The hamlet was also bigger. Today there is nothing more than Water Eaton House itself. There are three public footpaths to it, but the Thames Path crosses the river on a new footbridge close to where another footbridge replaced the original ford. The Path joins the road from Seven Bridges to Castle Eaton, a distance of over two miles, and continues along it without being near the Thames. The river flows northwards from here, isolated in water meadows until it turns east again at Castle Eaton. This must have been a desolate marshy area bounded on both banks by raised, straight roads. If any fords existed along this stretch they are now forgotten and no rights of way still exist to indicate where they might have been.

Place names incorporating the word 'eaton' occur on the Upper Thames, and also downriver at Eton opposite Windsor. A recent study suggests they indicate a place where a ferry service was available, but possibly these particular ones also had a special function. Navigation on the river before the advent of the Thames Conservancy was difficult and hazardous, with many water mills and their attendant weirs to negotiate. Flotsam and other debris would build up at certain points and would need to be cleared regularly, especially from fords; this function would be carried out from these places. It follows that the operation would be most needed in the upper river, where names such as Water Eaton, Castle Eaton and Eaton Hastings occur.[11] There is another Water Eaton in Oxfordshire on the River Cherwell which strengthens this theory.

Castle Eaton (Exp.169 144 958) is a large compact village approached from the north by a causeway over low-lying meadows to a rather ugly metal trough-like bridge more suited to a railway than a very pretty river. Along The Street, lined with old and new houses, is the large Manor Farm and the church is up a path alongside, sited on a knoll. The church was Norman with additions in other periods, and restoration in Victorian times. The bell turret is its distinguishing feature. The churchyard slopes down steeply to the Thames which forms its northern boundary. To the east is the site of a timber castle on a mound. As this part of the village is at a corner, the road coming from the south appears on the map to be aligned with its counterpart on the north, indicating that the latter was diverted to the west to the present bridge crossing. Therefore, it is suggested that the original ford was next to the church where the river takes a sharp bend and is then joined by a small stream. As this stream is the parish boundary there is a strong possibility the Thames was diverted here, possibly to allow for a wharf for the village to be built.

The bridge in its present position does not 'feel right'. It is too close to The Street. The public house, the Red Lion, is just a few yards away to the left and was built in Georgian times, not an old establishment as is often found next to an ancient crossing and church. However, a bridge was given on old county maps in the seventeenth century and was replaced by a timber one on five stone pillars with a handrail. This was in use until the early twentieth century. Mr and Mrs Hall described it as 'a pretty bridge, more than sufficient for its traffic'.[12] A picture of it is hanging in the Red Lion among other old prints and photographs of the area. Castle Eaton, they said, was 'a secluded and most pleasantly situated spot, where the "busy hum" is rarely heard'... Quite so, but today airplanes are! When the village was a staging post on a drovers' road, as is thought, there would have been plenty of noise.

At Kempsford (Exp.169 162 965) on the Gloucestershire side, the Thames also flows past the church and churchyard, forming their western boundary. The manor house and farm shared the same complex. One of the names given to the village was Kynemeresforde. One Kynemere was the hero of a battle fought in AD 800 between the Mercians and West Saxons whose kingdoms were separated by the Thames here.[13] The Anglo-Saxon Chronicle records that the battle took place on a 100-acre field on the south bank of the river, still called 'the Battlefield' today. A fortress or castle defended the crossing place to the field opposite the church, which was a sort of elongated ford along the river bed. The ford followed a gravel bank and did not cross straight across the river because of a deep pool on the south bank. Deep pools in the river have been detected at other settlements along the river, where it is thought excavations for building materials took place. So the fording place went upstream for about 150 yards following the north-east bank where the water is shallow and avoiding other holes in the bed which are clayey, rather than gravelly. It ended where a flight of stone steps ascended to a garden, but is now part of the extended churchyard. The steps are shown on a watercolour which hangs in the church, presented in the 1980s. The ford then crosses to the south bank in shallow water.

Following the battle, won by the men of Wessex, the fortress was obsolete and a moated manor house of some renown was built there instead. Within the moat a garden was made, with a bower or summer house by the Thames. It looked out along a terraced walk raised above the river by a walled bank about 50 yards long. The manor was owned by some high-ranking families, and at times it was owned by the Crown. When the future Duke of Lancaster was staying there in 1351 his only son and heir Henry was drowned at the ford. It was thought he had mistaken the unusual nature of it, and fell into the deep pool. The Duke was so upset he fled on his horse, vowing never to return. Legend has it that his horse cast a shoe, the villagers found it and nailed it to the church door. Henry had two sisters, Maud and Blanche, who then became the Duke's heiresses. Both were very upset at the loss of their brother. Blanche married John of Gaunt, father of King Henry IV, and she died in 1367. Maud died in 1362 and is said to haunt the green terrace walk. As the 'Lady of the Mist' she 'floats above the river in the pale moonshine' awaiting the return of her brother Henry. It is said she appears only to women, calling them by name.[14] Other versions of this legend differ about how the persons were related, but the story is the same.

The way to the ford (it is unlikely it was superseded by a ferry) was by a road that crossed the Provost's Garden to the river by the summer house. Some called it the Gunner's Room, as the wall with the large window was thought to have been part of a tower of the castle.[15] The ford had some importance from being recognised as a route from Fairford and Lechlade to the Roman road at Cricklade, a salt way perhaps. A track once led across the meadows to Castle Eaton but floods have eradicated it. River dredging in 1976 resulted in the fording place being destroyed.[16]

Kempsford has now turned its back on the river, and there is no right of way to it. The old manor house was demolished before 1784 and a new one built in 1846. Lady Maud's walk still existed in 1976 but has now disappeared along with the wall of the summerhouse, buried beneath a garden and a tennis court. Even the churchyard has been made smaller by the building of what seems to be a new vicarage and garden – all very private. You can see the river, and beyond, the meadows of Wiltshire, by looking over the church wall. The daffodils are lovely.

Leaving Kempsford by a road leading south-east to Highworth, an old hilltop town on the Wiltshire Downs overlooking the valley, the Thames is crossed by Hannington Bridge (Exp.169 174 961). As the river here is the boundary between Wiltshire and Gloucestershire, the bridge was the link between them and each was responsible for the upkeep of the bridge on their side. By 1439 the bridge already existed and superseded a ford, although the ford beside it continued through the ages to take coaches, wagons and carts. In 1574 the Duchy of Lancaster took out a court order against the people of Kempsford because they had not repaired the north end of the bridge, which was their responsibility.[17] The bridge was destroyed in the Civil War and rebuilt in 1647 in stone, the previous one being timber. Proposals and specifications for a new carriage bridge were made in 1828, but it was not built until 1841.[18] It proved too narrow to take carriages, so in 1852 subscriptions were called 'concerning the proposal to widen and enlarge the footbridge over the River Thames between Kempsford and Hannington to take carriages'. To allow for construction a licence was given to the Bridge Trustees to have free access to the bridge site over their land at the Freke estate by Capt. J. S. W. Johnson RN and his wife, the former Mrs Freke. The bridge was rebuilt in brick with three arches and causeways leading up to it on both banks.[19]

Kempsford. Lady Maud's Walk, with the fording place over the Thames below. From a postcard by Percy Simms of Chipping Norton.

Kempsford. The dipping place by the church with the ruins of the summerhouse or castle tower in the background, From the Halls' *Book of the Thames*, 1859.

Road sign on the Gloucestershire approach to Hannington Bridge, Winter 2010.

In 1941 Hannington Bridge was rebuilt again, in stone but still with three arches, and still on the skew, making it rather difficult to navigate beneath it. Actually it crosses two streams of the river which join again a few yards downstream. The one to the north is narrow and forms the parish boundary, that to the south is straighter and would be the navigation channel. Standing on the bridge little islets and fallen trees are seen in the river which presents different aspects on each side. Upstream to the west it is a quiet country river, but downstream to the east is a fast-flowing but shallow serious young river.

Writing in 1910, Charles G. Harper declared Hannington Bridge to be the first bridge of any importance on the Thames.[20] A small settlement grew up at the crossing on the Wiltshire bank with Bridge Farm, said to have existed in 1281. The Hannington Bridge Inn used to brew its own ale but closed in 1858 when another inn took over. Two cottages built of rubble with stone quoins are listed. The listing schedule states unusually that they are probably a late nineteenth-century replica of a late seventeenth-century house on the same site. Just over the bridge at a crossroads the road continues straight uphill to Highworth as a track. The road itself turns right then rounds a sharp corner to the bigger settlement of Hannington Wick on higher ground, consisting of six farms. Did the importance of the bridge owe itself to a salt way?

The Thames continues its sinuous way through open countryside until it reaches Inglesham on the outskirts of Lechlade (Exp.170 205 988). It is not followed by the Thames Path mainly because there was not a towpath beside it after Inglesham. Instead, the Path has to use the very busy road A361, a former turnpike between Burford and Highworth, until it reaches the turning for Inglesham at the site of a deserted medieval village (DMV) of that name. Close to the river bank at Inglesham is a farm and a delightful little early church, beloved by William Morris who saved it from the ravages of Victorian restoration. Perhaps even more famous is the entrance on the left bank to the disused Thames & Severn Canal, with a lock and a round lock house unique to this canal. The canal, opened in 1789, joined with the Stroudwater Navigation, opened in 1779 at Stroud. Potentially the canal was very good for trade on the Thames to Oxford and London, therefore the Thames & Severn Canal Company was instrumental in badgering the Thames Commissioners to improve navigation on the river. Just beyond the canal entrance the Thames receives the waters of the River Coln, which rises at Withington in the Cotswolds and from here onwards the Thames is a major river.

Lechlade on Thames is a small town which grew in importance after it became the head of navigation. Before that time in the eighteenth century it was important not only for being at the junction of four counties: Gloucestershire (in which all the ancient town itself lies), Wiltshire, Berkshire and Oxfordshire. It also lies at the junction of major routes from east to west and north to south, with a marketplace and lovely church in the middle. There are two bridges now crossing the Thames, one in the town, the other being St John's Bridge about one and half miles further east where the River Leach joins, thus giving the town its name, passage over the Leach. Both bridges began as fords.

Adin Williams who wrote the standard history of Lechlade in 1888 gives the first mention of the old ferry as 1627.[21] Previous to this there was a ford,

Inglesham. Junction of the Thames & Severn Canal coming in to the Thames from the right. The round houses built for the lock-keepers are a unique feature of the canal. From the Halls' *Book of the Thames.*

called Tidford – was this the first name of the settlement? When navigation was improved by dredging, the river would be deeper and a ford made impracticable. The way to the crossing place was down a narrow medieval lane named Tidford Lane (Exp.170 212 994) leading from the main street and now called Bell Lane, near the traffic lights. A few yards on the left, before the water's edge, is a small house facing east to the large wharf with a small kiosk by the side. Although there is no positive evidence, a suggestion is made that this was a ferryman's house and ticket office. Looking from the ferry place across to the opposite bank, is seen a track and hedge to match the alignment with Bell Lane. The ferry came to an end when the toll bridge, the Ha'penny Bridge, was built close by in 1792. A straight road called the new road was made 1½ miles long towards Highworth until it was joined to the old 'Barker's Lane' from Buscot at Lynt Bridge. This lane also took the heavy traffic which had to go round by St John's Bridge

What became of the landing place at Tidford is a problem, as it may be for other former ferry landing places along the river. An enquiry was held at Gloucester on 10 July 1974 by the Chief Commons Commissioner. The purpose was to determine the ownership of a piece of land called Old Town Ditch, maintained by Gloucestershire County Council although no owner was registered. In his report the Commissioner describes the land as a long, narrow strip which abuts on to the river on the south and to Bell Lane at the north.[22] On the east side it abuts a property known as Park End Wharf, which had belonged to the Thames & Severn Canal and on the west was another wharf known as Free Wharf, which most likely was the original wharf for the Thames Navigation and was held by the Parish officers of Lechlade. The land was an extension of the lane to the ford or ferry although nothing of them remained after 1839 – the date of the tithe map which in fact showed there was an inlet of the river in that place. The inlet was manmade as demonstrated by a wall on each side separating it from the wharves, and thus earned its appellation of 'ditch'. Later the inlet was filled in, or was silted up although it is still apparent today.

Park End Wharf was sold in 1959, the former owner had used the inlet for mooring boats in connection with his business but it was not included in the sale. The Parish Council had looked after the land and had planted bulbs. There was no firm evidence that the owners of either wharf had also owned the land in question. Nor was there evidence to support a claim to a possessory title to any part of the land. The decision was made that the land would remain subject to protection under the Commons Registration Act of 1965. Allegedly the firm bed of the river which formed the ford was dredged away in 1960.[23]

At best the ford and ferry, which probably existed side-by-side, were difficult. The trustees of the Burford and Highworth Turnpike obtained permission to build a toll bridge to replace them.[24] It opened in 1792 with a toll house at the town end, which still exists although tolls were abolished following a petition in 1839. The charge for pedestrians was one half-penny, so the bridge gained its name of 'Ha'penny Bridge'. A toll gate for beasts was not removed until 1888. The new road built by the trustees incorporated a causeway on the Highworth side.

The bridge made road travel much easier but many people were not satisfied. Revd William Alleyn Evanson MA, vicar of Inglesham, wrote a letter to *The Times* in April 1852 complaining about 'the enormity of taxation under the name of tolls at turnpike gates. 'No town in Europe is more stockaded with them at all points of the compass than my post town, Lechlade'.[25] He states that the road along its length of 21 miles is very bad and not kept in repair. The Act of Parliament setting up the bridge expired in 1813 and was renewed for a further twenty-one years, and again in 1834. The Acts permitted some Commissioners to mortgage the tolls and, after necessary payments were made, they were to apply the surplus to the relief of highway rates in the area. Having been forced to abolish the toll for foot passengers, the Commissioners proceeded to double the tolls on all the other users. The vicar claimed the trustees never paid the contractor, who did not pay his workers. Then he became bankrupt and walked away. 'Notwithstanding this, the Commissioners gallantly went on "taxing and tolling, and fleecing and flaying" us Christian pilgrims'. Evanson had found out that the Trustees were £4,000 in debt, although they were still collecting tolls, he believed, with no right to do so, and nobody had seen their accounts. He wrote to Lord John Russell suggesting that Turnpike Trusts be consolidated, but he got only a 'brush-off'. The letter ends with a plea, 'nobody hesitates to believe that turnpike trusts are universally hotbeds of corruption ... and nobody hesitates to say that the Lechlade Bridge Trust is a rare specimen of the genus.'

Over one hundred and fifty years later the Halfpenny Bridge is still not giving satisfaction. It is used heavily and made dangerous for pedestrians by heavy lorries. In December 2007, Lechlade History Society posted an item on the web. 'The most ambitious project for the future is a new footbridge that would separate pedestrians from heavy vehicle traffic over the 216-year-old Ha'penny Toll Bridge. For pedestrians this will put the clock back to when they passed down Bell Lane to Tidford Ferry at the Free Wharf, whilst carts and carriages heading south towards Marlborough and Portsmouth would have to take the long detour via St John's Bridge'.[26]

CHAPTER THREE

# Running the River Part 1: The Thames Navigation Commission

Since at least the time of the Norman Conquest, navigation of the Thames has been of primary importance to trade for the conveyance of heavy goods to and from London. As trade increased and the size of vessels became larger, navigation became increasingly difficult. Impediments were caused by weirs or kiddles built across the river. The first were supposed to aid navigation but in fact they were used by owners of water mills to hold back the water to power their own mills. This resulted in barges being kept awaiting the convenience of the millers, who were allowed to charge boatmen for passing. A flash of water would be necessary and was provided by removing part of the weir by hand. The barge would then float down and, if lucky, would also be carried over shallows. Kiddles were basket-work constructions created for the fishing trade and barges had to pay to pass those too. In most cases the weirs, mills and fisheries were controlled by the monastic establishments and manors, the riparian owners.

Given these circumstances, regulation of the river was very difficult, and therefore haphazard. Thacker, in his first volume, *The Thames Highway: General History* gives a good comprehensive account of the different methods by which the river was regulated before the first permanent commission was created as a semi-public body. An attempt had been made by the twenty-third clause of the Magna Carta in 1215, which stipulated that all kiddles (meaning also weirs) were removed from the Thames. Largely, this edict had been ignored.[1]

At the beginning of the seventeenth century the Thames was fairly satisfactorily navigable from London upriver as far as Burcot, a small village with a natural wharf near Dorchester-on-Thames. From there navigation to Oxford was prohibitive; apart from obstructions, the river was too shallow. Goods had to be unloaded and conveyed to Oxford by road, a costly operation. In the third year of the reign of James I an Act (*c*. 20) recited that by the removal of some impediments and obstructions the Thames could be made passable to Oxford.[2] The vice-chancellor of Oxford University and some other eminent gentlemen arranged in 1607 to survey the river between Clifton (Hampden) ferry and Cricklade to ascertain what improvements would be needed. They found that west of Oxford the river was quite good. However, the Act did not give sufficient powers for any progress to be made in the hazardous stretch of the river and eighteen years later the Act was repealed.

Pressure for another Act was exerted by the University and the City of Oxford because it was in their interests for the conveyance of heavy goods to be made easier and cheaper. For instance, building stone from quarries at Headington was needed in London and coal was brought up from there for Oxford. The Act passed in 1624 allowed for the Thames to be made navigable between Burcot and

Oxford for barges, boats and lighters. The Oxford-Burcot Commission was set up with eight commissioners, four each from the university and the city. They were empowered to borrow money to construct pound locks (then known as turnpikes).[3] The Commissioners were to keep the river clean and maintain it. For this they could levy taxes on the university and city as the improvements were for their benefit. The university used a large legacy on the improvements as their part.[4] The city neglected to pay for some time. Progress was slow and the first barge did not reach Oxford until 1635. A wharf had been constructed at Folly Bridge on the north bank around 1629. It included a wet dock and later an oak crane.

Charles I was particularly interested in the function of the river and in 1631 noted that the Act passed in the reign of his father James I in 1624 had not been entirely successful and ordered another survey. He was concerned about the cost of timber being carried from Burcot to build his naval establishment at Dartford. The Commissioners had succeeded in opening the channel by 1638 and built locks at Iffley, Sandford and Swift Ditch. Undoubtedly there was a made towing path for men halers or even horses, but in the absence of the Commission's records, this cannot be checked. Possibly the Commissioners merely negotiated with riparian landowners to create the path over their land, without actually buying it themselves.

The Oxford-Burcot Commission continued to exist under a manager even after a new body was set up by an Act of 1751. Although based on the Oxford-Burcot Commission, the new body was unwieldy, having 600 members consisting of representatives of Oxford University, the mayors of riverside towns and riparian owners who owned lands worth over £100 annual rateable value.[5] They had jurisdiction over the river from London Bridge to Cricklade in Wiltshire, except for the stretch between Burcot and Oxford. The orders and constitutions made by the commissioners in 1730 were revived but still the powers invested in this new body were not sufficient to give them enough control of the river. They sought a new Act which was passed in 1770. Numbers were increased again to include all Members of Parliament for counties bordered by the river but a quorum was only eleven. For the better management of the river it was divided into six districts. The first was from London Bridge to the City Stone at Staines. Soon afterwards this section was returned to the jurisdiction of the City of London. The second district was from Staines to Boulters, the third to Mapledurham, fourth to Shillingford, fifth to Oxford, and the sixth to Cricklade. Each district held regular meetings at a specific place in their area and made regulations and organised tolls to be paid at the locks. Another Act of 1775 amended the previous one, sorted out some anomalies and gave more powers to the Commissioners. The official name for the body was The Thames Navigation Commission.

Meanwhile, the powers of the Oxford-Burcot Commission were diminishing, along with their trade. After the Swift Ditch, a manmade cut which bypassed Abingdon, was reopened, most barges used that route instead of unloading at Burcot. In 1789 the Oxford-Burcot Commission was no longer viable and was sold to the new body at a reduced price of £600.[6] All of their land and hereditaments were included, except the Folly Bridge wharf at Oxford. However, coal and flints continued to be brought to Burcot wharf until 1914. When the river became a favourite place for the leisured classes in the late nineteenth and early twentieth centuries, Burcot, which had remained a hamlet clustered round the church and the inn, which may have had the right of ferry attached to it, then became an unspoilt desirable residential spot.

From being a busy trans-shipment point and the head of navigation on the river, Burcot, with its farms, timber-framed thatched cottages and seventeenth-century Chequers Inn was ripe for development.[7] Jabez Spencer Balfour (1843–1916) bought Burcot House in 1886 to become the squire of Burcot. Having enlarged and altered the house he proceeded to buy up most of the village and farms, demolished a row of old cottages in Occupation Row and rebuilt them as eight pairs of semi-detached estate houses set back from the north side of the road and named Balfour Cottages. On the south side he did away with the wharf and divided the land into long strips on which were built large houses with gardens reaching to the water's edge. Some of these have now become hotels and rest homes, John Masefield, the poet, lived in one of them in the 1930s.

Balfour came from humble stock, the youngest of seven children. His family was strictly nonconformist and they were temperance campaigners. Jabez began work as a parliamentary agent and made many good contacts. When only twenty-five, along with his brother John and some nonconformist friends he created the Liberator Building Society, after the Liberation Society, a movement of nonconformists who naturally presumed the two bodies worked together. After his marriage Balfour settled in Croydon and expanded his business enterprises by setting up companies with money invested in the building society by ordinary working class people who thought to receive a mortgage in due course. As a public benefactor to Croydon and entrepreneur, Balfour stood for the Liberal Party in the general election of 1880, winning one of the seats for Tamworth. But he lost the seat when the constituency was reorganised. This coincided with Croydon becoming a Borough and, although not a councillor, Balfour became Mayor. He still aimed to become an MP and after three failed attempts he won the seat for Burnley in 1889. Burcot became a Mecca for the great and good in political life and lavish parties were held there. As a gesture of goodwill to the village he gave a recreation field.[8]

Behind the bravado were rumblings that all was not right with the Balfour group of companies. They were operating a scheme of 'robbing Peter to pay Paul', which came to be known later as a Ponzi scheme, first exposed by Charles Dickens in *Little Dorrit* when Mr Merdle was the Balfour-like character. In 1892 the Liberator Building Society collapsed, followed like a pack of cards by the other companies. Balfour quickly resigned his seat and escaped to Argentina, which did not have an extradition treaty with the United Kingdom. He took with him two young ladies, described as his wards. Diplomacy having failed, Scotland Yard sent an inspector to bring back their fraudster, which he did by kidnapping him. At the trial where Balfour was described as 'The Champion Hypocrite of England' he was sentenced to fourteen years' imprisonment, the longest time for a sentence for fraud. He was an inmate of Portland prison but received a three-year remission for good behaviour. When released in 1906 he sold his story to a London newspaper and set himself up as a consultant engineer, no doubt using his expertise as a builder and owner of London hotels and luxury blocks of flats. Having ruined many honest people, some of whom had committed suicide, Balfour died a poor man, with only £1 19s 4d in his pocket, of a heart attack on a train to Swansea in 1916.

Following his downfall, Balfour's frauds had amounted to the equivalent of more than £450 million in today's money. The police found his cellar at Burcot House to contain huge quantities of fine claret and best champagne. His effigy was burnt on bonfire night, (he was described as a short butter ball of a man). The recreation committee of Burcot received a bill for the rent of the field from the true owner! By his machinations Jabez Balfour had deprived posterity of the legacy of a valuable part of the heritage of the River Thames, 'the liquid history'. Nothing tangible is left at the waterside at Burcot to show the wharf which for centuries was so important to the lifeblood of the river and the head of navigation. There is not even a right of way to the river for the public to admire its beauty.

At least four Acts concerning the navigation of the Thames were passed in the early years of the reign of George II, who was keen to develop water transport. The Act passed in 1788 was to enable further improvements and to complete the navigation of the Thames. It stated that the Commissioners had raised £38,900 and spent most of it making pound locks, ballasting the channel and making horse towing paths from Staines to near Cleeve in Oxfordshire, resulting in the price of carrying goods being reduced.[9] They were now empowered to borrow another £25,000 in addition to the £50,000 already authorised against the proceeds of the tolls. All vessels and rafts on the river were to be charged and also payment had to be made for any horses used in towing and for passing through any gates on the towing path or over any bridge or ferry made or established by the Commissioners. They were allowed to alter tolls at their discretion, but were limited to no more than 2*d* for each horse passing over any bridge, across any river or being carried over any river by any ferry boat belonging to the Commissioners. This was the first time in any Act so far where ferries were mentioned specifically.

Persons were to be employed to collect tolls, but those for the towing paths, bridges and ferries were to be kept separate. Boards giving notice of the tolls were to be erected at the places where they were collected. All private owners of the old locks would have to charge the same amount as laid down by the Commissioners. Only cargoes of manure were given free passage.

A measure of safety was introduced by regulating the draught of the vessels; the gunwales were to clear the water by at least two inches. The Commissioners now had powers to make bye-laws 'for the well-governing of the river and bargemasters, bargemen, watermen, lock-shatterers, pound-keepers, horse-towers [*sic*] and drivers of horses and other beasts'. Rates were to be laid down for the price of towing, haling or drawing of barges and other vessels and for the use of towing paths both now and hereafter to be used, including the number of horses to haul on each stretch. No tolls or the toll collectors would be subject to taxes.

Following this Act of 1788, the directors of the Thames & Severn Canal were anxious that the necessary improvements to the Thames Navigation were not being carried out quickly enough. On 8 May 1789, Joseph Pitt, their clerk, wrote from the canal's headquarters at Brimscombe Port near Stroud to Henry Allnutt, Clerk of the Commissioners for the Rivers Thames and Isis. He wished to inform them that the Thames & Severn Canal would open in six months and requested that the Thames be in a fit condition as per the Acts 'in order that the public trade of the Thames & Severn Canal passing into and out of the rivers Thames and Isis may not be impeded or injured for want of the above mentioned improvements being made'.[10]

The Commissioners were prompted to action and called in the engineer William Jessop who recommended eight pound locks to be built and fifty-five timber bridges be constructed for the towing path.[11] The canal did open on time, although only seven locks were completed by 1791. Within four months, four of them were showing signs of collapse although they probably did not do so. Another engineer, Robert Mylne, took over as engineering consultant to the Commissioners at the instigation of Edward Loveden of Buscot Park, who was himself a Commissioner and shareholder in both the Thames & Severn Canal and the Gloucester & Sharpness Canal. He was a riparian owner and charged a heavy toll at his Buscot Lock. Mylne recommended that the Commissioners take over the private weirs, buy up the old locks, make a continuous towing path and deepen the channel. These works the Commissioners proceeded to do, but progress was slow and in 1793 they were indicted for neglect of the river. Throughout its existence the Thames & Severn Canal was beset by adverse conditions of navigation on the Thames and this circumstance and the shortage of water at the summit level contributed to its failure in the early twentieth century.[12]

The body of Commissioners was made up of a diverse set of people, not necessarily with an interest in the Thames. One was Sir John Call, of Whiteford (now demolished) near Callington, Cornwall, who was father-in-law to Loveden. Others were drawn from the fields of politics, banking, investment, clergy, business and the more affluent barge owners who also owned land.[13] Principal families from each of the five districts were represented on the Commission. The Blandys of Reading who had connections in Madeira owned wharves and barges. Owen Williams of Temple Mills near Hurley was both a commissioner and MP for Marlow 1796–1832. One Commissioner, taken to task for not attending at his district's annual meeting, declared that unless there was important business to be done, he considered it 'to be useless to travel a number of miles for the sake of any eating and drinking'.

Staff employed by the Commission consisted of four general clerks and, in the later years, four general treasurers. Henry Allnutt an attorney of Great Marlow served as the first Clerk for forty-nine years until his death in 1820, at an annual salary of £160. He was succeeded by his son Zachary Allnutt. Most noteworthy is the Treacher family of Sonning and Reading who served the Thames Navigation Commission for almost ninety years. Beginning in 1773, John Treacher (1736–1802) was a builder and carpenter with little formal education and who specialised in mills, which gave him what was described as 'a practical knowledge of the ways of running water'. From around 1786 he was made responsible for the programme of building locks above Reading, under the Commission's surveyor John Clarke. Treacher became General Surveyor for the upper district in 1791, and four years later he was promoted to be General Engineer of the whole Thames Navigation Commission area.[14]

John Treacher Jnr succeeded his father in 1802 until his death in 1836. Under a reorganisation of the Commission in 1821, Treacher was also appointed General Surveyor of the whole navigation from Staines to Cricklade, and in his own right was surveyor of bridges for Berkshire. George Treacher, his son, a highly skilled builder and engineer, was his assistant and took over as General Surveyor from his father on his death. From 1856 George also took on the post of General Receiver (of tolls etc.) for the Commission. Unfortunately, he had to resign in October 1862 because of illness caused by stress, and died in 1863. The extensive Treacher papers are deposited at Berkshire Record Office in Reading.

Before John Treacher Snr took over the locks downriver, they were the responsibility of Humphrey Gainsborough, elder brother to painter Thomas Gainsborough. He served as Congregational Minister at Henley-on-Thames from 1748 to 1776, but was also a very competent engineer and inventor.[15] When first he arrived in the town he constructed to it a new access road by cutting off the top of White Hill and filling in a valley to make a causeway. He built the picturesque arched bridge to take the Henley to Wargrave road over Happy Valley, where it falls to the Thames at the bottom of the grounds of Park Place, by using stones taken from Reading Abbey. More significantly, he designed and superintended the construction of the pound locks in the neighbourhood of Henley. Boulter's Lock was the first in 1772, and by the end of 1773 the locks at Marlow, Temple, Hambleden, Hurley, Marsh Lock at Henley, Shiplake and Sonning were completed. The locks were built of wood with turf sides strengthened at intervals by timber piles. Of course they were vulnerable so if the barge masters damaged them by levering against the sides with barge poles, they were fined 2s 6d. Soon the locks fell into disrepair and were replaced by stone, but meanwhile they were a great boon, allowing easier navigation and saving time for the vessels. Gainsborough was appointed by the Commission to be Rate Collector of the locks from Hambleden to Sonning. When he died on the river bank in August 1776 it is said he was carrying in his pocket £20 of river tolls.

Records show that under the Treacher family much work was undertaken to improve the navigation, the major part being the provision of towing paths (to be the subject of the next chapter). One Robert Treacher began in 1789 to record in a ledger all the work done for the 'gentlemen commissioners of the Thames navigation' as the family called them. Robert was paid one guinea a week for his meticulous work. John Treacher himself was paid two guineas a week for the period from 27 June until Christmas 1789, possibly in a lump sum at the end. Whenever Mr Allnutt sent a letter, seven pence had to be paid by the office receiving it. When surveys were carried out at the Commissioners' orders, a man and a boat had to be paid for. In 1819 John Treacher produced on handwritten sheets the results of a survey he had undertaken to list all the land and towing paths owned by the Commission. On it is inscribed in pencil 'Read. Zachary Allnutt'.[16]

Altogether the Thames Navigation Commission built thirty pound locks, (sometimes in the early years they were called turnpikes), including the eight already mentioned. Some had a ferry alongside: Temple, Caversham, Hurley, Goring, Bell Weir, Clifton, Sonning and Marsh Lock, which had two ferries. John Clarke the surveyor submitted the account for tolls collected at locks to John Treacher at Sonning for June 1789. There were ten locks altogether in the account, of which four of the above with ferries were included. The total amount collected was £24 10s 6d. Most locks being isolated, it became apparent that the keepers would need shelter. At first 'small wooden houses' costing £12 each were provided at Temple, Hurley, Hambleden and Sonning locks. Obviously they were not substantial and were probably like the white ticket offices provided by the Thames Conservancy, of which many are still *in situ*. Eventually small brick cottages were built, although for some it took prolonged negotiations with landowners to secure the site and access by land would have been a problem. In 1802, Robert Mylne, the consultant engineer, was insisting that a keeper and cottage must be available at every lock. Sometimes the work was done by the nearby miller or a fisherman. As the purpose of having a keeper was to keep an eye on the activities of such people, this was not a satisfactory arrangement; also they did not always attend to their duties. Until 1831 the position of pound keeper was open to both men and women, but then employment of women was forbidden. The wages of the keepers were poor, the highest at the important locks being £5 a month and decreasing according to work done.[17]

The City of London, who had jurisdiction over the Lower Thames, desired to take control over the Upper Thames as well and occasionally acrimonious encounters would take place. To investigate this possibility, a deputation of nine men from the City made a tour in 1816 by waterway from London via the Thames and Kennet and Avon Canal to Bristol, up the Severn to the junction with the Stroudwater Navigation which joined with the Thames & Severn Canal and brought them back to the Thames at Inglesham. Pertinent remarks were made about ferries in their subsequent report. 'Much inconvenience also arises from the frequency of ferries in this district', speaking of District Five, from Oxford to Shillingford. In the fourth district, Shillingford to Mapledurham, ferries were too frequent. The locks were often unattended so 'the lock-keepers should reside at them, or be so arranged as to assist effectively at the numerous ferries'.[18] The ferries referred to would be those horse ferries set up to take horses over when the towing paths needed to change sides. At Caversham in the third district the travellers were perturbed by the ferry being kept locked.

A new threat to the viability of the Commission came in 1818 when steam propulsion began to take the place of haling by men and horses. Messrs Parsons of Newbury applied for permission to use a steam vessel, probably a tug 'for the purpose of Towing their Loaded Boats'.[19] This was granted 'by way of experiment', but it meant that no tolls were eligible to be paid for horse ferries, nor for using the towing paths. Therefore the Commission received no income for maintenance. However, the use of steam on the river suffered a learning curve. John R. Denyer, the young manager/agent of the Thames & Severn Canal, wrote to his colleague, the treasurer John S. Salt of a report seen in an Oxford newspaper.[20]

An account of Mr McCurdy's attempt to navigate the Thames to Oxford by means of a steam boat which has proved a compleat failure, his four horse-power engine which he used upon the occasion, being unable to perform that which two real horses accomplished – I am sorry the first attempt of the kind has been so unfortunate as it may tend to deter others.

Measures were taken by the Commission to lessen their commitments in the face of lessening trade. A new arrangement was made in July 1848 whereby 'all barge and other horses and all persons employed in the navigation might pass toll-free over the Commission's ferries'. At that time steam was catching up! To pass up and down the river was toll-free anyway. Even more drastic was the notice issued on February 26 1854 by William Graham, the General Clerk from Abingdon, announcing alterations to the salaries and duties of the pound lock-keepers and ferrymen.[21] Some had increased duties to perform with additional salary. Others had their salary reduced but were given extra work. At least one man was summarily dismissed. As a sweetener, men who were just pound lock-keepers with no extra duties were allowed to keep the tolls taken for pleasure craft, which were increasing in number, but instead were to take a cut in salary. William Graham himself volunteered at Christmas 1861 to take only half his salary of £400. He died shortly afterwards.

By 1835 the Commission was suffering increasing losses and was fearful of the threat of competition for freight travel by the railways. They had successfully opposed one Great Western Railway Bill and the next one was passed. George Treacher was given the supervision of the construction of a railway bridge for the Oxford branch of the railway to be built over the river at Nuneham in 1852.[22] No money was available for repairing the locks and the upper reaches became unnavigable. Little traffic now entered the Thames from the canal. Moreover there was more difficulty caused by towns discharging sewage into the river. The Board of Trade had to make a decision about the future of the Thames Navigation Commission. It was passed over to the Thames Conservancy in 1866, the body which in 1857 had taken over jurisdiction of the Lower Thames from the City of London.

# CHAPTER FOUR

# Running the River Part 2:
# The Thames Conservancy

The Act transferring the navigation of the Upper Thames to the Thames Conservators came into force on 6 August 1866. Its official title is the 'Thames Navigation Act 1866 for vesting in the Conservators of the River Thames the conservancy of the Thames and Isis from Staines, Middlesex, to Cricklade, Wiltshire, and for other purposes connected therewith'. According to the *Oxford English Dictionary* Conservators were persons having charge of a river, its embankments, weirs, creeks etc. and supervision of the fisheries, navigation, watermills etc. thereon. There were ninety-one sections in the Act and two schedules annexed. The preamble is long and begins by setting out the previous Acts and explaining the role played by what the Act calls the Upper Navigation Commissioners. The Commission had been badly constituted and was not a body corporate, meaning that individually they were exposed to liabilities.[1] Problems mentioned above were cited as further reasons for the change of administration. Now, the new body was charged with 'the preservation and improvement of the stream, bed and banks of the upper part of the Thames as a matter of great local and public importance'.

As the river between Teddington and Staines was already vested in the Conservators of the Thames it would be of advantage to have both parts under one management, so the Commission would be discontinued. Commissioners and staff were to be compensated where loss of income was established. Most importantly private owners of locks, dams and weirs were discharged from their obligation to maintain them, but they were not to receive any tolls as hitherto and they were to forfeit their property. An exception to this clause was Robert Campbell Esq. of Buscot Park who retained his rights to Buscot and Eaton weirs and locks and works connected with them because he used the weirs for driving the water wheels he had at Buscot and Eaton Hastings. But he no longer had to repair them and was not allowed to levy tolls.

A very welcome clause was that which prohibited pollution of the river. No discharge whatsoever was to be allowed and sewers already built had to be removed. The surface of the river was to be scavenged to remove substances 'liable to putrefaction'. Further Acts on this topic were projected.

One of the drawbacks to the Commission's work had been that it was overloaded with members, most of whom had no direct interest in the river. The Conservancy was to have an extra five members to join the existing eighteen members. One of them was to be a delegate from the Board of Trade and elections were to be held for the other four. Their duties were detailed in the Act, including the power to borrow money. They were to have the same powers over the Thames and Isis above Staines as they enjoyed below Staines. The document was not signed by individual Conservators, but the Common Seal of the Board was affixed.

After the Act was passed there followed a period of shaking down. First there was an inspection of the works between Oxford and Windsor when all lock-keepers were informed there would be no tolls charged by the private owners. A table of the new tolls for all journeys up and down was fixed, including a payment of tuppence (2*d*) per ton at each lock. Steam tugs were still free unless they carried passengers or cargo. Lock-keepers were restricted in their activities and later a booklet, *Instructions to Lock and Ferry Staff*, was issued. Notices for the sale of refreshments were not to be exhibited at the keepers' premises and they were not to take lodgers. Nor were they to receive gratuities and for the first time pleasure craft had to purchase lock tickets for sixpence. In future no old names were to be used of locks and weirs and the locks were to be kept clean and neat and the keepers to be mindful of taking tolls from all vessels at the locks; there were often cases of evasion.

The Conservators proceeded to work towards getting navigation restored and inserted an advertisement in the *London Standard* of 24 January 1868 giving notice that the navigation was then open from Oxford to London and from the Duke's Cut on the Oxford Canal to New Bridge and also from the Thames & Severn Canal at Lechlade to Radcot Bridge. It also reminded readers that all old lock tolls had been abolished and listed the charges payable on through routes to London. Full information could be obtained from the Superintendent of the Upper Navigation at Reading. John Taunton of the Thames & Severn Canal replied on 31 January to Capt. Burstal, Clerk to the Thames Conservancy, asking for verification of the tolls. He had observed that the portion of river between Radcot Bridge and New Bridge (Oxfordshire) was not included in the notice. He asked if he was to 'Presume that the

Thames Conservancy staff pictured at the Reading Headquarters early in the twentieth century. Some ferrymen are holding their punt poles. Reproduced by permission of English Heritage.

Conservators intend to maintain the navigation on this portion of river and to improve it as from time to time they may decide'. 'Will you say if that is their intention and for any information you can give me as to the probable period when this exception to the satisfactory announcement of your Conservators may cease, I shall be obliged.' Capt. Burstal replied, 'There will be no tolls charged in future for any weirs above Oxford and the only tolls on craft will be at Pinkhill Lock, Buscot Lock and St John's Lock at tuppence per ton. It is the intention of the Board to open and maintain navigation between Radcot Bridge and New Bridge and the Conservators will be obliged if you can furnish as to what traffic with any information is likely to be put on that part of the river'. This information was passed on by Taunton to W. W. Kearsey, solicitor to the canal company, on 18 February 1868. He added that the stretch in question was about 9 miles long and could with some difficulty be navigated by means of flashes.[2]

Others were also disenchanted by the work of the Conservators. William Morris had taken a lease of Kelmscott Manor in 1869 and describes it as 'the old house by the Thames' in *News from Nowhere*. Often he would travel up by boat from London and was not impressed by the way the river was being run. He dismisses the Conservators as 'heedless London bureaucrats who simply cut down the trees, ruining banks and indulging in unnecessary dredging while all the time drawing a salary for 'masterly inactivity'.[3] He should have mentioned the stream was being choked with weeds. Even the Conservancy screw launch was stopped by them and the Inspector called for a paddle launch instead. By 1876 the tremendous task of pollution by sewage had not been sorted satisfactorily, towns who persisted in their old systems but which were situated on tributaries had been forgotten about. Railway embankments were interfering with natural drainage, resulting in increased flooding.

By 1878 the state of the upper reaches was no better and a Bill was put before Parliament for conferring on the Conservators of the River Thames further powers and for extending the Thames Acts of 1857 to 1870 and other purposes. The Acts were to be put together and certain clauses repealed, but the new powers now requested were not ground-breaking. Clause ten stipulated that persons cutting weeds, grass etc. from any stream connecting with the river shall remove them immediately after cutting and not throw them into the river. The Conservators hoped that this would prevent rubbish from piling up by lock gates. Other clauses allowed for changes in the structure of charges, such as cheap day returns, reductions for annual licences, and steam pleasure boats had the option of paying eighteen pence daily or £5 a year. Double fare would be charged for various non-propelled vessels if towed by horse or any other animal.[4] The Thames & Severn Canal Company wished to have a clause inserted in the Bill appertaining to the improvement of navigation on the upper reaches of the Thames. They wished to set up a petition and instructed a firm of Parliamentary agents to act on their behalf. For one month's work in May 1878 they paid £24 18s 2d.[5]

John Edward Dorington of Lypiatt Park Gloucestershire wrote on behalf of the County on 9 April 1878 to Admiral Sir Frederick W. E. Nicolson Bt. CB, deputy Chairman of the Thames Conservancy, to set the ball rolling. He described the incidents of a voyage made in the previous December from Gloucester by a vessel loaded with 25 tons of timber. Its purpose was to test the possibility of merchants trading regularly between Gloucester and Oxford. The vessel, drawing 2 feet 10 inches, started from Gloucester at 1.30 p.m. on 10 December 1877 (Monday) and arrived at Lechlade wharf on the afternoon of the 13th. The least depth on the Thames & Severn canal had been 3 feet 11 inches. The Thames was bank full on the day they arrived. On the 14th Tadpole Bridge was reached after a journey of 7 hours from Lechlade (10 miles). On the way, below Radcot Bridge 'the horse had to be sent round owing to the insecurity of the towpath bridge over the old stream'. 'At the entrance to Rushy Lock the boat was hauled through mud with difficulty'.[6]

The river was in flood after Tadpole Bridge. Thames Conservancy dredges were in operation at Shifford where the two towpath bridges were in such bad condition they were rendered useless. They stopped at Skinner's Weir and reached Oxford on the 16th (Sunday) at 12.30 p.m. The cargo was discharged on the Oxford Canal and they returned empty to Lechlade, taking three days. The cost of the voyage both ways including the journey on the Gloucester & Berkeley Canal, the Stroudwater Navigation, Thames & Severn Canal and the Oxford Canal as well as lockage to the Thames Conservancy amounted to £14 13s 0d.

This amount could possibly be reduced to £11 5s 0d if a public wharf were provided at Oxford instead of vessels having to enter the canal to unload at one shilling per ton. This did not allow for competition with the railways. 'If the River Thames were in such a condition that vessels might count on getting through when the river was not in flood – the Gloucestershire Committee believe that a trade would spring up and be of benefit to the Conservancy. But the River is not at present navigable throughout except on special occasions.'

Dorington also cites a more recent voyage by James Smart, barge owner and canal carrier of Chalford, near Stroud. It involved two boats, each drawing 2 feet 4 inches with a cargo of timber, and began at Duxford on 22 March 1878 (Friday). After a mile they were grounded between the fords at Shifford and Sansom's. They were detained there all Saturday and Sunday, finally getting away by 9.30 a.m. on Monday. They had assistance by using blocks and ropes, four donkeys and twenty men, and breaking £4 worth of ropes in the meantime. 'At this point a channel had been dredged (in the previous December?) but it was only about 4 feet wide and had been done rather for drainage than navigation. These shallows (according to the trader) are owing to the removal of Townsend's Weir.' The boats then passed in 10 hours to the Duke's Lock at Oxford. A further homily rounded off Dorington's letter. Trade could be developed if a return cargo was carried: 'if the Conservators will assist by placing the river under their charge in a condition in which it was intended to be kept when handed over to their care.'

Other petitions were handed in, one from Robert S. Hawkins, the secretary of the Thames Valley Drainage Commissioners, who declared the total neglect of the river in some parts between Oxford and Cricklade was 'a natural consequence of the management being invested in a Board composed as is the Conservancy Board and holding all its meetings in London'. Another petition was signed by James Smart, the Ford Brothers, mealmen of Ryeford, Stroud, who had a large business, and fifteen others.

Even if the petitions did have an effect on the condition of the early river, it was not a lasting one because again in November 1895 the Thames Conservancy was asked or rather presumed to be improving the river upstream from Oxford. By an Act passed earlier that year the Thames & Severn Canal Trust had been set up by five navigations and six public bodies working together to keep the canal open and allow trade to prosper. One of the chief promoters of this move was J. E. Dorington, now knighted and MP for Tewkesbury as well as being the first chairman of the Gloucestershire County Council. As the Conservancy had already begun to make improvements for navigation, including a new lock at Radcot and another begun at Northmoor, the Trust entered into a mutual agreement that each body would improve its own navigation for the mutual benefit of them both. Therefore the Trust confirmed this arrangement with a memo: 'We the undersigned members of the Canal Trust appointed by Public Bodies hereby certify that we are satisfied there is a reasonable prospect of such works for improvement of navigation of the upper part of the River Thames as will enable a vessel drawing 4 feet of water to navigate the river from Inglesham to Kings' Weir near Oxford in the ordinary state of water, being carried out within a reasonable time.'

Signed by John E. Dorington, Wilfred J. Cripps and six others.[7] This memo was written in answer to a letter from the Thames Conservancy at the Victoria Embankment, London, on 14 October 1895. In it they stated their engineer had been in consultation with the Thames Valley Drainage Commission and improvements would be completed within three years. The official report of a detailed inspection made the previous April by four inspectors was printed. It bore no references to ferries; two were shown on the map which went with the report, Duxford and Bablockhythe. The towing paths between New Bridge and Oxford were found to be fairly good, but generally they were not ballasted so were listed for restoration.[8]

The Thames Conservancy did improve its make-up somewhat. In 1895 their number was increased to thirty-eight but in 1918 twenty-eight members were listed, with representatives for each county through which the river passed in their jurisdiction (plus Hertfordshire). Gloucestershire and Wiltshire shared one Conservator between them, and each of the big boroughs and urban districts were represented, with some sharing. Four persons were appointed by the Board of Trade.[9] An interesting insight into how Conservators were elected is gained from a document from the Ministry of Transport dated March 1921 and deposited in the National Archives. Proposals for a new Conservator were being called for and a list of MPs was sent with red ticks marked against the names considered suitable by the Minister. Will Crooks' name was included. He was well known in the lower river, a Woolwich ferry boat was named after him. But Crooks was a Labour party member and did not get a tick. In fact none of the London members had a tick.[10]

Each year the Conservancy issued a review of their work and affairs during the previous twelve months which was usually published in newspapers. In May 1887 they reported improvements had been made to the navigation above Oxford. Several drainage schemes were accomplished in conjunction with the Thames Valley Drainage Commission. They were intended to alleviate flooding and were paid for by levying a tax on land between Lechlade and Clifton Hampden, the only part of the river where a contribution was made by landowners for improvements. The newspaper comments on the inadvisability of some bye-laws in an Act passing through Parliament at the time. It was concerned mainly with boats being registered, whilst ignoring the fact that nothing was to be done about overcrowding or about irresponsible persons being allowed to hire light skiffs and racing boats, 'the incursions of 'Arry, of late so marked, are to continue unchecked'.[11]

*The Times* published the annual review of 1890 which was concerned mainly with affairs of the river below Teddington that the Conservancy still controlled. They had spent a lot of time and money in marking and bringing up wrecks, forty-six in all. On the upper river, dredging accounted for much of their work as well as further drainage schemes above Long Wittenham. When appearing before a Standing Committee of the House of Commons with the Drainage Commissioners, the Conservators agreed to spend £2,500 p.a. on restoration and maintenance of the works between Cricklade and Long Wittenham.[12]

Estimates were printed for Thames Conservancy expenditure each year. They are difficult to understand, not being in the double-entry accounting system. For instance, in the 1908 estimate is an amount of £180 for enlargement of Cookham ferry cottage, but the amount actually spent was £24 11s 09d. It appeared again in the 1909 estimates. The same happened with general repairs to cottages – in 1908 it was an estimate of £200, and was shown again in 1909 as £300. New punts for ferries were estimated in 1908 as £25 for Roebuck, £15 for Spade Oak, a new horse punt for Lashbrook was to cost £70, and general repairs to horse punts £50. The only one which appears to have materialised was a new ferry punt for Cookham at £70.[13]

Lock-keepers and ferrymen were beset by a myriad of bye-laws they had to abide by. One was 'No person without the consent of the ferryman first obtained, shall take away any or use any ferry boat or any pole or tackle belonging to such ferry'. How was he to stop them? They were kept busy in many ways, particularly their gardens. The custom of awarding prizes for lock gardens was first introduced in 1898. Competition was fierce and results were published in newspapers. The Sir Reginald Hanson Challenge Cup for the best-kept lock, weir or ferry garden was given in 1930 to the overall winner, E. E. Light of Sonning Lock. The incumbent of Keen Edge ferry near Shillingford was often the winner of the ferry section being J. R. C. Overy in 1930, W. Cunningham in 1932 and in 1936 it was J. West.[14] This tradition is carried on to the present day, the gardens and surroundings of the locks are always lovely. During the Second World War employees of the Thames Conservancy joined a special section of the Home Guard – The Upper Thames Patrol. Their duty was to guard the locks, weirs and bridges. The Thames was regarded as a vulnerable through route into central England and some of the pill-boxes set up then are still to be seen close to the river.

After the First World War concerns were expressed about the excessive expenditure of the Conservancy – a figure of £60,000 was recorded. There was a question of the Conservancy being taken over under the Ministry of Transport Act, so that a direction to increase rates and tolls could be issued. Conservators gave their consent, but this reform was to come later.[15] Further consideration was made in 1937 when the Works and Navigation Committee gave its report on a recent inspection of the river. They found that there was a decreasing use of the ferries set up originally by the Board to assist navigation by the towing path crossing the river. Now that horses were no longer used for haling, the ferries were being used by people crossing for other unremunerative purposes. There were then only nine ferries still under the Conservator's control: Keen Edge, Chalmore Hole, Gatehampton, Roebuck, Spade Oak, Lashbrook, Aston-Hambledon, Cookham Upper and Cookham Lower. One ferryman was employed at each ferry, usually with a house attached. After the meeting an official spokesman said, 'The merits of each one of the ferries will be considered separately before any decisions are reached'.[16] All these Conservators' ferries were closed eventually, thus making difficulties for the Thames Path, a National Heritage Trail which was being planned at the same time.

At their Annual Board meeting in April 1946 the Conservators approved a scheme for new engineers' headquarters at Reading at an estimated cost of £94,000 of which £35,600 was for the offices. The chairman welcomed Mrs M. M. Ashdown as Labour representative for Heston and Isleworth, the first woman member of the Board since its reconstitution in 1909. 'He thought they might congratulate Father Thames on the arrival of a daughter'.[17] The Conservancy finally moved into their new skyscraper headquarters at Reading in April 1973.[18]

Another Thames Conservancy Act was passed in 1950 which was mostly concerned with finance, and secured its revenue for the future. The number of members was increased by four, to thirty-eight. At the annual meeting held in January 1951 the chairman reported that the standard of maintenance following the war had been restored. Three hundred people were now employed, plus contractors. Pollution and sewage were still major problems but were being dealt with, as well as bathing.[19] As regards the Thames Path (or river walk as they called it), a survey was called for.

The River Thames Conservancy was disbanded in 1974 to become the Thames Water Authority, but it continued as The Thames Conservancy Division under that Authority. In turn it came under the umbrella of the National Rivers Authority in 1990. Then, in 1996 the Environment Agency took over the management of the Thames as part of their far-reaching portfolio. They operate the affairs of the river from their purpose-built offices at King's Meadow House in Reading, close to the river. Environment issues are of paramount importance, and recently the Thames has

Buscot Lock. Metal marker post *in situ*, 21 February 2009.

won an award for their achievements in this field. The Thames Division also deals with soundings of the river bed and dredging, boat licences, fishing licences and hydrology. Regular checks on quality of water are made by experts at set stations along the course of the river. Some say the Environment Agency has too much responsibility and there is a movement afoot to put conservation of rivers under the aegis of a general waterway authority in the future. Whatever happens, the Thames will remain a separate entity because of its beauty and its unique role as the second longest river in this country.

# CHAPTER FIVE
# Following the River (Towpaths)

To take advantage of the River Thames as a highway between London and the West for the passage of goods in both directions, the propulsion of vessels would need to be aided in some way. Rowing was the obvious method for light vessels carrying passengers, but as trade increased and larger barges were built, manpower was used. Thacker found a reference in an Act of 1623 to towing by horses, but this method was not used generally until much later.

The teams of men engaged in the work of pulling the boats along were called 'bow hauliers' or 'halers'. There is some dispute about the exact meaning of the term. Some believe it refers to the way of pulling – by a rope attached to the bow (pronounced bough) of the vessel. Others consider it refers to the harness occasionally worn by the men on their shoulders which was in the shape of a bow (as in ribbon). Actually some engravings show the rope attached to the mast, but again, why was there a mast when sailing on the river was not possible? The men evoked pity from those who witnessed them at work. They were strong and stocky and being of a low class were poor, with no chance to better themselves. Their work was spasmodic and on a daily basis according to demand and the state of the river. If the river was in flood, there could be no work for weeks. No work, no pay! Speaking of the bow hauliers by the River Severn at Ironbridge, Shropshire, the Swiss-born vicar of Madeley, John Fletcher (c. 1729–85) compares the men with horses doing this strenuous work.[1]

> How are they bathed in sweat and rain. Fastened to their line as horses to their traces, wherein do they differ from the laborious brutes? Not in an erect posture of the body, for in the intenseness of their toil, they bend forward, their head is foremost, and their hand upon the ground. If there is any difference it consists in this; horses are indulged with a collar to save their breasts; and these; as if theirs were not worth saving draw without one; the beasts tug in patient silence and mutual harmony; but the men with loud contention and horrible imprecations.

At first the practice of bow hauling was performed on an ad hoc basis, with no defined path on the banks. The teams would pass through a riparian owner's land free of charge and where it was necessary to change banks, it is supposed another team would be waiting on the other side and the rope was thrown to them.[2] As trade on the river increased so did the difficulties of navigation, especially from the mills and weirs. Owners were charging exorbitant tolls for passing them, causing the cost of water carriage to rise. Legislation sought to redress this by the Act of 1730 and stated that persons were now charging for bow hauliers using their land 'which paths used to be free for men to tow'.[3] The barges were larger, so 'towing requires such numbers of men as renders it very chargeable, and it is found much more convenient to tow with horses'. An estimate of the cost of taking a loaded barge from Mapledurham upstream to Oxford was compiled around 1770.[4] This included charges for towing by men and by horses in different sections; forty hirelings (bow hauliers) to Day's Lock, taking two days at 5/- each cost £10. To provide the men with provisions, beer and one night's lodging cost £4. For another forty men towing from Culham to Oxford cost 2/6d each, equalling £5. To make the same journey using horses instead of men was estimated at £3 15s less.

In matters concerning the improvement of navigation, all the eminent surveyors called in to report emphasised the importance of having horse towing paths, but this ideal was not easy to achieve. The Act of 1771 was a step forward and recognised the difficulties encountered by bow hauliers when they were replaced by horses. Item twenty-four states, 'forasmuch as the drawing of barges by horses instead of men, on all or many more banks than at present have horse towing paths, may deprive many men who are now employed in drawing such barges of their usual livelihood, as several such men are or may become through sickness, age or bodily infirmity, disabled from earning their daily bread by any other sort of labour … it is to be enacted that the Commissioners may bring such a case to the general meeting and the Treasurer is to relieve the disabled man by a sum not exceeding four shillings per week.'[5] By 1780 the horse towing path had been made as far as Pangbourne but the old track for men still existed. Perhaps bargemasters for a time had a choice – men or horses? No matter which, riparian owners still charged and were compensated whenever the towropes destroyed their osier beds, willows were a lucrative crop.

Various reports were made in the 1790s on behalf of the Thames Commissioners on the progress made after the Acts to improve navigation were passed. Henry Allnutt, General Clerk to the Commissioners, reported in 1792 that the Commissioners had made a continuous horse towing path upstream from near Staines to Oxford, about 64 miles.[6] However, there were still about 15 miles of other horse towing paths 'in various disjunct parts with gates, bridges and other works necessary' These were in private hands and tolls were charged for them. Allnutt gives the total mileage between Staines and Lechlade to be 105 miles, leaving 26 miles presumably unimproved. Some private surveyors had made reports, but the only ones working for the Commissioners were John Treacher, who was responsible for the fourth, fifth and sixth districts, and John Clarke for the second and third districts. Treacher stated there was no proper towing path between Nuneham and Oxford in the fifth district. Apparently the reason was due to Lord Harcourt not allowing towing through his meadow at Nuneham, so the horses had to cross to the other side and ferries were set up for the purpose. Concern was felt over the state of the towing path between Oxford and Godstow where it passed through low-lying Port Meadow, the common land owned by the City of Oxford since time immemorial. The towpath had been made on the left (east) bank at the river's edge of the meadow, but the banks were insecure and it had been washed away in the floods. Treacher disagreed with Robert Mylne who considered it would be better to use the parallel Wytham stream further away from the river on the west bank as the main navigation channel. It would be less expensive and the towing path would be built on higher, more solid ground and be nearer to the deep navigable water when it joined the river again. The only problem was the willow trees which would need to be cut down. Treacher and Josiah Clowes agreed the navigation channel should continue to be the one skirting Port Meadow. Surveyor Robert Whitworth voiced the opinion that as the Port Meadow was one of the shallowest places it would be better to construct the towing path on solid ground rather than raise it out of the bed of the river, where horses had to walk through water, as this would cost less. At the General Meeting of the sixth district held on 27 July 1791 some were of the opinion that the towing path from Godstow to Osney should be expedited while the water was low. That part, already begun on the south side of the meadow, should be continued further into the bed of the river where the horses tow at present. However, an estimate for £102 10s was accepted to make the towing path on the Binsey (west) side. On the east side the work to construct a bank to 'keep the river in bounds' was to be included.

Thomas Court, a bargemaster of Oxford, gave a long account of the workings of the towpath to a Thames Commissioners Committee in 1793. Asked how many horses were used in towing a barge of seventy tons against the stream from Staines, he replied as follows.

> From Stadbury (at Shepperton) to Windsor 10 or 12
> From Windsor to Hamlington Bank 8
> From Hamlington bank to Boulters 10 and 12
> From Boulters to Poulters' Horsey 6
> From Poulters' Horsey to Edsor (Hedsor, near Cookham?) 8
> From Edsor to Spade Oak 8
> From Spade Oak to Marlow 8
> From Marlow to Henley 5 or 6
> From Henley to Kennet's Mouth (Reading) 8
> From Kennet's Mouth to Geddington (Gatehampton?) 10
> From Geddington to Chamberhole (Chalmore Hole) 6
> From Chamberhole to Benson 7 or 8
> From Benson to Abingdon 10 or 11, sometimes 12

Horses towing Thames barges upstream on the Cliveden Reach by using a rope attached to a mast. Engraving from the *Copper Plate Magazine*, 1792.

From Abingdon they used five of their own horses to Oxford. Between Oxford and Lechlade it was necessary to transfer the cargo into three separate boats, each with three horses to haul them. For each of the above stages the horses would have been hired either from private riparian owners, the Thames Commissioners or their agents. To traverse the towing paths there would be another toll. Court explained that on top of these charges would be the cost of the horse lines, or towing ropes. They would last only for three voyages at a cost of £10–11 each.

When heavy goods were carried downstream, usually a single horse was needed to draw the barge out of the different pounds and along the reaches that lead to the pound locks. Then such commodities as iron, copper, tin, manufactured and pig iron, brass, spelter, cannon, cheese, nails and other iron goods and bomb shells were taken. A barge master would be lucky to get such a load. Coal was too expensive for Court to handle. His cargoes taken upstream included groceries, deals, foreign timber, merchandise of every kind, a few coals, raw hides for Tewkesbury and Worcester and gunpowder for Bristol and Liverpool.

At the same meeting one of the Commissioners reported that in the second district the towing path had been made and bridges and gates erected for towing by horses throughout the district. Both the third and fourth districts were able to report similar progress. In the fifth district the towing path had been made as far as Nuneham but orders had been given to complete it to Oxford immediately. The sixth district had towing paths only in the upper part but little had been done to improve it just above Oxford. After hearing the reports the Commissioners were of the opinion that navigation would not or could not be improved until all the obstructions were removed and all the locks, weirs etc. were purchased or leased so that the whole navigation was under the absolute control of the Commissioners. Consideration was given to the possibility of setting up a new corporate body. This did not happen for another seventy years.

None of the reports seem to have given a list of the places where horse ferries needed to be set up for when the towing path changed banks although there was an appended list giving places where tolls were collected on the upward journeys. The list included most of the places that had locks and ferries, like Boulters, Hurley, Hambleden, Sandford, etc. Jessop had stated earlier that towpaths which were in low and wet places needed to be raised above the water for convenience and safety. Also trees on the banks must be cut down to allow the towing path to continue along the bank for as long as possible, to avoid the necessity of carrying horses frequently across the river, a costly business. Jessop stressed a piece of land 9 feet wide was sufficient for a towpath used by horses. If it had to be raised, 18 inches would be high enough This may upset landowners on the opposite bank, but he said 'it should oblige them to raise their banks also, it will do them most essential service'. The cost, Jessop opined, was not prohibitive to landowners at only ten shillings per acre. There were about 12 miles where the towpath needed to be raised by the Commission and this could be achieved for about £50 per mile for the raising and covering with gravel. Fifty-four horse bridges were necessary to cross over drains, with an average of £5 each. To cross one river and four streams would cost about £60. The money for such work could be raised by an annual rent. Robert Mylne agreed in general to Jessop's recommendations and drew a red line on a map of the river along which bank the towing path should run.

The 1751 Navigation Act had forbidden the Commissioners to alter, change or remove any of the towing paths or landing places which were in use at the time, without consent of the owners. The 1771 Act gave the Commissioners more freedom in the matter, except they were not to make any new towing paths or landing places over or through any land belonging to Richard Mitchell of Culham Court near

Wargrave.[7] Nor could they build any bridge, nor station any boat or float within 200 yards of any island or lands belonging to him. Not all riparian landowners were so unsympathetic, most were willing to sell land to the Commission, whilst others retained the land and charged rent for the towing path and perhaps hired out the horses as well. The early minute books of the Thames Commission, between 1771 and 1784, show that its main concern was the horse towing path. With regards to width, the towing path for men would be 9 feet wide, but for horses it should be widened by 9 feet, to give a width of 6 yards to accommodate horses and their driver.[8] Evidence of this width can still be seen both in the approaches to the one-time ferries and the path along the bank, as at Old Windsor, opposite Wraysbury.

Robert Treacher kept a ledger of all the work he had supervised for the Commission. On 21 October 1789 he records that work had begun on two stops (gates?) for the towing path at Clifton ferry (where the banks are steep).[9] Three carpenters worked for 5½ days each and received £1 15s 9d between them. Four labourers worked for five days each and shared £1 6s 8d. More work and ballasting was done the following week. It is not clear how much of the construction work was undertaken by the Commission themselves or if outside labour was engaged. The first towing path toll was taken in 1771 for the completed path between Windsor Bridge and Maidenhead Bridge at 3d per ton. When the Boulter's Lock section was completed the price rose to 7d. The toll collector at Boulter's was allowed 4s 6d a week for taking care of and driving the horses for towing the barges there.[10] It was in addition to his former allowance. 'Luddites' expressed their anger at the horse towing path at Windsor by pulling down the gates. A reward was offered for information about the culprits.

A new Act passed in 1795 ratified those issued previously and gave more powers to the Commission. A horse towing path was now most urgent. 'It would greatly conduce to the benefit and advantage of the navigation if a free, continued, uninterrupted and public horse towing path were made and established throughout the whole of the navigation, so that barge masters or other persons might employ their own horses or cattle in the towing of barges, boats and vessels either upward or downward, without interruption or impediment.[11] Now it shall be lawful for the Commissioners to purchase and make any such horse towing paths, roads and ways for the haling of barges, boats and vessels or for passing from any public road to any horse towing path as the commissioners shall think convenient and necessary over and through any lands or grounds whatsoever (except those on which a messuage or tenement is built)'. The Commissioners were to give notice of all places where they planned to build a horse towing path by compulsory purchase to owners. They were to pay recompense for any losses or damages incurred. However, they were not allowed to erect any campshot (fencing) 'for the purpose of haling barges or vessels on the navigation before or against the Park, Paddock, inclosed Lawn or planted Avenue, belonging to Anthony Morris Storer Esq. at Purley'. Storer (1746–99) was a collector and man of fashion, a member of the Dilettanti Society who had inherited great wealth, made in Jamaica, from his father.[12] When he bought the Purley estate he engaged Humphrey Repton, the landscape architect, to improve the grounds beside the Thames. No doubt he campaigned in Parliament through influential friends to have the clause inserted in the Act in order to preserve his newly laid-out grounds. Henry Allnutt had written to Storer on behalf of the Thames Navigation Commission on 25 January 1794 concerning the status of the land proposed to be used for the towing path at Purley.[13] Three days later another letter from Matthias Deane was sent to Francis Annesley MP. Storer, an old Etonian, had friends in high places, thus he was able to make an impact on the plans of the Thames Commission. His relations with the Commission were still not good for on 11 July he sent a letter to Allnutt giving the Commission notice to quit a 'yeate' (ait?) which had been taken from a meadow adjoining the towing path. When he died, Storer left money to his nephew to build a new mansion along the lines of neighbouring Basildon House. The estate then became Purley Park.

Despite many entries in the cash books detailing work done on the towpaths – for instance those sections between Oxford and Lechlade undertaken in 1797 – the situation continued to be unsatisfactory. A report given in July 1811 of a joint survey undertaken by a Committee from the City of London and the Commission from Lechlade to London stated that that particular section had been improved by pound locks but still 'needs a substantial and uninterrupted Horse Towing Path'.[14] Allnutt kept a Towpath Rental Book between 1797 and 1813 in which payments and receipts for various sections of towing paths are listed, including some 'Ferry Lanes', the approaches to the ferries. An item of £2 10s 2¼d is entered for Ferry Lane, Pangbourne, in 1795, and one for King's Meadow Reading in 1801 is £10 7½d.[15] The method of accounting does not make clear which are debits and which receipts – probably half and half. Among the Treacher papers is preserved a small *bilet doux* which is a handwritten note inscribed on the front, 'Mrs Hewett's account for towing path'.[16] It is addressed from The Commissioners of the Thames Navigation to John Hewett and John Nicholas Esq. and was for five years' rent of the towing path from Gatehampton Meadow to Goring Mill from Michaelmas 1818 to Michaelmas 1823. Also, for one year's rent of the towpath from Gatehampton Meadow to Streatley Ferry (about 100 yards shorter) from Michaelmas 1823 to Michaelmas 1824. The amount paid is not given, but obviously the Commission were in arrears. John Hewett was the tenant of Quernes Farm at Goring.[17] He was mentioned by Arthur Young in *View of the Agriculture of Oxfordshire*, 1809.

Inevitably the mis-management of the towing path led to some disasters. The Thames & Severn Canal Company was ever mindful of the way the path was looked after because it affected the efficiency of its business – the canal could not exist without the proper navigation of the Thames. On 13 March 1827, John Denyer, the Agent/Manager, wrote to the Treasurer of his company: 'The want of "Guide Posts on various parts of the Towing Path on the Thames as noticed in my letter to the Committee (26 February) was exemplified last week, two horses being drowned near Rose's Weir and their drivers nearly sharing the same fate'.[18] Landowners were also unhappy. In 1840 Sir George Young of Formosa, Cookham, wrote to the Commission asking that a fence be erected to prevent encroachment onto his land by towing horses.[19] Not only would the horses be wearing down his grass, but would be eating it too. The quality of the towpath surface was not robust. James Thorne described it in *Rambles by Rivers – The Thames* in 1849, writing, 'It is not a narrow winding path, worn out of the soft green grass … but a broad towing path for horses, formed of flint stones and flanked by a ditch – generally. At times the surface is sound, others mud.'[20]

Following the setting-up of the Thames Conservancy on the Upper Thames in 1866 it was expected that conditions for navigation and the proper management of the towing paths would improve. This took a long time to happen, as a case before the Court of Common Pleas held on 5 July 1872 testifies.[21] The plaintiff was one Winch, the defendants the Conservators of the River Thames. The case followed on from an action brought by Winch at the Surrey Spring Assizes for compensation as three of his towing horses had drowned in the river when the towing path bank gave way. One horse fell first, dragging the other two after him. The plaintiff was given damages of £100 but the ruling was 'nisi', meaning 'not finished'. Therefore the case was then brought to the other court. The Winch family were based in Shepperton on the Lower Thames and were the largest owners of barge horses in the district.[22] Their monopoly began in 1787 when George Winch set up as a farmer and haulier. He died in 1805 and his eldest son, also George, was killed by a fall from his horse in 1835, by which time the family was described as 'people of some consideration in the neighbourhood'. The exact place where the accident happened is not given, but it could have been anywhere as far as Windsor or its neighbourhood.

The defendants were charged with negligence in the management and conduct of a portion of the banks and towing paths on the River Thames and not keeping them in a reasonably safe and proper condition for towing barges. The question of law was whether, under the various Acts of Parliament and the application of common law, the defendants were under any legal liability for the repair and maintenance of the towing paths on the bank. The history of the Conservators and the points about the towing paths given in the Acts were outlined to the Court. It was pointed out specifically that prior to the Act of 1866 which set up the Thames Conservators, the owners of certain locks and weirs were entitled to take tolls on them, provided they undertook to keep them in repair. This Act abolished these private tolls and the private structures became the property of the Conservators, along with the need to repair them, and the defendants could charge tolls to pay for the repairs.

There was some ambiguity. It was announced 'there are no words directly imposing the obligation to repair banks and towing paths on the defendants as in the case with locks etc.' but the towing paths and the right to take toll for passing along them was not absolutely transferred to the defendants in the same manner as for locks etc., so there was no necessity for any such express enactment with respect to towing paths and the defendant's rights and liabilities. As a reference to this point the attention of the court was drawn to the former Acts 'as well as to the general scope and language of the Act'. It was pointed out that the Thames Commissioners had obtained powers to make needful repairs and to improve the navigation, which included banks and towing paths. All these powers had been confirmed by the 1866 Act.

58 The Towing Path, Pangbourne.

Photo by Tidbury

An example of a typical Thames conservancy five-barred gate on the towing path with a substantial bridge over a small brook. From a postcard.

After their inauguration the Conservators had made arrangements to secure the banks at certain places, and they then paid an annual rent to the owners of the towpaths per rod. At Teddington Lock where the territory of their jurisdiction is entered they could take an aggregate toll for the entire navigation and the towing paths. They have now acquired and have use of the whole of the towing paths along the river and the right to take toll over them. It was explained that the arrangement made with the owner of the towpath was by parol (word of mouth) only. However, in this case the owner must have known what powers the Conservators had to enable the public to have and enjoy the use of the towing path, including repairing them.

The question was asked, 'What is the Towing Path?' The court was told it was impossible to confine it to the 'mere beaten track described to have been made principally by single horses towing downstream, for in towing upstream the horses cannot always be in a direct line, and there must be space for them as well as the driver and proper use of the tow line. We think the towing path must include so much of the bank as necessary and proper for the use of towing barges and is reasonably and properly used as such'. The defendants had acquired the towing path for the use of the public, subject to payment of toll (Winch had paid toll), then invited the public to use it and pay them. Also they employed a superintendent and engineer to inspect and report and the 'faults were part of the engineer's job to identify'.

'The jury found the towing paths and banks were not in a fit and proper condition for proper use as towing paths. This was the cause of the accident. There was no neglect in the navigation of the barge or in the management of the horses'. They stated that 'it would be very strange if the defendants were at liberty to make orders upon the owners to do repairs whilst they received the tolls from the public'. Furthermore, the defendants contended there was no right of towing on the banks of the river, but the court maintained that there is (according to a previous case) on most navigable rivers, by custom. But there is no objection to the dedication of a way to the public for a limited purpose but that a towing path may be a highway to be used only for the purpose of towing barges or other vessels. The decision of the court was in favour of the plaintiff and the rule was discharged.

With the advent of steam tugs to tow the barges and some barges becoming motor driven, together with less freight traffic on the river, the towing paths fell into disuse at the beginning of the twentieth century. In 1920 the Conservators paid out £149 in rents for the towpaths they did not themselves own.[23] A minute dated 17 March 1920 in the Ministry of Transport records concerns a report on the expenditure of the Thames Conservancy. They spent a total of £60,060 p.a. at their headquarters. It was suggested they 'should seek legislature to relieve themselves of the maintenance of the banks and towing paths and place it under local authorities, on the grounds that towing from the banks is now obsolete and the towpaths have become footpaths' for the general public. This matter was not settled until after the Second World War when the Thames Path was created.

Although by the end of the nineteenth century trade on the Thames had dwindled considerably, there was increasing use of the river by the leisured classes. In the decade of the 1880s alone at least five important books on the Thames as a leisure resort were published: *Our River* by George Leslie, son of the biographer of John Constable; *A Trip on the Thames* by Julia Isham Taylor; *The Lazy Minstrel*, poems about the river by Joseph Ashby-Sterry; *A Dictionary of the Thames* by Charles Dickens Jnr; and that all-time favourite, *Three Men in a Boat* by Jerome K. Jerome. Ashby-Sterry (1838–1917) was a journalist, painter and novelist who was passionate about the River Thames.[24] In an article he wrote for the *Graphic* on 18 June 1898 he expresses his indignation on learning that the Thames Conservancy were considering allowing cyclists to use the tow path.[25] 'Are we all to be crushed beneath the wheels of this Modern Juggernaut? ... Are the placid delights of the towpath of the Upper Thames to be invaded by the whirr of the wheel and the ting-tang of the bell? Is no place to be reserved for the pedestrian?' He goes on to explain that the towpath, although flat, it is not safe to cycle on, being full of stones, potholes and tree stumps and dangerous for both the cyclist and pedestrian. Perish the thought that some may ride abreast! However, he need not have worried too much, because the towpath, now the Thames Path, is not a cycle track; cyclists have no rights to ride on it, although they are permitted to do so if special precautions are taken to ensure the safety of walkers, who have priority. Cyclists must dismount when passing groups with children, animals and elderly or disabled persons. Riding through lock gardens or riverside public parks is strictly forbidden. In fact it is officially recommended that cyclists use the Sustrans Thames Valley cycle route instead.[26]

The proposal for a long-distance path beside the Thames was first mooted in the 1930s when the cost of keeping up the towing paths and the associated ferries was becoming unjustified. The year 1926 was generally accepted as the date when the towpaths had 'definitely ceased to be a necessity for purposes of navigation'. In 1937 the Conservators began plans to close some more ferries, some had closed already, but fourteen remained. Nothing was done during the war years, 1939–45, and when the plans were taken up again in 1948, the fourteen ferries still remained. However, the National Parks Commission rejected the plans put before them in 1952 and the subject was postponed indefinitely. But it did not go away. Ferries closed and by 1955 when things began to stir again, only five ferries were left. They were Benson, Temple, two at Cookham, My Lady and Cookham (Upper) ferry, and Bablockhythe which was a private ferry. The plan was revived by the ubiquitous 'letter to the Times' published on 13 August 1955.[27] Actually this one was a long *Three Men in a Boat* type account of a walk by the river from Reading to Oxford, entitled *Two Men on the Towpath to Oxford*: 'A Summer Pilgrimage Along the Deserted Banks of the Thames'. The anonymous Correspondent writes amusingly of the trials and tribulations he and his companion, Walker, encountered, including the lack of ferries to continue walking the towpath on the opposite bank. Sometimes they had to retrace their steps to cross at a bridge, another time they borrowed a boat from a friend. At times the path was like a jungle and impassable so they had to take to the road more than once.

Five days later, 'A Special Correspondent' picked up on *Two Men* and laid some facts about the ferries before the public in a brief résumé explained that two of the remaining ferries, Benson and Temple, were by locks and accordingly were worked by lock-keepers.[28] The other three were worked by ferrymen who had a Conservancy House close by but each was working at a considerable loss, and were kept for their amenity value. Sometimes the river could be crossed at a lock, or weir as at Rushey. The cudgels were taken up by the the River Thames Society and by the Rambler's Association, led by their vice president, David Sharp, who campaigned assiduously for the path and gave it much publicity. After the path opened he wrote the best guide on behalf of the Ramblers' Association and the Countryside Agency.[29] In 1977 the Ramblers published a new concept for the walk which obviated the need for ferries, that being the main bone of contention. This statement is borne out by a report published by the Countryside Commission (now the Countryside Agency) in 1987 where they say to build a new footbridge or negotiate a new right of way would be far cheaper than reinstating a ferry.[30] Nevertheless, they were hoping some private ferries would be able to set up along the route. To avoid old ferry routes new footpaths could be made, especially where rights of way already existed, as at Buscot and others could be negotiated. New footbridges were planned, at Spade Oak by attaching a girder

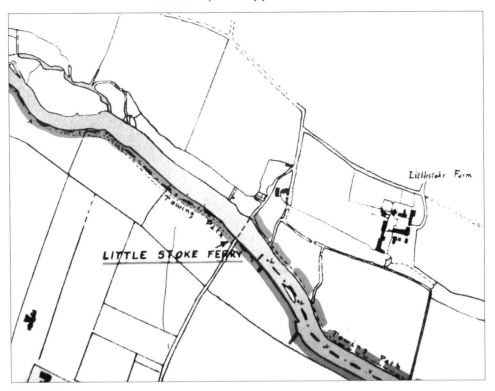

Plans showing how the Thames Path was made. At Little Stoke, a horse ferry had taken horses from the left bank to the Cholsey side. Now the towing path was to be continued on that side to Moulsford downstream. From a book of plans courtesy of Gloucestershire Archives.

extension to the railway bridge at Bourne End, and at Temple, where a splendid single arched timber bridge was nearing completion.

In 1989 the Thames Path was declared a National Trail and since then thousands of people have used it each year, summer and winter. It is 184 miles long, from Thames Head, near Kemble to the Thames Barrier near Woolwich. Although the path is designated as a public footpath, it is actually on private land and should be treated as such. Cyclists may use it on some short sections, otherwise they are trespassing. The Countryside Agency and the Environment Agency both work to administer the path in association with local authorities. It is well kept and free. Unfortunately, the several deviations are necessary; some are along busy roads, as at Roebuck, and at Keen Edge near Shillingford, where the access to the road is positively dangerous. From time to time the authorities do make improvements.

Following the river but almost hidden from view in the undergrowth is a line of concrete gun emplacements or pill boxes hastily erected in 1940 between June and August due to the threat of German invasion. Built under the auspices of Sir Edmund Ironside (1880–1959), they were meant for use by the Home Guard, although they were not much used, and not at all after Sir Edmund stepped down and no more pill boxes were built.[31] Ironside had intended them to serve as a delaying tactic, but there was not enough artillery to go round and the volunteer forces were hardly trained at all. Technically this line along the Thames began at Pangbourne and known as Stopline Red, it proceeded westwards, towards Bristol. It is thought about fifty pillboxes were constructed along the Upper Thames, all of type FW3/22 and all surrounded by an anti-tank ditch. Some also had adjacent 'dragons'teeth', a pattern of concrete pyramids about three feet high, intended to act as a barricade against tanks. Most pill boxes are still *in situ* because it has proved difficult to destroy them. Enthusiasts spend time finding and recording them and those of the Stopline Red are regarded amongst the best preserved.[32] They have served as farm buildings, storage sheds and shelters or unspeakable rubbish dumps. Occasionally they have become inhabited, as at Duxford in a coppice beyond the ford. There, where it is difficult to work out why a pill box was built because the Thames at that spot was no longer the navigable stream, lived an eccentric, Arthur Merrick, in the 1950s. By repute he was a very, very good fisherman. He had a boat and a motorbike and travelled to work as a porter at the Radcliffe Infirmary in Oxford each day.[33]

## CHAPTER SIX

# Ferries Between Lechlade and Newbridge

## LECHLADE

The original crossing of the River Thames below the town of Lechlade was a ford at or just above the present St John's Bridge (Exp.170 222 990).[1] A piece of land there was recorded as The Lade in 1246.[2] As the crossing served the main route between the City of Gloucester and mid-Gloucestershire to London, the ford was soon replaced by a bridge, known to have been in existence before 1228. Close by on the north side of the bridge the owners of the manor built a hospital or priory dedicated to St John the Baptist, to serve the travellers and wayfarers. The hospital was responsible for the maintenance of St John's Bridge and the prior received grants of pontage in 1338, 1341 and 1388. It had a long causeway of twenty arches leading towards Buscot on the south bank.[3]

When the priory was dissolved in 1472 some of the materials from its buildings, including the chapel, were used to repair the bridge. The priory site is now occupied by a mobile homes park. The Lords of the Manor became owners of the hospital and took over the right to take toll on barges passing beneath the bridge. The Thames Commissioners, as part of their business to improve navigation, bypassed the bridge and its toll when they constructed a new shortcut in 1791 with a lock. This is now the main navigation channel, and the Thames Path runs along its southern bank and passes the statue of Father Thames which formerly guarded the spring in Trewsbury Mead. The famous Trout Inn abuts the bridge on its Northern approach. An inn has stood here since before 1692 when it was first recorded. First named the Baptist's Head, after the priory, it was sold by the manor in 1800 together with fishing rights and the name changed in 1831.

Crossing the road from St John's Lock, the towpath – now the Thames Path – follows the meandering river and crosses a side stream to Bloomers Hole where there was once a ferry from Bloomer Meadow. Ireland relates a strange phenomenon in this stretch of river. He said that watermen had asserted the river in this vicinity started to freeze firstly at the bottom. They frequently found 'icicles adhering to the keels when there is no appearance of ice on the surface'.[4] Dr Plot, the eminent natural historian of Oxfordshire, confirmed it was caused by salts in the water at this point. Nothing is known of this ferry except it is shown as a crossing place on the plan made for the alterations to the towpath required for the Thames Path to be made. Probably it was intended to avoid the bridge which was always difficult to manoeuvre. The initial plan shows the path crossing the bridge, then taking a right turn along Kelmscot Lane just after the Trout Inn until it turned right back to the river by a new path to be made alongside a drain. Because of difficulties in using this new way it was decided

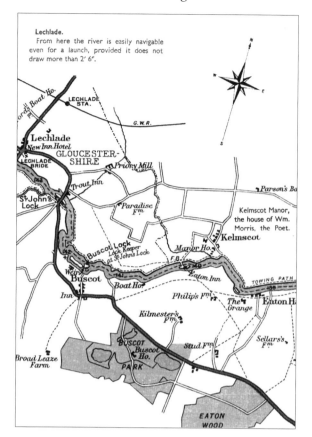

Map showing the river from Lechlade. St John's Bridge is situated by the Trout Inn. From *Stanford's New Map of the River Thames, c.* 1900.

Lechlade. The Trout Inn from St John's Bridge. Postcard issued before the Second World War.

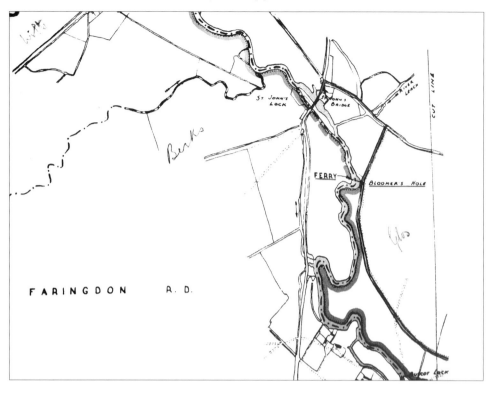

Plan showing the position of Bloomer's Hole ferry, now replaced by a footbridge. From a book of plans for the Thames Path, 1947, courtesy of Gloucestershire Archives.

by the Countryside Agency to build a footbridge instead. It was commissioned from Oxfordshire County Council who constructed it in steel and cladded it with timber, to give the appearance of a timber bridge, like others on the Path. Two 28-ton steel beams were lowered into place by helicopter in the year 2000. From Bloomers Hole the path continued using the towpath on the left bank until Buscot Lock was reached.

## BUSCOT

On the way the river sweeps towards the main road to Faringdon from Lechlade, the A417, where a little grassy parking lot marks the site of a cheese wharf. Apart from the passing traffic its peacefulness today belies the hustle and bustle of the past. From here were shipped vast quantities of Gloucestershire cheese destined for the London trade. A little further on the Path reaches Buscot Lock (Exp.170 230 981) There is no historic evidence for a ferry or ford, but there is much to interest the visitor. The pound lock was built originally by Edward Loveden Loveden (*c.* 1749–1822) of Buscot Park.[5] He was born in Cirencester to Thomas Townsend and his wife Martha, née Loveden. When Martha's brother died in 1749, the male Loveden line died out and the infant Edward succeeded to large estates, including Buscot and Eaton Hastings and a fortune. He changed his surname to Loveden by Royal Licence. Two of his wives were heiresses who also left him a fortune but he cancelled the proposed divorce from his third wife because of financial concerns. Loveden spent his time in public life, serving as MP for Abingdon between 1783 and 1796, then for Shaftesbury from

1802 until 1812. He was also a very active but controversial Thames Commissioner, regrettably not always acting in the Commission's interests, but following his own agenda to protect the large income (the largest toll on the river paid for passing both up and downriver, against the normal practice of just up journeys) he received from tolls taken at his private lock. 'Old Father Thames' was his nickname, earned by his fiery and litigious personality. Loveden held shares in the Thames & Severn Canal, opened in 1789, and caused friction when he opposed the junction with that canal and the Wilts & Berks Canal.[6] The Buscot and Eaton Hastings estates were sold in a run-down state by Loveden's great-grandson, Sir Prysse Prysse, in 1860 to Robert Tertius Campbell (*d.* 1887)

Campbell, a Scottish entrepreneur, came to the area from Australia, where he had acquired enormous wealth in the goldfields. He set about turning his 4,000-acre estates into a prosperous industrialised farm, changing it from sheep farming into dairy and arable. The chief crop was sugar beet, processed in a large distillery built in 1869 near the lock, which produced alcohol spirit for export to France for the brandy industry. By-products of sugar beet were processed for other uses, like fertiliser, which was distributed around the estates by a system of narrow gauge railways powered by tank engines. Other innovative ideas included a gasworks, concrete barns and farm buildings, a brick and tile works and a malt house. Campbell's own private wharf was made by cutting a pill connected to the Thames. His workers, who included some Frenchmen hired to work in the distillery, were given a 9-hour day. In 1863 a reservoir covering 20 acres was constructed on the hillside close to Buscot House and fed by two large pumps driven by water wheels on the Thames at Buscot Lock and another at the weir at Eaton Hastings, sometimes called Hart's Weir after the family who kept it. An irrigation system was developed to run from the reservoir.

Charles Bravo, a London lawyer, died at his house, The Priory in Balham, of poisoning in 1876. There were two inquests but never a trial and the case remains unsolved. The chief suspect was his wife Florence, who was the eldest daughter of Campbell's seven children. After her first husband died, she had an affair with Dr Gully who ran the famous spa treatment at Malvern, 'three weeks in wet sheets'. She became pregnant by him and he performed an abortion. She was a social outcast until she married Bravo who, it is said, had an eye on her fortune. His death occurred only a few months after the marriage and she never recovered her status in society. Only two years later she died of alcohol poisoning aged thirty-three and was buried at night by the porch to Buscot church.

Her father became a broken man. The French workers had returned to France so the distillery on what became known as Brandy Island was sold in 1879. Campbell's enterprises were regarded as under-capitalised and the mortgages were crippling. Gradually the estate diminished and in 1887 Campbell died and was buried with his wife in the churchyard at Eaton Hastings, bordering the river. Most of the property except Brandy Island is now in the care of the National Trust. It includes the house, most of the village, farms and land and some cottages used for holiday lets. Brandy Island is at present subject to controversy.[7] It was bought for £11 by compulsory purchase in 1949 for use as a pumping station. Thames Water became the owners and offered it for sale unsuccessfully, until in October 2009 it sold at auction for £380,000 to the owners of the boatyard and mobile homes park by the Trout Inn at Lechlade for development as a marina. This would destroy a valuable wildlife habitat for kingfishers, otters, water voles and other species as well as spoiling the setting of one of the best churches in the country, listed Grade I. Local residents have set up 'Save Brandy Island Appeal'. They claim the sale was illegal and hope the National Trust will be able to acquire the site to keep as a wildlife reserve. No further progress has yet been made.

## HART'S WEIR

Several footpaths converge at a place just before Kelmscott (Exp.170 245 986) on the left bank of the river. The Thames Path passes by, following each meander of the river; a footpath strikes off northwards to join with another towards the village, and a footbridge crosses to an island and from there three separate footpaths cross fields to scattered farms, eventually joining the main road. The island has a white shed or outhouse, a bridge over a backwater which provides mooring for a few boats and lots of humps and hollows and some ancient gnarled stumps of trees. All in all, a classic site for a ferry. This was Eaton Weir, also known as Hart's Weir and formerly known as West or Lower Farmer's Weir. Pedestrians would have crossed by a walkway above the weir. It was a famous place in the days of navigation, part of the Eaton Hastings estate and owned by Loveden and then Campbell.

Mrs Hart was the keeper of the weir in 1802 when Robert Mylne wrote 'At Mrs Hart's Weir the tackle and the whole construction of this old Wear [sic] is in very bad order and belongs as a freehold to a poor woman, who cannot afford to reconstruct it at all'.[8] She still held it in 1821, but it is doubtful if she still owned it then. Mr Campbell retained this weir and Buscot Lock when the Conservancy took over in 1866. The lock-keeper at St John's also had care of the weir and the two locks, cycling between them as necessary. Thacker was very fond of this weir, 'with its white rymers and paddles and fresh tumbling water filling the air all day long with murmurous sound'. The weir and flashlock were removed in 1936 and the timber bridge made to carry the public footpath. Alongside the weir was a popular inn, the Anchor, again extolled by Thacker who said, 'viewed from the meadows below under summer evening light (it) presents the softest imaginable grouping of mossy roof and leathery willow'. He described the interior as 'bare, sturdy, stone flagged'. When J. Penny took

Hart's Weir near Kelmscott, showing the timber bridge over the weir. The keeper has removed some rhymers to allow a flash for a fishing punt. Facing south with the Anchor Inn on the right bank. From the Halls' *Book of the Thames*.

Hart's Weir, looking downstream from the direction of Buscot. Only one of the buildings, the small white one in the centre, still exists. Photograph by Taunt, *c.* 1870. Reproduced by permission of English Heritage.

over the tenancy in January 1891 he was given charge of the weir as well. Sadly the inn burnt down on 21 January 1980 and the landlord lost his life. It was rumoured that two people who were there at the time also died. They were to be married the next day.

## EATON HASTINGS

Passing downstream, Kelmscott village is just away from the river on the left bank. A bridle path connects the Thames Path with the entrance to the village at Kelmscott Manor, the country home of William Morris and his family. Following round a bend in the river is the church and parish of Eaton Hastings, a good example of a DMV (deserted medieval village). As the river is quite shallow here and there is a slight difference in depth in the bed at Eaton Hastings, it can be assumed a ford existed many centuries ago (Exp.170 265 986). Situated on a raised platform beside the river the church, dedicated to St Michael and All Angels, has some Norman and Early English features.[9] The name Eaton Hastings suggests a crossing place where the river needed to be kept free of debris as mentioned in an earlier chapter. Being on a bend where steep banks would slump into the river from the force of water the explanation seems feasible.[10] In August 1842, Revd J. Rice, being a riparian owner, was given permission to remove an island which had formed opposite to his land.[11] Hastings was the name of the family who held the manor in 1086.

That year, the Domesday Book records a holding worth twenty shillings given by a former lord to Westminster Abbey.[12] There were then twenty-nine households centred round the church. To the south of the church, now open fields with humps, is a field named 'Old Town' which was the site of the village and traces of foundations have been found there. When a lord died in 1333 thirty-nine households were recorded but the population was diminishing even before the Black Death wreaked its havoc in 1349. By 1542/43 only four men were paid small sums in subsidy, an indication the village was then deserted. The trend in agriculture had moved from arable to pasture, requiring a smaller workforce. One pasture in Kelmscott was recorded as belonging to Eaton Hastings, thus suggesting there was communication over the river between the two places, but no ferry is mentioned until much later.

A series of indentures concerning Revd Richard Rice and two pieces of land, Mill Mead and Old Town begin in February 1837 when he took out a mortgage with Miss Martha Halcup, spinster of Falfield, Oxfordshire.[13] It mentions the pasture ground called Old Town, with a lane adjoining and two cottages with gardens in the occupation of Joseph Wiggins and Thomas Clack. A garden in the occupation of Revd Rice together with a small close and a fishery were also included. The whole was re-conveyed in 1860 by the will of Miss Martha. In 1863 Revd Price mortgaged pasture ground in Old Town to another spinster, Miss C. E. Hewlett of Mytton Lodge, Tewkesburry. The next indenture in 1865 shows Revd Rice occupying the two cottages himself. He died on 29 September 1868 and the property was left to his sons, Richard and Henry, the will being proved on 16 October 1868. Instructions were left as to the disposal of the estate, the first crop of 10 acres of hay to be taken from Mill Mead were to be sold before the sale of the Ferry House, stable, barn and other buildings.

This was the first time the ferry house had been mentioned. The executors sold the properties to Edward Sheppard and Miss E. J. Sheppard, spinster, both of 18 Durham Villas, Kensington, for £1,450. Included were the two cottages in the sole occupation of Joseph Wise and the garden attached. The Tithe map attached to the document showed Joseph Wise as tenant of the Ferry Cottage, with stable, coalhouse, barn, pigsties and garden, an area of 1 acre, and five perches in all. The ferry must have been run as a private concern by Wise, for people wanting to reach Kelmscott or to follow the towpath running on the opposite bank.

The ferry house, once two cottages, is on an island next door to the churchyard but separated from it by three short streams running from some ponds to the west and forming a semicircle round the cottage, which has its back to the river. Now listed Grade II, it was built as a small house in the seventeenth century but has had several extensions since then.[14] It is of limewashed rubble stone with a gabled thatched roof with brick chimney stacks at each end. Two stone mullioned windows survive, but no internal features. However, it gives a good idea of the appearance of the type of house which made up the village.

The Thames now cuts across a vast open plain with no settlements, only isolated farms and many smallish fields, both pasture and arable. Much of the area has now been drained, with ditches following the hedgerows. On the south bank linking Eaton Hastings with Duxford, a small hamlet of Hinton Waldrist, is a footpath, which becomes a wider bridle path some parts of the way, and which runs close to the river. Apart from that no roads use the valley bottom here. Communication between Oxfordshire on the north and Berkshire on the south would not be needed, except in summer at harvest time. Long-lost fords were then available, as portrayed by Stapleton.[15]

> And through the banks a little rural road,
> Dips to the ford, through which the lumbering wain,
> Dry o'er the water bears its towering load,
> And mounted herdsmen urge their lingering kine in vain.

Grafton Lock (Exp.170 272 992) was a likely place for a ford before the lock was built. It has several footpaths converging on it and measurements of depth of the water show that from being 2.49 it changes to only 1.26 metres near the footbridge. A large nearly rectangular field on the right bank is marked on the map as 'access land'. At one time it must have been very marshy.


## RADCOT BRIDGE

Actually three roads do cross the Thames and proceed from north to south and vice-versa. All are very busy and fast. The first is A4095 from Witney to Faringdon and crosses at Radcot Bridge, or rather bridges (Exp.170 285 995), claimed to be the oldest bridge on the Upper Thames. The hamlet of Radcot itself is mentioned in Domesday but the crossing point, a ford or primitive bridge, must have been older, connecting Mercia and Wessex. It was defended by an earthwork, thought to be Norman, just to the north, now marked on the map as 'The Garrison' and the alignment of the road was straight through it. No date is known for the bridge being built, except that it is from the fourteenth century. Jervoise describes it as 'one of the best examples of a medieval bridge over the Thames'. Records for it begin in 1312 when pontage was granted. Down the centuries Radcot Bridge has featured in various episodes of British history, leaving the bridge damaged. Following the Peasants' Revolt in 1381 the bridge was sabotaged and guarded by the Earl of Derby against the Duke of Gloucester in 1387.

After the death of Henry I in 1135, the throne was taken by Stephen, his nephew, instead of Matilda of Anjou, his daughter.[16] There followed a civil war (1139–54) in which Matilda sought to depose Stephen. In 1141 when her support was waning Matilda built a fortification or 'castle' on top of the earthworks to thwart Stephen who was holding Oxford. It meant that the road was diverted slightly to the east. The detour was retained by the Faringdon & Burford Turnpike Trust when they took over the road in 1770, and remains the same today. During the Civil War of 1642–48 the bridges were held by the Parliamentarians but taken by the Royalists who survived a skirmish by the bridge in July 1645, only to be forced to surrender in April 1646. Once again the bridge had to be reinstated, with the result that although it was the oldest founded bridge of the upper river, its fabric was much younger and its historic status was challenged by Newbridge, further downstream. Radcot Bridge crossed over the main stream of the river, but another a few yards to the north a bridge was built over another stream which led to a weir and to a millstream, now filled in, which served Monk Mill. In anticipation of extra traffic to be supplied by the Thames & Severn Canal the Thames Commission was prompted to build a new navigation cut in 1787 with a new bridge. Many alterations have taken place, making it difficult to determine where the towpath ran. Traffic lights now control traffic flow over the bridges, but they remain in constant use, with the ancient Swan Inn surviving for the convenience of travellers.

The site of Old Man's Bridge (Exp.180 299 002) as shown on the map indicates that here was an ancient ford. The former weir, known as Old Man's Weir, had a footpath across it, which it would not have unless a right of way already existed. Several footpaths come from the north and the village of Clanfield, which has a medieval

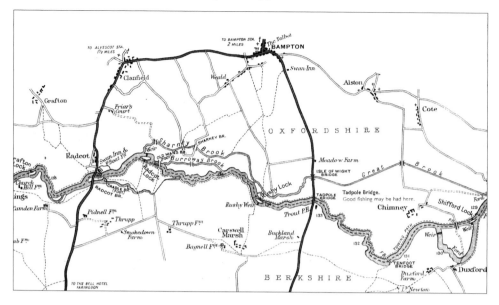

*Stanford's New Map of the River Thames, c.* 1900. Grafton Lock to Shifford Lock.

Radcot Bridge, drawn and published in aqua-tinta by Samuel Ireland in *Picturesque Views on the River Thames,* 1792.

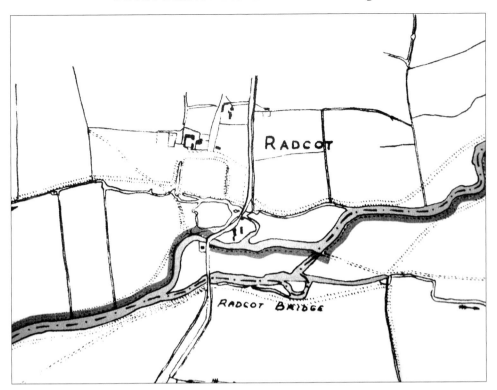

The Thames Path at Radcot bridges which uses the original towing path. The first bridge as illustrated above is the one to the south on the plan. From the Book of Plans for the Thames Path 1947. Courtesy of Gloucestershire Archives.

moated site, a former preceptory of the Knights Hospitallers.[17] The footpaths, some rights of way, some private, all converge at the wooden footbridge which was constructed in 1868 when the weir had become dilapidated and removed.[18] At least twice has the bridge been replaced at a high level. The depth of water beneath it is fairly shallow.

## RUSHY LOCK & WEIR

Rushy Lock and Weir (Exp.180 323 001) is a unique place on the Upper Thames. The main channel is crossed by a paddle and rymer weir based on a frame secured on the river bed with beams set above the river. It is listed Grade II by English Heritage and although it has been adjusted and replaced several times since first built in 1790 it remains basically the same.[19] The paddles and rymers (timber uprights) are removed manually when necessary and stored in racks in the traditional manner, thus giving a good impression of how the river and the weirs were managed. The only additions in modern times are the railings put on to the gangways as a 'health and safety' precaution. This is another case of a ford crossed by footpaths from north and south and converging at one spot. Thacker mentions a ferry, slightly upstream of the lock, as belonging to the Thames Commissioners in 1816, but it could have been much older.[20] The gangways were made to take the towpath where it changed banks instead of running the ferry. The Thames Path also crosses here and continues downstream on the north side along a metalled track to Tadpole Bridge.

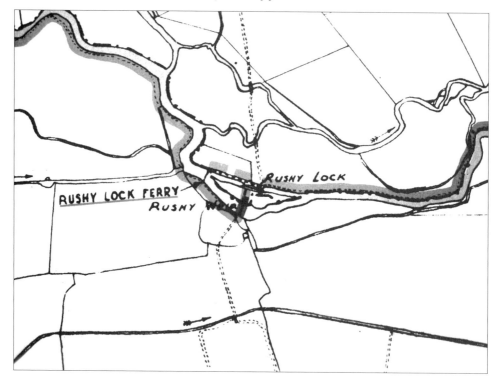

The Book of Plans for the Thames Path shows how the original towing path came from Tadpole Bridge downstream and passed behind the Conservancy house to the ferry place. When the towing path was discontinued provision was made for a footpath to cross over the weir and

## TADPOLE BRIDGE

Tadpole Bridge (Exp.180 334 005) carries a minor road from Bampton to the north and on to Buckland or to the main road A420. Bampton was an important market town and boasted a castle, some remains of which can be seen. The minor road is still very busy and has the appearance of being a turnpike road, but this cannot be verified at present (turnpikes are a subject waiting for historians to research in depth). Tadpole Bridge has one elegant arch, dated by Jervoise to 1802, which would seem likely to make it a turnpike bridge. Thacker found it on Robert Whitworth's map of 1784, and suggests there may have been an earlier bridge.[21] Although the water at this bridge crossing is not deep, it is much deeper just eastwards of the bridge where there was a weir. Thacker suggests there is no evidence for a ford, but there is a likelihood that an ancient track from the Downs would have terminated at the river near the point where the weir was later built. The Trout Inn stands by the bridge in the age-old tradition.

## TEN FOOT BRIDGE

About 1¾ miles below Tadpole is the oddly named Tenfoot Bridge (Exp.170 353 996). Various suggestions have been made for the derivation but none are really convincing. The most plausible is that when a weir was built at this location it incorporated a ten-foot flash opening. Jessop referred to it in a report of 1791 as 'the 10 feet weir'.[22] The

Thames Conservancy in 1867 found the weir to be non-functional and demolished it. As local people had established a right to cross at the weir, the Conservancy built a timber bridge to carry the footway although at first they had disputed the right. No footpath is marked on the map on the north bank, but on the south is a right of way connecting with the hamlet of Duxford and the DMV of Newton. A tumble-down thatched cottage is shown on the right bank in old prints. Access would have been required to reach the towpath on the left bank. The Oxfordshire Historic Environment Record has a question mark against Newton Deserted Medieval Village.[23] They found insufficient evidence of a village but certainly there was a settlement near Lower Newton Farm (Exp.170 357 991) which was close to the Eaton Hastings to Duxford medieval bridle path mentioned earlier and some building materials from the sixteenth or seventeenth century were found there. The ground was very low-lying.

## CHIMNEY

The small, almost inaccessible hamlet of Chimney (Exp.180 363 005) which is situated close to the river on its left bank, as seen today belies its ancient history. It is a closed community and allows no access to the river except for a poorly maintained bridle path which runs eastwards, then turns southward for 1¼ miles to reach Duxford. The OED offers no definition of the word 'chimney' to explain this place name for an Oxfordshire hamlet, so it must be a corruption, probably phonetical, of another name. One explanation is that the name was 'Ceomma,' meaning 'Ceomma's Island'. By 1069 when most of the lands formerly belonging to the Saxons had been confiscated by the Normans, Chimney with its surrounding low-lying lands was an established township.[24] A ferry existed then, probably at the point where the Thames takes a meander to the south towards Duxford and a weir was built later. It is claimed in old documents that the ferry boat was sunk in 1261, with a loss of life.

Robert Mylne, in his report printed in 1802, calls the place 'Chimley Town' and talks about the weirs in the neighbourhood which often needed a man with a cabin and a gauge to look after them.[25] In a later addition to the report Mylne advocated a new cut be made across the top of the meander between Chimney and Shifford and stated 'at Chimley is a folding footbridge and a ford for cattle through it'. Furthermore Mylne predicted that 'A new cut will leave Duxford totally deserted'.[26] However, this did not happen until nearly a century later. In 1897 a new lock was completed on dry land where the meander to Duxford resumes the direction of its normal course. Then what became the Shifford Lock Cut was made by widening a side channel and connecting the new lock to it.[27] A footbridge was constructed about halfway along the new cut to take the very old bridle path from Duxford. Later the Thames Path also adopted this route.

## DUXFORD

The Chimney Water Meadows Nature Reserve surrounds Shifford Lock and includes the entire island formed above Duxford when the new cut was made. It was developed from 2003 when Chimney Farm was bought by the Trust. A weir and a footbridge have been constructed at the western end of the loop of the river which leads to Duxford (Exp.180 360 001). To reach the ford from the north it is necessary to cross the footbridge over the new cut and follow the bridle path through the nature reserve until the river is reached through a spinney. To approach the ford from the south is like going back in time. A lane leads from the village of Hinton Waldrist to Duxford

Farm, which is a dead end. On a corner a track is signposted to the right leading to the ford. It goes past some very old timber-framed cottages, one of which has the date 1659 carved on a wooden corbel under the end of a beam.[28] Wild roses grow in the old hedge on the left. The track is metalled but has not been cleared of mud, so it would be difficult for any motor vehicle, other than a tractor, to go down it. Passing some buildings which were part of a farm, you arrive at the water's edge, overhung by weeping willows. A more tranquil spot is difficult to imagine in the twenty-first century. If you had not encountered large agricultural machinery in the lane, hardly anything has changed since the eighteenth century. This is the only surviving purpose-built ford.

The Domesday Book of 1086 gives Duxford as 'Dudoch esforde', taken from a personal name, 'Duduc's Ford'.[29] A suggestion is made that the Romans used the ford as a cross-country route, certainly it would have given access to the ancient town of Wantage to the south. It was quite a safe crossing, as far as fords go.[30] Hinton Waldrist an ancient market town, was a very important place, being part of the Honour of St Valery, a large association of estates belonging to the St Valery family. It had a motte-and-bailey castle, supposedly to guard the Thames crossing place a mile away.[31] The manor house was built on a raised and moated mound in the twelfth century and other earthworks and fortifications are evident. Longworth is the next village to the east and is where a congregation of Baptists originated in 1703.[32] Later they worshipped at the chapel at Cote in Oxfordshire and Duxford would have been their nearest crossing point.

Duxford. The bridle path to the ford is still a right of way but it would not be easy to cross the ford except perhaps in high summer. Winter 2010.

Oliver Cromwell and his forces crossed at Duxford on Monday 14 May 1649.[33] They were chasing the Levellers and caught up with them at Burford. Cromwell had already tried to cross at Newbridge but found it too strongly held. Thacker further explains that one of the Levellers on that occasion was Miles Sindercombe who escaped from Burford and went on to devise several plots to assassinate Cromwell. He was betrayed, captured and imprisoned in the Tower where he took poison in 1657. Cromwell died the following year.

Until local government reorganisation in 1974, the ford marked the county boundary between Oxfordshire and Berkshire. It is not known which county was responsible for it but it was well marked.[34] A bed of large stones covered in concrete made a firm base about 25 feet wide with wooden posts placed on either side about 6 feet apart.[35] Most of these are now washed away. In winter the posts could be submerged, making the ford dangerous. Therefore a ferry was set up nearby in what became Ferry Farm in 1827; although it was marked on a map of Berkshire in 1767.[36] It could have been a mistake for ford. The fare to cross the ferry in 1861 was sixpence. There are two lovely photographs of it reproduced in a book of stereoscopic views taken by Thomas Richard Williams in the 1850s of *Scenes in our Village* which was Hinton Waldrist.[37] One shows the ferry punt which could also have been used to bring goods to the wharf alongside the farm. Other photographs by Taunt show the same scenes, but obviously the ferry was no longer running then. Thacker recalls he met 'an aged woman in Duxford (who) told me the craft was swept away in a great snowstorm years ago, and has never been replaced. There is one, however, down at the lock'.[38]

## SHIFFORD FERRY

The lock Thacker meant was Shifford Lock (Exp.180 371 010), the youngest on the upper river, built in 1898 when the Shifford Lock Cut was made. The ferry was just downstream of the lock, and had operated from there since the fifteenth century.[39] A document from 1426, an Inquisition, claimed that the 'fferybarge' at Shyffordesfery should be maintained by the Abbot of Eynsham, and he was mildly reprimanded for not doing so, as it was part of his estate. The jury, however, reached the verdict that he was not bound to maintain the ferry barge. John Passour held the passage or ferry at the time. The name 'Shifford' suggests it was a 'sheep ford' which later became a ferry as well. Today there is only a cluster of buildings on the north bank named Old Shifford Farm with a small Victorian church, which replaced a Georgian one, isolated on a hillside a field or more away. The church is advertised as open for the Heritage Weekend in September each year but sometimes remains closed. A good view of the river is obtained, but there is no way down to it. Shifford as we see it today is strange. We learn that King Alfred (849–901) held a parliament here with 'many bishops, learned men, proud earls and awful knights'.[40] There must have been a town and certainly a large church, but nothing remains whatsoever. The place is so cut off, although only distant from Standlake, its nearest village, by about 1¾ miles as the crow flies, it takes nearly 3 miles to drive, the alternative being a walk along an old bridle path direct to Standlake.

## SANSOM'S FORD

Sansom's Ford once hereabouts is elusive. Thacker, between 1909 – the date of *The Stripling Thames* – and 1920, changed his mind about its location. It was somewhere between Shifford and Newbridge and Thacker found references to the place between 1829 and 1875. He settled for a spot below Standlake at the head of an island of poplar trees.[41] In recent years the landscape has much altered with more quarries being opened up for gravel extraction and then filled with water and no rights of way are now shown on the north bank. In fact the ford may have been where the constituency boundary leaves the north bank and diverts along a side stream close to Thames Side Farm (Exp.180 388 012) to rejoin the main stream and the Thames Path at a bend in the river. From here a long public footpath climbs Harrowdown Hill southwards and descends to Longworth beside a line of trees, then proceeds to the Downs and the Vale of the White Horse. In other words, Sansom's Ford may have served an ancient long-distance path. In just over a mile the Thames is crossed by Newbridge.

# CHAPTER SEVEN
# Ferries between Newbridge and Oxford

## NEWBRIDGE

Newbridge (Exp.180 402 013) was built in the thirteenth century and got its name as the youngest of three old bridges on the upper reaches of the Thames, the others being Radcot and Lechlade. Nevertheless, this bridge has withstood the ravages of time best of all. It carries the A415, a very busy and important route north–south between Witney and Abingdon. Concerns have been felt about its safety but the heavy traffic is controlled by traffic lights and there are very long-term plans to build another bridge alongside.[1]

Whether Newbridge was preceded by a ford is not known, but quite likely it was, the road being so important. The modern map shows the road was realigned to cross the bridge and perhaps a ford originally crossed west of the bridge. Recent recordings of the depth of water show it to be shallow, whereas to the east it is fairly deep. This might be explained by the confluence of the River Windrush being close to the bridge. Originally it was a little further upstream, but debris carried down by the Windrush formed an island and it found a new course. The old course is followed by the parish boundary. The road crossed the marshy ground by long causeways either side of the bridge, which has six pointed arches built of Taynton stone. This stone was also shipped from a wharf here to Oxford for building some colleges. It was a very busy place.

In 1644 the Parliamentary forces under Sir William Waller were held back in battle at Newbridge, and were defeated at Cropredy Bridge not far away when they tried to reach Oxford, then the headquarters of the Royalist army. The bridge was damaged, but held. Adjustments to it have been made from time to time, including the alignment, and alterations in the eighteenth century, but it remains steadfast.

Two old inns served this crossing point, both well known. The Rose Revived on the left bank in Oxfordshire dates back to the sixteenth century, but it developed from an earlier alehouse called the Chequers and belonged to Lincoln College, Oxford. The inn on the opposite side, The Maybush was built as a post house in the seventeenth century. Both are still flourishing.

## RIDGE'S FERRY

Some confusion exists about the next crossing point below Newbridge. Even Thacker seems unsure of its name and location. He gives it as being 1¼ miles below the bridge at (Exp.180 420 011) and names it as Ridge's, being the name of one weir keeper.

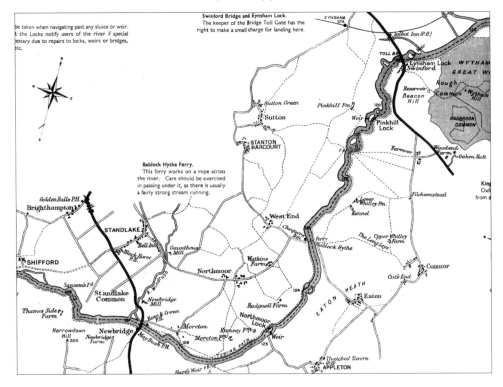

The Thames from Shifford to Swinford showing the area now covered by Farmoor Reservoir. From *Stanford's New Map of the River Thames, c.* 1900.

Newbridge. Looking towards the Rose Revived from the west. A shallop is travelling up river. Drawn and published in aquatint by Samuel Ireland for *Picturesque Views on the River Thames,* 1792.

Newbridge as depicted in the Halls' *Book of the Thames* 1859. The bridge was strengthened by cutwaters. As it was narrow, pedestrians were still carried across by ferry.

On his sketch-map he marks it as a 'footbridge (weir and ferry)'. Other authorities named it differently as Langley's, Butler's, Cock's, Old Hart's, Rudge's and the map for Rocque's Survey of 1761 marks it as Hart's ferry.[2] The modern Ordnance Survey maps have escaped the issue by marking the footbridge and several public footpaths connecting with it, but not naming the place at all. All this confusion may suggest there was once another weir, higher upstream, possibly at (Exp.180 420 010) below Moreton, and Hart's Weir itself was below Moreton Farm, which is not shown on the modern maps. A ferry was attached to Fyfield manor in the fifteenth century and may have been the one in the seventeenth century which was accessed across Moreton meadow, that is Hart's Weir.[3] The isolated footbridge, known as Hart's Weir Footbridge, was built in 1879 to preserve the ancient rights of way which used the weir or the ferry to cross, although they no longer seem to go anywhere.

This is a true 'rags to riches' story. Thomas Ridge was keeper at this weir and lived in a cottage alongside with his daughter Elizabeth, who was born 18 July 1746. Reputedly she was very beautiful, but shy and retiring.[4] She helped her father in his work, possibly by running the ferry, and she also worked at the inn at Bablockhythe. One day a young student from Christ Church College, Oxford came by and was attracted by Betty and vowed to marry her. He sent her away to a gentleman's house to be educated, and then they were married in Northmoor Church in 1766. He was William Flower, 2nd Viscount Ashbrook (1744–80) of the Irish peerage. Their signatures are recorded in the parish register. Betty became Elizabeth, Viscountess Ashbrook. The couple lived briefly in a riverside house until the Viscount took a tenancy of the manor of Shellingford, near Faringdon. There they had some children but only two boys lived, both to become Viscount Ashbook in succession after the death of William, aged thirty-six. The younger son, Henry Jeffery Flower, 4th Viscount Ashbrook had a daughter, Charlotte Augusta Flower (1818–50) who married the 6th Duke of Marlborough as his second wife in 1846 to become the Duchess of Marlborough of Blenheim Palace.

## BABLOCKHYTHE FERRY

After Hart's Weir, the Thames changes course northwards to avoid the hills surrounding Oxford, mainly the very steep hill of Wytham Woods which slopes down to the river on the north. The Thames Path follows the river on the left bank until, after passing Northmoor Lock, it has to veer away at Bablock Hythe (Exp.180 435 042). Here is the best-known ferry on the Upper Thames, linking by road the villages of Stanton Harcourt on the left bank with the large parish of Cumnor on the right. It was a quick way of getting to Oxford by avoiding low-lying land. Although now the ferry works only spasmodically, in co-operation with the landlord of the Ferryman Inn, it is still in private ownership, the only one working, ostensibly, on the Upper Thames.

There are signs of early settlement in the vicinity, particularly at Northmoor, but a suggestion that Romans forded here is disproved but not denied, the water is too deep for a ford at this point. Significantly, an uninscribed Roman altar of forest marble was dredged up at Bablock Hythe by the Thames Conservancy in 1932.[5] It is 27 inches high and 10½ inches wide but damaged. The altar depicts a nude figure holding a patera in the right hand and a cornucopia in the left; probably a goddess and erected originally against a wall. There was nothing to suggest it was a water deity. An authority suggests that if there had been an ancient ford and track connecting a route traversing the Thames Valley from south-east to north-west over Boar's Hill and crossing the river again at North Hinksey, then it was likely a shrine was set up at Bablock Hythe.

The early history of the ferry is lost in the mists of time, although the *Place Names of Oxfordshire* gives a date of 1212.[6] The name derives from 'Babba's stream' or 'Babba's

Bablockhythe Ferry. A simple raft-like ferry to carry cattle is depicted in the Halls' *Book of the Thames.*

cut' and the Old English word 'Iacu', meaning stream or brook is interpreted as 'lock'. Bab would have been a personal name or an adjective. In 1277 is a reference to 'Babbelack'. 'Hythe' means landing place or wharf and 'hyd' would have been added to the name sometime before 1581–82.[7] The earliest recorded reference found is for 1279 or thereabouts when John Cocus rented 'the ferry at Babbelak' from the Prior of Deerhurst, near Tewkesbury in Gloucestershire, for thirty-one shillings a year.[8] This seems a high rent but it also included some adjoining meadows. By the year 804 there was a monastery at Deerhurst which later became a Benedictine Priory, then a cell of the Abbey of St Denis, Paris.[9] The monastery owned the whole parish of Deerhurst but in about 1060 the property was divided between Westminster Abbey and the Abbey of St Denis. The abbot sold those properties in 1250. However, he kept land in Northmoor and the ferry at Babbelak in la More as, in 1318, a grant was made by King Edward II to John, son of John le Keu to retain a messuage and land in Northmoor and the ferry of Bablockhithe acquired by his father from the Prior of Deerhurst to himself, Agnes his wife and their heirs.[10] This time the rent was reduced to £1 per year but John had to undertake to ferry the Prior and his servants free of charge, and the Abbot of St Denis and his servants likewise. Not only them, but bodies being taken to the early fourteenth-century church at Northmoor (dedicated to St Denis) for burial had to carried for nothing. As tenant, John undertook to maintain the ferry boat and keep in repair a causeway nearly a league and a half long (this could mean the track from Cumnor which is about 1½ miles long).

Ferrymen were notorious for being parsimonious. For centuries the usual toll for foot passengers was one halfpenny per journey. The charge for horses varied between one penny and threepence. Carts and carriages which required a 'great boat' were being carried across in 1692 at Bablockhythe at great expense. Robertson quotes a story from *A Hundred Merry Tales* of 1526, a book known to Shakespeare. 'A courtier and a friar happened to meet together in a ferry boat, and in communication between

From Robertson's *Life on the Upper Thames*, 1875. The ferry boat is now more sophisticated and the rope is pulled across by a winch. Looking from Bablockhythe towards Cumnor on the right bank.

Bablockhythe ferry boat in a semi-derelict condition photographed by Taunt. Postcard posted in 1908 but probably produced earlier.

Bablockhythe from the Cumnor side. The ferry punt is now replaced and the Chequers Inn is advertising apartments. Postcard *c.* 1910.

them, fell at words angry and displeased each with the other, and fought and struggled together, so that at the last the courtier cast the friar over the boat, so was the friar drowned. The ferryman, who had been a man of war the most part of his life before, and seeing the friar so drowned and gone, said thus to the courtier, "I beshrew thy heart thou shouldest have tarried and fought with him on land, for now thou has caused me to lose an halfpenny for my fare".' When the river was popular for walking and rowing at the end of the nineteenth century, one guidebook advised the walker to go prepared with a pocketful of change, because for some reason, ferrymen were never able to give any!

The village of Cumnor was a nice walk from Oxford, over Boar's Hill and was frequented by students. Tourists also came to see the place where Amy Robsart had met her mysterious death at Cumnor Place. Many would walk down the lane called Long Leys to the ferry, stopping at the Physic Well (Exp.180 443 044) for a 'pick-me-up'.[11] The well was described in some diaries dated between 1717 and 1728 as being 'esteemed as a very good medicinal purging water'. John Butler was the first keeper of the well, followed by his son, also John, who lived at a place on the way to Filchampstead called Tumbledown Dicks.

Matthew Arnold (1822–88) memorialised Bablock Hythe ferry in his long poem *The Scholar Gipsy* (1853) based on the legend described by Joseph Glanville (1636–80) a Rector of Bath Abbey in his book *The Vanity of Dogmatizing*. It tells of a poor Oxford scholar who gave up his studies to join the gipsies, learn their lore and roam the world with them. He is said to roam the countryside around Oxford forever.

> For most, I know, thou lov'st retired ground.
> Thee, at the ferry, Oxford riders blithe,
> Returning home on summer-nights, have met
> Crossing the stripling Thames at Bablock-hithe,
> Trailing in the cool stream thy fingers wet,
> As the slow punt swings round;

The Chequers Inn has extended its buildings and cleared the landing place of trees and bushes. Postcard *c.* 1916.

Unimaginative critics have said of this poem that the 'slow punt' does not 'swing round', but goes straight across.[12] Another points out the crossing takes only 3–4 minutes anyway and because the gunwale is only a few inches high it would not have been possible to trail his fingers in the water. Laurence Binyon also immortalised the ferry as *Bab-Lock-Hythe* a poem in his collection *England and Other Poems* published in 1909 and set to music by Martin Shaw in 1919. The poem focuses on the beauty of the scene and the bird and plant life around the tranquillity of the place.

Many other writers have written about this ferry including Robert Bridges, the Poet Laureate. In a letter to his mother from Christ Church College written on 11 March 1851, T. E. Brown wrote, 'We proceeded to Bablockhythe ferry where we crossed the Isis (Thames) and kept on through very pleasant rural scenery to Stanton Harcourt where there is a rum Old Manor House.'[13] Pope used to stay at the manor house, so did Byron, but it is not thought they wrote about the ferry. The scenery is now marred somewhat by a large car park for the Ferryman Inn and a large mobile homes and camping and caravanning park just downstream. The enterprise takes so much space that the Thames Path has to make a substantial diversion around it.

By the 1950s some students were able to afford cars and a trip to Bablockhythe, crossing the ferry for a pint was a typical excursion. A student of that time described one such outing.[14] One of his friends had a Mini and invited him and another chap. On arrival at the spot opposite the pub they had to flash the car lights and a very old man came over to fetch them. Afterwards, when you left, the operation was done in reverse. Asked how much it cost, the answer was it was free, paid for by the pub because, after all, there was no other reason to cross, other than to visit the pub. The old man had made a strong impression on the students for he was remembered clearly after fifty years. Was he John, the Polish man, also remembered by locals? He might have been paid by the pub in pints.

The vehicle ferry met its Waterloo one Saturday night in June 1964 as reported in the *Oxford Mail*.[15] At 11 p.m. a Land Rover drove on to the moored ferry boat, followed by a Morris 1000. Almost immediately the boat started to fill with water and sank quickly with about a third of its length still showing. There was no time for the Land Rover to reverse, so the driver climbed into the back, opened the rear doors and swam to the bank. By then only a few inches of the top of his vehicle were still visible. The other car reversed along the sinking ferry to reach the bank. A breakdown vehicle winched the Land Rover off the ferry in the early hours of Sunday morning and a boat was used to take a cable out into the stream and hook on to it. The ferry owner was the landlord of the Chequers Inn, as it was then named, Leonard Miller-Mead. He said, 'I decided we needed a new ferry and had ordered one, the first since 1934. Now this has happened. The ferry was moored while the ferryman was collecting the last load for the night. It was built to take three vehicles. The only thing I can think is – the ferry was tied up tight. The Landrover drove to the extreme tip and water started coming over at that end.' In other words it was not loaded sensibly and tipped up.

Writing in 1910, C. G. Harper in *Thames Valley Villages* Volume 1, describes the 'still, quiet scenery' at Bablockhythe but along with many others has reservations about the method of propulsion, the rope or chain. 'At Bablockhythe remains the last of the old river ferries, capable of taking a wheeled conveyance across and of giving an unwary oarsman or punter a very nasty check with its rope, permanently stretched athwart the stream'. Other writers commented similarly; Robertson in 1875 explained that the rope had to be raised when a barge or a large vessel needed to pass.[16] 'The rope would be just at the level of the rower's neck and could cause severe injury.' Garotting is what he was thinking about, but no records exist telling of such a tragedy at this place. The ferryman would stand in his boat and pull on the rope hand-over-hand to propel the boat across. Thacker describes how in October 1894 the Thames Conservancy wished 'to substitute a submerged chain for the benefit of modern degeneracy'. A chain was bought for £8 and installed with a winch on the bank to wind up the chain and pull the vessel along. The chain rested on the river bed. When it came up the chain would be wet and dripping into the ferry punt. One winch can still be seen by the pub and the seating for the other is seen on the Cumnor side. The chains were anchored on the banks and passed though guides at each end of the boat. But Aubrey Harcourt of Stanton Harcourt decided the chain was too dangerous and reinstated the rope in 1898. At that time a journalist from the *Lock to Lock Times* published an article together with a drawing of the punt and rope, stating 'a curious rope ferry still exists, the only specimen of this numerous class which now survives on the Thames'.[17] The Conservancy took away the rope again and returned the chain in 1900. How long it then lasted is uncertain, but the rope was soon back. However, with the increase in motor vehicles which got heavier and more cumbersome, the chain became necessary again.

Another member of the Harcourt family wrote in December 1869 to an unknown recipient asking for information about the Earl of Abingdon's bridge at Eynsham.[18] Basically he wanted to know if there was any prohibition on building another bridge within a limited distance of that bridge because he was contemplating building a bridge at Bablockhythe. Harcourt received a reply which must have been non-informative as he wrote again a few days later. That time he declared he knew no ferries were permitted within two miles of Eynsham Bridge and had heard of a 'five mile prohibition' but did not know to what it referred. Whatever it was, the bridge did not get built. An earlier attempt to build a road bridge by Act of Parliament had failed in 1855 through too much opposition which came mainly from the Earl of Abingdon who wished to safeguard his income from the Eynsham Toll Bridge.

Close-up view of the winch mechanism preserved on the bank at Bablockhythe. It may have been re-erected higher up than its original position, 7 September 2000.

Pressure from cycling factions led to a public meeting in July 2002 about the construction of a pedestrian/equestrian/cycling bridge at Bablock Hythe.[19] Aided by funding from various sources, Oxfordshire County Council undertook to provide a bridge by 2005. Apart from obvious reasons for supplying a bridge was another. It was 'to prevent inbreeding in the villages on each side of the river'. Subsequently the County Council issued a statement through the Sustrans site. They had re-assessed the case and resolved the bridge was no longer a scheme to attract priority funding. It was not rejected out of hand because if a significant grant was forthcoming from elsewhere, then the project could move forward. Meanwhile the Council would investigate the possibility of a ferry service!

People of Cumnor were not fazed by the aspersions cast against them. Judging by their Historical Society website they have fond memories of the ferry and particularly the Ferryman Inn. Like most river ferries an inn was always situated at the ferry landing, which makes this inn almost one thousand years old. In the 1850s when it was the Chequers Alehouse someone described it as 'much frequented by the lower classes'. Of course it has undergone many changes since and was rebuilt in the 1930s as an hotel. Today the buildings cater for a large number of customers. There is still a bell nailed to a willow for summoning the ferryman and still a broad-beamed punt-like ferry boat although it was beached in 2008.[20] Contributors to the oral history section of the history society speak of boys swimming in the river at the ferry, although the stream was fast flowing. On Sundays folks would walk down Long Leys to what they called 'Bablockhigh' or just 'Bab'.[21] There they would have lemonade and a packet of crisps. Mrs Trinder who lived in Long Leys said on Sundays the inn would cater for Sunday fishermen. When she was a girl of seven in the early years of the twentieth century Mrs Mildred Hale moved to the Chequers with her family. They kept it as a hotel with a few rooms to let and also ran the ferry. During the First War she helped with the ferry, the house, the smallholding and the cooking. She left to get married in 1928. Mrs Hale's parents when they gave up the hotel had a bungalow built on the other side and lived there.

John Askins wrote that his mother Eleanor and stepfather Munro Stevenson owned and ran The Chequers between 1953 and 1959.[22] He helped out, as a teenager, especially in operating the ferry. John, the wartime Polish refugee, worked the ferry between 8 a.m. and 11 p.m. with one day off a week, when Mr Askins would fill his place. He said it was easy to operate the ferry using the winch which then controlled a steel rope. It was busy and the fare was quite small, although worth paying for the shortcut to Cumnor and Oxford.

## SKINNER'S WEIR

About 1½ miles below Bablock Hythe was Skinner's Weir (Exp.180 437 062). Here the Skinner family kept the weir and a little inn, The Fish. Judging from the evidence on old maps of footpaths converging at this point there must have been a ford. Thacker used a white footbridge here which obviously replaced the ford, and he saw ruins of the inn.[23] Today the Thames Path rejoins the riverbank here, but the whole scene has been changed by the Farmoor Reservoir. This occupies a large stretch of land which was Farmoor Common in the tything of Stroud, an open field bordering the Thames on the west. The reservoir was built in 1967 to serve Swindon and extended in 1976. It is used for water sports and has nature areas, but it obviated the need for footpaths to reach the Thames.

# SWINFORD FERRY OR EYNSHAM FERRY

Passing Pinkhill Lock, the river continues its northward course until it reaches the toll bridge at Swinford (Exp.180 443 086). This crossing point has always been one of the most important on the Upper Thames and profitable, even to the present day. The prosperous small town of Eynsham grew up away from the river on rising ground slightly to the north. A huge late Neolithic enclosure surrounded by a ditch and a bank previously occupied the site. Some traces of Roman occupation have been found followed by an early Saxon settlement, which later became the centre of a royal estate.[24] A site overlooking the river to the south was chosen to build a minster and a Benedictine abbey was set up around 1005 and refounded possibly in 1086. Extensive remains are *in situ* and show that the abbey commanded the fording place approached by a causeway. Swinford was the name given to the place, derived from one of its functions, swine ford, and situated at the foot of the steep Wytham Hill. This is pronounced 'white ham' and derives from an Old English word 'wiht', meaning a bend because after flowing past Swinford the Thames takes a bend around the north of the hill before turning again to flow southwards to Oxford.

The ford, being a natural phenomenon was available for all to use, being part of the King's Highway. The adjacent ferry which was set up to take carts, coaches and pedestrians was a private enterprise. The landing places belonged to the abbeys, Eynsham on the left bank in Oxfordshire, and Abingdon on the right. The latter was much bigger and richer than Eynsham, having a gross annual income at Domesday of £462 3s 3d as opposed to that of Eynsham Abbey being £40 9s 0d.[25] It happened that Abingdon ran the ferry and took a good profit from it but Eynsham as it became wealthier resented having to pay toll to Abingdon for using the ferry and landing opposite. There were many disputes during the thirteenth century until a rather complicated treaty was made in 1299.

Arguing practically, Eynsham stated that no ferry anywhere could be run without utilising the land at both ends. It followed that 'at the very moment when Abingdon boats touched Eynsham land, and still more when men and beasts came off the boat and when mooring posts were dug in and perhaps a landing stage made, the ferry (no matter how much it was owned by Abingdon) became indebted to Eynsham. Also it was not possible to get back to the Highway from the landing stage on the Eynsham side without crossing Eynsham land'. A pact was made between the two religious bodies at Swinford on the boundary between the counties of Oxfordshire and Berkshire on Tuesday of Easter week in the twenty-seventh year of the reign of King Edward I (on a boat in the middle of the river?) between the abbot and community of Abingdon and the abbot and community of Eynsham. The latter recognised that the whole of Swinford ferry with all that pertained to it was for all time the rightful possession of the Abbot of Abingdon and his church of Abingdon. Moreover, on behalf of themselves and their successors Eynsham gave up and relinquished to their opposite number any right and claim which they had had or in any manner could have had in the ferry.

In addition Eynsham agreed it was permissible for the Abbot of Abingdon, his entourage and his ferryman (*passoribus*) to cross (*passere*) at all times with barges and boats, both large and small and to land and moor without charge or claim made against them, 'as was their customary right in times past'. There was one condition – that Eynsham was not to suffer any loss or damage in their meadows and pastures adjacent to the ferry through the Abbot of Abingdon and his ferrymen, except those which were involved in the ferry and without which it cannot reasonably be operated. If the Abbot of Abingdon or his ferrymen wished to dig or work in the soil of Eynsham outside of the said limits, then special permission must be obtained. The annual payment of twelve pence per annum by Abingdon's ferrymen, which they had been accustomed to pay for landing, crossing and mooring on Eynsham land outside the King's Highway, was to continue.

The Abbot of Abingdon, in recompense for this concession, allowed that the Abbot of Eynsham, his community, household and family should cross free of all ferry toll as often and whenever, whether on horseback or foot with their belongings, victuals and all beasts. But the ferryman himself was not to lose for when the Abbot of Eynsham himself or his cellarer or steward chances to cross they were to give the ferryman, in the name of the Abbot of Abingdon, two loaves called 'peysloves', and two gallons of second-best beer on every occasion. This was a custom already set up before the treaty. It was agreed that in future, the Abbot of Abingdon would not be able to make any further claims against the Abbot of Eynsham or his successors. All ill will between the parties was to cease and be set aside completely. The document was sealed with the common seal of both abbeys and witnessed.

The charge of twelve pence (one shilling) was still being paid to Eynsham in 1538 when Henry VIII ordered the dissolution of the monasteries. The king gave a pension of £200 pa to the Abbot of Abingdon, Thomas Pentecost, who resumed his patrician name of Rowland.[26] He then retired with his followers to the mansion of Cumnor, later Cumnor Place, where he died in 1540. The property was sold by Henry, together with the lordship of the manor, to his physician George Owen. John Wortle took a lease of the Swinford ferry and it became the custom that the ferryman should pay a tithe to the vicar of Cumnor. The Owen family chose not to occupy the manor and let it out to Anthony Foster, steward of Robert Dudley, the Earl of Leicester, favourite of Queen Elizabeth. Forster bequeathed the house to Leicester, who sold it to Sir Henry Norreys of neighbouring Rycote.

Allied to the annual payment of a shilling rent to Eynsham was the custom of 'beating the bounds' at Rogationtide by the vicar of Cumnor and his parishioners.[27] On their perambulation round the parish boundaries they would arrive at the Thames at Swinford. There they continued to claim the whole breadth of the river as far as the Eynsham bank. In order to confirm this, the vicar and his party had to cross the river to grasp the reeds on the opposite side. Then the ferryman, carrying a napkin, would present the incumbent with a bowl of water in which he had placed *6s 8d* (a third of one pound). The tithe money was taken from the bowl and the vicar having sprinkled the water on the bank among the people returned to the Cumnor bank. The parish of North Hinksey, (once part of Cumnor parish) the other side of Oxford downstream, also practised a beating the bounds ceremony. Even in the middle of Oxford the church of St Mary the Virgin in the High Street held the ceremony on 13 May 2010, Ascension Day.

Roads around Oxford were always difficult; there were so many watercourses to cross. The main road to the west from the city went from Botley up the steep Wytham Hill and diagonally westward through the wood to Beacon Hill where it descended very steeply by a fenced track to Swinford. Harper described it as 'a plaguey bad road, a very beast of a road'. There are no rights of way at all over Wytham Hill, which is an SSSI but permission to roam can be obtained from the Secretary of the University Chest to whom the area was bequeathed in 1943. After crossing the ferry the road crossed the meadows on a causeway to enter Eynsham by Abbey Street and Mill Street to join the ridgeway which still carries the main road (A40) to Witney, and on to Gloucester. When the Witney to Woodstock road (A4095) was turnpiked in 1751, the old horse road over Swinford ferry became just a minor branch of it. 'A great boat to bear a horse over' was noted in 1692 and again in 1764.

Intrepid traveller John Wesley experienced a horrifying crossing on 17 January 1764. 'Between 12 and 1pm we crossed Ensham [*sic*] ferry. The water was like a sea on both sides. I asked the ferryman, "can we ride the causeway?"[28] He said, "Yes Sir, if you keep in the middle". But this was the difficulty, as the whole causeway was covered with water to a considerable depth; and this in many parts ran over the causeway with the swiftness and violence of a sluice. Once my mare lost both her fore feet, but she gave a spring and recovered the causeway, otherwise we must have taken a swim, for the water on either side was ten or twelve feet deep. However, after one or two plunges more we got through and came safe to Witney' (where he had special friends).

This state of affairs could not continue, and Lord of the Manor, Willoughby Bertie, the 4th Earl of Abingdon determined to build a toll bridge. Aided by his steward, Sir William Blackstone, who did the negotiating, Abingdon had to buy back the ferry and the adjoining land at a very high price, £2,473. 10s.[29] An Act was obtained for building the bridge in 1767 and included the right to repair Botley Causeway at the entrance to Oxford, and to reconstruct a turnpike road from there around the foot of Wytham Hill, the so-called Seven Bridges Road, now B4044, thus providing a much easier and convenient way from the west into Oxford. The difficult road over the hill was abandoned finally in 1835. Unfortunately for future generations, Abingdon and Blackstone struck a good deal. The Act, which has never been rescinded, allowed for tolls to be collected in perpetuity free of all taxes and death duties. Willoughby Bertie, (1740–99) was an important landowner in Berkshire and Oxfordshire and an MP.[30] He was described by Walpole as 'a singular young man, not quite devoid of parts, but rough and wrong-headed, extremely underbred but warmly honest'. Another acquaintance, Lord Charlemont, wrote, 'a man of genius but eccentric and irregular almost to madness'. Eccentric maybe, but astute beyond all reasonable expectations he certainly was!

The bridge, described as 'Lord Abingdon's magnificent new bridge' was opened in 1769.[31] On 4 August of that year the *Oxford Journal* reported the Stroud Water Coach travelled for the first time along the new turnpike to Witney and went over the

Swinford. The original Eynsham Toll Bridge with toll house, seen from the Oxford side looking north. From the Halls' *The Book of the Thames*.

bridge. Built in stone, it is thought by Sir Robert Taylor, the bridge is very handsome and listed Grade II*. A large mansion-like building was constructed at one end of the bridge, intended to be an inn, but was not used. Eventually it was converted into cottages, and is now demolished. The toll house is on the north side of the bridge. It looks small from the road but actually it is built up from the river bank and is quite high.

When Lord Abingdon took over the ferry, the lease was held by John Winter whose father William held it before him. John paid the same rent of £80 p.a. until the bridge opened. Thomas Parker then became the toll keeper at the bridge. In 1809–10 the total taken in tolls was £410. By 1901 the tollgate keeper was Henry Floyd aged forty-one who was born at Swinford.[32] His wife Sarah was thirty and born at Chippenham in Wiltshire. Their daughter aged thirteen was born in Eynsham.

Users of the bridge and former turnpike which give a shortcut into Oxford still resent having to pay a toll, although the charge for foot passengers only was abolished on 7 June 1835 in celebration of the marriage of the then Lord Abingdon's eldest son. Users made application to Oxfordshire County Council to take over the bridge, but they could not afford to buy out the rights. Protestors claim the toll bridge is an anachronism and an anomaly and is resented by all and sundry. In May 1964 William Hamilton, MP for West Fife, asked for permission to bring a private member's Bill into Parliament regarding the tax-free toll bridges and to have them nationalised without compensation.[33] Swinford was the first of five toll bridges cited. The MP disclosed that Swinford yielded about £6,000 annually which the Earls Abingdon sat on. He stated, 'I understand the Earl is greatly in favour of an incomes policy in the national interest (Laughter)'. Leave to introduce the Bill was refused.

*The Times* reported on 29 July 1981 the bridge was for sale.[34] It was then owned by Michael Cox who had been the manager under the Abingdon family. Lady Abingdon had bequeathed the bridge in 1979 to friends Mr and Mrs Ronald Hole of Dorset who had sold to Mr Cox. It was revealed that between 15,000 and 25,000 vehicles cross every week, each paying two pence, giving an average income of £100 a week. Some people were exempted from paying toll – doctors, ambulances, fire engines and service vehicles. Others evaded payment by speeding past the toll-keeper. If he wished the owner of the bridge could claim their vehicles if offenders did not pay within four days. Cox claimed the original Act did not impose the liability to maintain the bridge, although the owners had always done so at their own expense. The bridge was advertised for sale again in May 1985 when the price was £275,000 and the toll per car was still two pence. The new owner was Mr Graham Smith.

When Mr Smith died in 2009 his family had no interest in keeping the bridge and put it up for sale at £1,650,000.[35] The toll for a car was then five pence, with fifty pence for a lorry. A campaign was started to persuade the County Council to purchase the bridge, and stop the 'highway robbery'. Every day there was a tail-back of a mile in the rush hour, but the campaigners were defeated.[36] In December in that year the bridge, with land and the house sold at auction for £1,080,000 to a private buyer.

# CHAPTER EIGHT
# Oxford

Oxford is generally thought to have derived its name from 'the oxen ford', perhaps on a drovers' road, in fact there were many fords in the area. A suggestion is made that the 'ox' part of the name may derive from the Celtic name for 'river', as in Ouse, Ock, and Osna. The River Thames, after turning to flow southwards from Eynsham, formed the boundary of the town and a line of defence to the west. On the east Oxford was bounded by the River Cherwell. The town grew up on a gravel bank of rising ground between the two rivers and to a certain extent was able to avoid flooding. However, it is criss-crossed by numerous watercourses, some natural branches of the Thames, some manmade, like millstreams and drainage ditches. Each would have necessitated a crossing of some sort.

Dr Robert Plot, keeper of the Ashmolean Museum and Professor of Chemisty at the university, declared the town had been putrid and the healthiness of its waters was in question.[1] One of his jobs was to test the chemicals in the water. Writing in 1705, Plot credits Bishop Richard Fox (*c.* 1448–1528), the founder of Corpus Christi College in 1517, with having cleansed Oxford's rivers and cutting more trenches, 'for the waters' free passage'. The town had been healthy ever since, whereas before, cattle were killed in the streets which had dung lying in them. Owing to the carelessness of the townspeople, the Rivers Isis and Cherwell became filled with mud. Isis is the name given to the River Thames in the area around Oxford. On Ordnance Survey maps it is marked 'River Thames or Isis'and as such it occurs in legal documents. The name is associated with Oxford in particular and probably comes from 'Thamesis', a supposed Latin version.

## BINSEY FORD

An old bridge at Godstow (Exp.180 483 092) was mentioned in 1692, and would have replaced a ford used for access to the nunnery.[2] The manuscript also records 'here by ye help of foards and other bridges both horse and foot do pass into each county'. Bridges were also built later to take the new navigation channel and the Wytham stream. The Thames Path continues to follow the river on the right bank until it reaches Binsey (Exp.180 496 076) known for its poplars, treacle well and boat, not forgetting its hostelry, the Perch. There was a ford at Binsey, with lesser ones nearby, used for moving cattle when the water was low.[3] Thacker, writing in 1909, described the ford as still clear with a hard gravel foothold. Within living memory he said it had been 'used when horses at grass on Port meadow became wild and impossible to catch. They were headed over the ford to Binsey Green where they were caught more easily.'

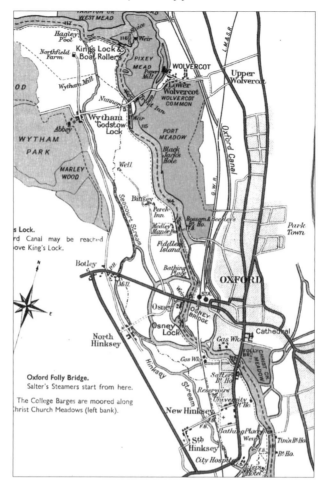

The River Thames as it flows from north to south past
Oxford. From *Stanford's New Map of the River Thames,*
*c.* 1900.

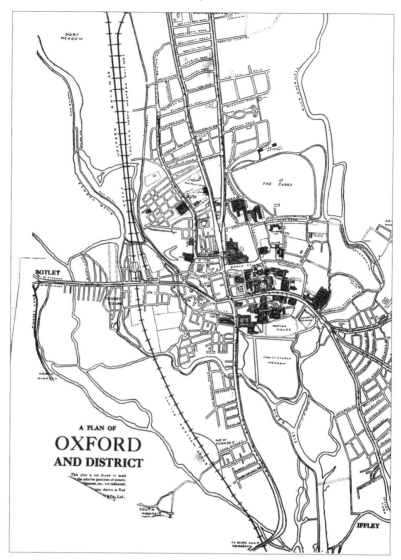

Plan of Oxford, not to scale, showing the numerous watercourses that thread through the city. Jericho is the planned development just north of the railway station. Early twentieth century.

Binsey Green was a large area of common land over which the causeway to the ford ran. Today a metalled track leads to about the same spot. Robert Mylne in his report printed in 1802 recommended the ford at Binsey 'should be done away'.[4]

At least by the 1880s a ferry was in operation, possibly private, to supplement the ford. One farmer of Binsey who held rights of inter-commonage possessed a boat to ferry his animals to Port Meadow across the mainstream of the Thames.[5] These were free waters, administered by the Mayor of the City. Lawsuits often concerned issues arising from the rights, mostly fishing, and uses of Port Meadow. Freemen have been allowed to graze horses and cattle for nigh-on one thousand years but who actually owns the land is a mystery – the City of Oxford? Whatever, it is a valuable asset, often flooding, it provides sport, open-air facilities and as a SSSI it preserves a unique environment for wildlife and plants, never having been ploughed.

A vessel which became known as 'The Binsey Boat' was discovered in 2003 sticking out from the bank where Port Meadow borders the Thames, opposite Binsey.[6] The banks here are continually eroding, and the river has changed considerably in the vicinity since the nineteenth century. The archaeological report describes it as punt-like, about 20.6 metres long by 2 metres wide with a clench bolt construction. Both ends were square, built possibly in the late eighteenth or early nineteenth century. It was found seemingly abandoned in reed beds, not in a separate channel. Various suggestions were made as to its likely use. A later report gives detailed measurements and the method of construction.[7] Inside were found the base of a bottle and a horseshoe post 1825. Here is a classic description of a punt horse ferry boat, but this is not mentioned in either report. Clearly when the ferry service was discontinued, the ferryman left his boat where anyone who wished could use it and it got forgotten.

Passengers preparing to be taken across to Port Meadow in the ferry punt are depicted in the watercolour by William Turner of Oxford (1789–1862), 'An April Shower'.[8] It looks capable of taking only one horse. Also shown are stumps of the so-called poplars, actually aspen trees, bordering the Binsey bank. Gerard Manley Hopkins wrote about them in *Binsey Poplars* when he found they had been felled in 1879, 'My aspens dear, whose airy cages quelled'.[9] These aspen poplars are different from the Lombardy poplars for which the banks of Thames are famous, particularly growing by ferries, and they shimmer in the light breezes. Every 150 years or so they have to be cut down, but at Binsey they have always been replaced.

Binsey Church is isolated in farm land at the end of a lane about ¾ mile from the settlement. In the churchyard is a spring or well, popularly known as the Treacle Well, dedicated to St Margaret.[10] Pilgrims journeyed here to worship and experience its healing powers, crossing the river by fords and ferries. This is reflected in the name of the place. Often surrounded by water in times of flood, 'ey' signifies island and 'bin' or 'ben' stands for prayer. The well is now muddy but the dormouse at the Mad Hatter's tea party in *Alice's Adventures in Wonderland* explained to her that it was treacle. '"You can draw water out of a water-well", said the Hatter; "so I should think you could draw treacle out of a treacle-well".'

The Perch is an inn dating back to the seventeenth century but it is likely there was an earlier alehouse for watermen and fishermen on the site. Being very popular it has some interesting legends and folk tales associated with it. Although fire in the thatched roof in 1977 and again in 2007 damaged the building severely, it has been carefully restored to its original state.

One of the fords between Port Meadow and Binsey Green being used to bring hay wains across. The Perch Inn is in the distance. From Robertson, *Life on the Upper Thames*.

Children using an abandoned punt for a game of pretend using a punt pole cut from a hazel bush. Robertson titles this steel engraving 'The Wreck' in *Life on the Upper Thames*.

## CANAL FERRY

From Binsey the Thames Path continues southwards towards the city, passing Bossom's Boatyard. This family has been known in the area for centuries as boatmen and fishermen. At Medley the Thames sheds streams. The Old Navigation sweeps round to the east to run parallel with the Oxford Canal. A footbridge is signposted to the canal and the path joins the canal towpath where it forms the boundary of the suburb of Jericho, built to house workers at the Oxford University Press printing works nearby. A few yards further along the path, opposite the end of Coombe Road, an unusual feature on canals, a passenger ferry, operated. Ferry Road was renamed Coombe Road in 1959. The ferry was apparently used by workers attending the railway, gasworks and the many coal wharves which lined the canal. It was a short distance from Isis Lock where the canal connected with the Thames and was the location of wharves under the Thames Commissioners. When the foundation stone of Nuffield College was laid in 1949, the displaced coal merchants from the site were transferred to Juxton Street wharf upstream and the ferry was used to transfer the horses to the wharf from the towpath.[11] There had been a ferry house nearby which was sold in the late nineteenth century. Perhaps a full-time ferryman was not needed, for it seems passengers would be required to punt themselves over by handing along the rope. The ferry closed during the Second World War.[12]

Much speculation has taken place to ascertain which of the many fords gave its name to the town. Finally, researchers have settled on the one which leads south over what is now Folly Bridge at the end of St Aldates, formerly Fish Street. This is a very old crossing, dating perhaps to the eighth century when the Thames was the boundary between Mercia and Wessex. It would have served both north–south and east–west routes. The ford was in existence before the town when the place was merely a trading

*The Canal Ferry.*

Ferry on the Oxford Canal at Jericho. From Andrew Lang, *Oxford*, 1890 post on the river. Archaeological investigations undertaken around 1980 revealed that after accumulations of silt and urban refuse were removed a true ford of the late tenth or early eleventh century was found.[13] It could even have been a repair or widening of a ninth century construction. Thought to have been always below water level, the ford was found to be made of closely packed rubble, bonded with sand and silt. The surface was of small slabs of Corallian stone, only about 100–150mm thick and laid flat and showed signs of having been rolled. The width was estimated at about less than a metre. Following the abandonment of the ford because of silting and the building of a timber bridge, the river changed course, leaving the evidence of the ford beneath the frontage of the new Crown Court.

St Frideswide, the patron saint of Oxford, is commemorated in a shrine and stained-glass window in the Latin chapel of the Cathedral at Christ Church, just up from Folly Bridge. Many versions of her story are told, most embroidered, but here are the bare bones. She was born a Saxon princess to Didan, a ruler and his wife in Oxford about the year 665. Her beauty was renowned but she took a vow of chastity and rejected the advances of Prince Algar of the province of Leicester who wished to marry her. To escape him she obeyed voices which told her to take two ladies and go to the ford. There a boat was waiting, with a young oarsman dressed all in dazzling white. He took them downstream to Abingdon where they took refuge for three years. On hearing that her father was ill, Frideswide returned to Oxford. Algar heard she had returned and pursued her again. This time Frideswide felt she was trapped and in desperation prayed to the saints to help her. Immediately Algar and his followers were struck blind. Frideswide felt sorry for him and obtained his promise that if she would restore his sight, he would never bother her again. So she took him to St Margaret's Well at Binsey and administered to him. Frideswide was so grateful to be left alone she persuaded her father to help her set up a priory for nuns near the ford and a small

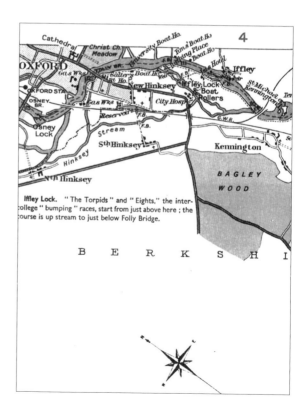

A section of *Stanford's New Map of the River Thames* showing Folly Bridge, North Hinksey, Iffley and Kennington.

chapel next to the well. At her death on 19 October 727, 735 or 740 (according to the various stories) she was buried in the priory. Later the priory was demolished and the Cathedral was eventually built close to the site. Her shrine was built in 1289 and destroyed in 1538, when the body was buried at an unknown spot beneath the Cathedral floor. The shrine was rebuilt in 1889 and again in 2002.[14] Only the base survives and has carvings of leaves to symbolise when Frideswide hid in a wood. The head of a nun and of a prince peep out from the leaves. The window by Burne-Jones has sixteen panels each depicting an episode of Frideswide's life, surmounted by the ship of souls transporting Frideswide to heaven.

## FOLLY BRIDGE

No reference has been found to suggest there was a ferry at the site of Folly Bridge. A pair of timber piles was excavated, which suggested a timber bridge was situated a little downstream of the ford and would have been supplementary to it, taking the heavier traffic. A long causeway was also built on either side of the bridge across the low-lying marshy ground.[15] Gradually the build-up of silt made the ford impassable. One of the timber piles was found having been displaced by part of a stone causeway. After the Norman Conquest, Robert d'Oilli or d'Oyley was given the township of Oxford and allowed to build a castle. He also built a bridge over the site of the ford, apparently by using part of the foundations of the previous Saxon timber bridge. It was called South Bridge and the very long causeway, about 700 metres long, associated with it was Grand Pont or great bridge. By the twelfth century the original river channel was choked by silt and a new channel was cut slightly to the north. Beneath Number 33 St Aldates has been found part of a causeway 4 metres wide, built of ragstone with arches like ones to the south of the bridge. In the sixteenth century there were more than forty arches.

View from Folly Bridge looking downstream, with a ferry punt intended for a large number of passengers. On the left bank are college barges, on the right is the site of Salter's boatyard. Engraving from the *Leporello Album of Oxford Views, c.* 1860.

Friar Bacon's Study on Folly Bridge as depicted in the Halls'
*Book of the Thames* 1859. It must be a copy of an old print
as the building was demolished in 1779.

At the north end of the Grand Pont stood a sort of gatehouse or tower astride the
bridge platform, known as Friar Bacon's Study. Originally it served as a medieval
fortification, but by tradition it was the observatory of Roger Bacon (*c.* 1214–92?) the
philosopher. In the mid-seventeenth century it had become ruinous, but was saved by
one Welcome, a local man who restored the building and added another storey, thus
making it a very tall building, which had the nickname of 'Welcomes's Folly'. Visitors,
including Samuel Pepys, paid to see it. Henceforward the bridge, its successor and the
surrounding area became known as Folly Bridge. It was demolished in 1779 when
the bridge was widened.[16] Hon. John Byng `passed over the bridge on 2 June 1781
and entered in his diary, 'Everyone must wish that the new bridge had been wider;
and I think that the old gateways of the town, which added dignity to the entrance,
and bespoke it to have been a place of arms and antiquity might have been preserved.
Amidst the general demolition, which the hurry of modern taste occasioned, fell Friar
Bacon's Study.' A new bridge, still in use today as Folly Bridge was built between 1825
and 1827.

## FERRY HINKSEY

Overlooking Oxford to the east is North Hinksey or Ferry Hinksey (Exp.180 496
055). Its ancient name 'Hengistesigge' derives from 'a pathway on the side of a hill'.[17]
This is evident on the ground but the village has been ruthlessly separated from the
hill by the western part of the A34, the fast Oxford Bypass. The view depicted in a
watercolour by William Turner of Oxford in 1852 of the distant city from above the
ferry is now obscured by trees.

From outlying areas to the west of Oxford the easiest way to bring goods into the
city was by tracks and a causeway across the flood-prone meadows to a ford or fords
at Hinksey. A track took this route in prehistoric times travelling from south-west to
north-east towards Banbury or Northampton. Romans also followed the same routes
and crossed the streams by fords. The Hinkseys were given to the Abbey of Abingdon
in AD 955 but they were not mentioned in Domesday, being then a chapelry of
Cumnor. Botley Abbey caused a stone causeway to be made to the ford which later
became a ferry by 1370. Dr Claymond, president of Corpus Christi College 1517–37
paid for improvements to the causeway.[18] Leland then described it as 'a causey of
stone from Oseney to the ferie and in this causey dyvers Bridges of Plankes'.

The estate, which included the ferry, of North Hinksey can be traced back to about
1500 when it was owned by William Balcombe and his wife Maud, who on his death
re-married.[19] In 1539 John Croke, Sergeant-at-Law obtained it from her son Thomas

Woodward. The estate then descended through generations of the Croke family until 1604 and was acquired with the ferry by William Fynmore when there was no other estate of importance in the parish except the manor. The Fynmore family continued as owners until 1924 when a descendant alienated the property to Brasenose College. Earl Harcourt became owner of the manor.

It is not certain which of the streams was crossed by the ferry, now the footbridges which cross the ferry place are over the Hinksey Stream and the Bulstake Stream, both branches of the Thames. Until the last decade of the eighteenth century when the Thames Navigation Commission made improvements to the river west of Oxford, the main navigation channel was the Bulstake Stream. Then the main stream was turned eastwards at Medley and a new cut was made to connect into Osney Mill Stream which was widened.[20] The Bulstake Stream was wider and faster flowing, so the ferry had some importance. It connected with the city by a metalled causeway as far as Botley Road.

The ferry was much used by local people, farmers going to market, students out for walks and scholars going to school. The boat was the usual Thames ferry-punt and capable of taking some horses and cattle and was pulled across by a rope in the fashion of hand over hand. If the boat was loaded, a punt pole would also be used. John Malchair (1730–1812) the German-born musician and drawing master who settled in Oxford regarded the ferry place at Hinksey as one of his favourite places to visit.[21] The Ashmolean Museum holds two of his pencil drawings, delicately coloured, one he describes as, 'a little drawing of the little Hovel and pigsty at Ferry Hingsley

Taunt photograph of 1895 showing the path to the ferry from The Fishes public house at North Hinksey. Reproduced by permission of English Heritage.

[*sic*]'. The other, drawn two years later on 13 June 1775 is inscribed on the back, 'This was the most favourit Villa of Mrs Malchair when livinge: here my miende is fullest of her, here I love to roam.' The buildings shown are at the water's edge, the edge of the boat is seen in the water and in the distance is the Sheldonian Theatre.

Beside the ferry path where it joins the main road in the village is the ferry cottage. Its outward appearance belies its antiquity. English Heritage list it as Grade II and describe it as early seventeenth century, one storey with attics and built of coursed and dressed limestone with ashlar quoins.[22] Much restoration has taken place in the twentieth century, but the interior retains some original building features. A previous owner, taking into account the internal layout with what was obviously a hall with central chimney and spiral staircase around it to the upper floor suggests it was sixteenth century.[23] The steepness of the roof indicates that it must have been thatched. Pevsner propounds 'Quite sophisticated for a house of this size, with mullioned windows on either side of the lobby entrance'. The garden at the back is very long, and extends to the ferry place. Perhaps the pigsty mentioned by Malchair was actually a hut for the ferryman. The ferryman in December 1803 was Mr John Stevens and Mr W. Hern held the post in August 1806.[24] An unknown writer of a book of rambles around Oxford in the 1880s gives advice to the rambler who arrives at the ferry. 'Should the boat be on the farther side a bell is provided to call over the ferry man or ferry lass, the handle to pull it is by a post to the right hand. Up through the garden brings us out almost facing the church.'[25]

The garden is big and belongs to the pub, The Fishes. The right of way to the ferry runs along a raised path beside a hedge and seems to be much used. The pub itself looks like a Victorian gentleman's house. Built in 1885 in red brick, tile-hung and high chimneyed, Pevsner describes it as a 'nice example of Domestic Revival'. It replaced a more conventional thatched alehouse called The Fish which was demolished because of flooding. The replacement is built on higher ground beside a walnut tree.

A special feature of North Hinksey is the delightful Willow Walk as it has become known. Branching off from the main street nearly opposite the church it is a metalled public bridle path which firstly crosses the Hinksey Stream by a railway-like bridge with cutwaters; then it proceeds beside a ditch or small stream bordered on either side by old willow trees which have not been pollarded for some while. It is a wildlife haven for plants, birds, frogs and fungi. Located a short distance upstream from the ferry place it brings people out to Hinksey Road and thence into Oxford as did the footpath to the ferry. Laurence Binyon, (1869–1943) watched a young lady making her way along the walk while he lingered at the bridge. His poem called *Ferry Hinksey* is dated 1909.

> Beyond the ferry water
> That fast and silent flowed,
> She turned, she gazed a moment,
> Then took her onward road.
>
> Between the winding willows
> To a city white with spires;
> It seemed a path of pilgrims
> To the home of earth's desires.
>
> Blue shade of golden branches
> Spread for her journeying,
> Till he that lingered lost her
> Among the leaves of spring.

Earl Harcourt in 1872 had plans to develop his land on the hill overlooking the village into an upmarket suburb and in 1877 architect Charles Smith made designs for 'a town in the woods'. Harcourt desired to make a private carriage drive as a shortcut to Oxford for himself and potential residents of his 'town'. However, he did not intend to put the burden of future maintenance of the drive, with two bridges, on his descendants.[26] So John M. Davenport, Clerk of the Peace and District Registrar of Oxford, was engaged to prepare an opinion and after consultation with his counterpart in Devon, Davenport produced a document in November 1877. He referred to an Act 43 of George III *c.* 59, known as Lord Gower's Act, under which a new public bridge built by a private person may be made a County Bridge if notice is given to the County Surveyor before its erection. If the bridge is built under the supervision of the surveyor and is substantial and commodious, then it could become a County Bridge. However it was found by visiting the 'locus in quo' that one bridge spanning the Bulstake Stream was wholly in the City of Oxford. The next bridge, near North Hinksey over the Hope Stream (Hinksey Stream), was wholly in the County of Berkshire, but in fact came within the municipality of the City; indeed it formed one of the boundaries of the city. Therefore Lord Gower's Act did not apply in this case as both bridges came within the bounds of the city. Davenport's conclusion was that 'no law can be found under which future maintenance of the bridges can be imposed on the City'. The residential suburb was never built but the Willow Walk, built in 1878, remained private until it was taken over by the City of Oxford and opened as a public path in 1923. The ferry closed officially in 1928 and the way to it became overgrown. In recent years it has been opened up and the path protected. A footbridge has replaced the ferry at the same site over a much narrower stream than before.

# CHAPTER NINE

# Ferries beyond Oxford to Culham

Many ferries on the Thames have existed without any of their history being recorded, perhaps because they were part of the landscape and the everyday life of the people, nobody thought to record them or mourn their passing. Such a ferry was Donnington over the Thames below Folly Bridge, of which very little of the history is known.

## DONNINGTON FERRY

It began as a ford on the Roman Port way running by Oxford in a south-west to north-east direction and was the Stone Ford or Stanford. By the fourteenth century the ford had become a ferry, owned by Sir Richard Abberbury (c. 1330–99) of a family well known in this part of the Thames Valley.[1] Abberbury was tutor to the young Prince Richard of Bordeaux, son of Edward the Black Prince. When the prince succeeded to the Crown in 1377 as King Richard II, Abberbury became Knight of the Chamber. He also acted as chamberlain to Anne of Bohemia, King Richard's first wife, and thus became very rich. He spent money on his estate at Donnington, near Newbury in Berkshire, by building a castle, a priory and an almshouse, Donnington Hospital, which still exists today as a Trust. Then he acquired other estates in Berkshire and Oxfordshire in 1393 including Iffley together with the river crossing. The ferry became Donnington ferry when Abberbury gave the income from it and other properties in Iffley to Donnington Hospital.

No further references are found until a mention is made by Rivington of a ferry punt shoved by a pole moored at the site, or just below, where the bridge was later built.[2] It was run as a free ferry service by Oxford City Council for foot passengers until replaced by a concrete footbridge in 1937. When it was opened on 19 May by the Mayor of Oxford after the ceremony the party returned to the east bank in the ferryboat, thus closing the ferry.[3] The last ferryman was Thomas Rose, landlord of the Isis Public House.[4] Then, in 1954 when the Council wished to erect a road bridge the Government refused to subsidise it, and took it on themselves. The new bridge opened in 1962 and the road, B4495, provides a busy link between the Abingdon and Iffley Roads (Exp.180 525 044).

## IFFLEY FERRY

It is easy to envisage what life was like in the old village of Iffley. Although now surrounded by suburbs of Oxford, it is still within the city and yet retains a countryside

Early photograph (*c.* 1880) by Taunt of an area just south of Oxford known as the Long Bridges. They were erected over a new cut for the Thames just below the new mouth of the Cherwell. Reproduced by permission of English Heritage.

atmosphere. The noted Norman church stands at the foot of Rose Hill overlooking the river. From the church, Mill Lane descends to the river where a bridge crosses over a weir to the island and continues on to the join the towpath on the opposite bank. The original bridge was the property of Lincoln College who let it out together with the mill and charged a toll.[5] According to local tradition a body being brought for burial in Iffley parish church from outlying parts of the parish could not be carried over the toll footbridge. The reason being that the path would become a right of way (it has now become one). Another reason handed down through folklore was that if a corpse was carried through the toll, the bridge would be broken forever. There are instances of the tollkeeper refusing to let a funeral party through.

Instead, a raft was provided to take the coffin and landed at a special place near the lock. From there it was carried up a wide grassy path now called Coffin Road.[6] The second part of the bridge connecting the island to the right bank was not built until later (Exp.180 527 036). The Isis Hotel on that side, very popular with the river trade, had its supply of beer brought by a special ferry boat until about 1977.[7] Further downstream is Rose Island (Exp.180 527 029) where a bridge gives access from the left bank over a backwater. Here is a boundary stone inscribed, 'Here end the Liberties of the City of Oxford' with the date 1786 on the back.[8] Now a private house, the former Swan Hotel on the island, formerly known as St Michael's Island, was a famous hostelry.[9] Taunt photographed it from the opposite bank showing a large ferry punt moored alongside about 1870. No records have been found of an official ferry at Rose Island.

## SANDFORD FERRY

Sandford-on-Thames (Exp.180 531 012) had a very important ferry. It is listed in early charters of Abingdon Abbey'.[10] The name suggests it began as a ford, a natural one.

Iffley. The lock, lock house and public footbridge to the right bank. Tall Lombardy poplars beside the Thames usually indicate a river crossing nearby. From a private photograph album *c.* 1870

The Swan Hotel on Rose Island with a ferry punt moored alongside. Taunt *c.* 1870, from a private photograph album.

Robert Mylne, the surveyor, in his report of 1802 notes, 'below the pound lock is a wide and long shoal which serves as a ford'.[11] He recommended it be done away with. A deed of *c*. 1294 shows there was then a ferry. Henry, son of Adam the ferryman grants the ferry to John Golding of Newnham [*sic*] and Scholastica his wife.[12] Other deeds of 1348 and 1361 list the ferry as part of a fee for masses said in Witney church. William Busshe was ferryman in 1514, having been appointed in 1506. The grant made then was, 'for keeping the passage or ferry of Sandfordhith in the counties of Oxford and Berkshire with *le fery botes*, then in the King's gift by the death of Thomas Hunt'. Busshe in turn was succeeded by John Dale in 1530. Writing in 1692–93, Baskervile, the antiquarian, said, 'At Sandford ffery when ye water is high, is a boat to carry horse and man over'. This suggests that when the water was low the ford could be used. In 1644 on 28 May, the day after the encounter at Newbridge, the Earl of Essex and his army crossed at the ford on the way to the battle at Cropredy.[13]

The ferry landing was just below the lock on the left bank, right beside the old established Kings Arms, which has always been associated with the ferry. It served as a place of refreshment for travellers between Oxfordshire and Berkshire and was sometimes known as the Inn at Sandford Ferry.[14] Thomas Hearn the Oxford antiquarian came this way on 27 April 1727 when he visited his friend Mr Powell. At that time the mill, horse ferry, fishery and inn seemed to be run together in the ownership of Mr Hill of Holywell Mill, Oxford. William Beckley in 1792 held the leases, except of the mill. An unknown writer eulogised about the inn in the following year. 'Beckley provides accustomed fair [*sic*] of eels and perch and brown beef steak dainties we oft taste twice a week'. He also provided games and rustic pastimes.

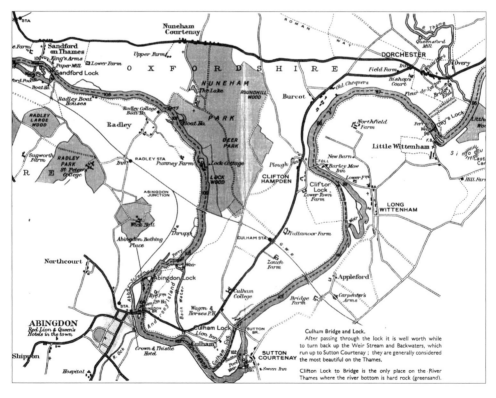

The river between Sandford and Culham from *Stanford's New Map of the River Thames*, *c*. 1900.

An indenture dated 14 October 1884 whereby £1,850 was paid to Gabriel Davis of Abingdon, corn factor and wine merchant, plus an annual payment of five guineas for land tax, a right of way and covenants in fee simple, refers back to a previous indenture of 7 July 1817.[15] The description of the property is the same in both documents. The Kings Arms is conveyed together with stables, fuel house, outhouses, buildings and gardens. There was also another garden, formerly a close of meadow land containing two roods, two rods and two eyots in the river, one called Baldon Mead Ham and the other a small ham. The ferry or passage was included together with all tolls payable in respect of all persons and all horses and cattle passing through or over the passage. A large fishery stretching north to the mouth of the River Cherwell was part of the sale. The purchasers in 1884 were Henry and George Simonds, brewers of Reading.

A bridge taking the towpath over a side stream on the right bank was being replaced in May 2010. This was probably the main stream of the Thames before the pound lock was built. A stone fashioned as a mounting block was unearthed here in the 1930s and set into the ground as a reminder of the ferry.[16] It has an inscription, 'A ferry existed at Sandford as early as the thirteenth century and this mounting block was used by riders to remount after crossing the river.' This

Sandford Ferry is in the foreground and beyond is the King's Arms and the paper mill owned by the Clarendon Press. Steel engraving by Percy Roberts from Shrimpton's *Rambles & Rides around Oxford, c.* 1886.

watercourse flows from the weir upstream known as the Big Lasher, with the deep Sandford Pool below, which sadly has claimed many lives, especially as it was used as a bathing place. Jerome K. Jerome described it as, 'a good place to drown yourself in'.[17] An obelisk is erected to commemorate some of the deaths, including in 1921 Michael Llewelyn Davies, the inspiration for J. M. Barrie's *Peter Pan*.

Today, the Kings Arms remains a favourite venue for townsfolk and students. The mill, which latterly made paper for the Oxford University Press, has been replaced by a modern lookalike building housing apartments. The ferry ceased supposedly during the war. A steel footbridge crosses the weir stream and the millstream, and the lock, which has the greatest fall on the Thames, is crossed over by the gates.[18]

## RADLEY FERRY

From Sandford the Thames Path follows the right bank of the river closely until it reaches Abingdon. When the second cluster of Radley College boathouses is reached there is a public right of way to the small tight-knit hamlet of Lower Radley. It is a very old settlement and retains some fourteenth-century houses. The lane to the water's edge led to the ferry place next to the boathouse (Exp.170 539 988). Over the river was the village of Newnham (now Nuneham Courtney) built on the side of a steep hill. A document exists which states that Agnes la Passeresse (ferry lady) held the passage since 1086 for the payment of eight shillings and a suit of court to the Lord of the Manor.[19] This meant she was a freeholder and was bound to attend the Manor Court twice a year. Her descendant Thomas le Passur of Newnham and his wife Agnes were mentioned in 1314. Later the Golding family, prominent land tenants hereabouts since the thirteenth century were engaged in ferrying until the nineteenth century.

It is not known whether the Radley–Newnham ferry continued in use during all that time, but it was certainly in service in 1707, about when the Harcourt family moved to the hillside from low-lying Stanton Harcourt further upriver.[20] Sir Simon

The 1st Earl Harcourt who landscaped his park and moved Newnham village to the main road, but could not abolish the Radley/ Newnham ferry. Portrait by Sir Joshua Reynolds, from Wikimedia Commons.

Harcourt bought the estate in 1710, as an investment, for £17,000. His grandson, the first Earl Harcourt (1714–77), who had been tutor to Prince George, grandson of George II, decided in 1760 when his pupil became King George III, to build himself a grand Palladian mansion.[21] His aspirations to grandeur had been further enhanced when he was sent to be proxy for the King at his marriage to Princess Charlotte of Mecklenburg and escort her back to the Coronation in England. Being a founder member of the Dilettanti Society, Harcourt was anxious to keep up with current fashion and engaged 'Capability' Brown to landscape his grounds. To this end the old village of Newnham Courtenay was demolished in 1760 and villagers rehoused in nineteen double cottages designed by Harcourt and which lined the turnpike road (A4074), out of sight (and mind). The name of the estate was changed to Nuneham Courtenay to avoid confusion with other Newnhams.

Many people were upset by Harcourt's machinations, particularly the writer Oliver Goldsmith who in his poem 'The Deserted Village', published in 1770, describes the destruction of the village of 'sweet Auburn', a thinly disguised Newnham Courtenay. In his diary for 1761 Revd James Newton, the rector, found difficulty settling into a new rectory and was especially sorry to lose the churchyard.[22] He could forgive the taking away of old gravestones to make into paths for the garden because he had done the same himself. It was the demolition of the churchyard boundaries and mounds to make into a smooth lawn which upset him. Earl Harcourt died on 16 September 1777 by falling into a well at Nuneham Courtenay and drowning while trying to save a pet dog. One obituary notice of Lord Harcourt reads, 'in the latter part of his life the love of money grew insatiably upon him.'

A well is marked on the map at the ferry place at Nuneham Courtenay. After the village was destroyed some of the old lanes were reused. They included the lane past the Home Farm and the Rectory down to the Ferry Cottage. The ferry to Radley did not stop when the village was moved and was still shown on a Stanford's map of the river dated about 1900.

The river as it flows southwards towards Abingdon beneath the hanging woods of Nuneham Park affords the most beautiful stretch of any part of the Thames. Many famous painters including Thomas Sandby and Joseph Farington were guests at the house and availed themselves of the fine vistas. Subsequent Earls allowed public access to the grounds occasionally and it became a favourite place for excursions in Victorian and Edwardian times. Visitors would see the Carfax Conduit, re-erected from Carfax in Oxford and then carry on down to the water's edge by a weir (called a lock) opposite an eyot. There some cottages were built for the weir keepers and an elaborate white wooden bridge was built about 1791 for people to visit the island. Teas were served in the gardens of the cottages. It seems another ferry, a private one, was run to the other bank at Pumney Farm (Exp.170 533 975). The towpath on that side would give access to Radley. Sandby in about 1760 painted in oils the view of the house from the Lock Cottages.[23] In the left of the painting is a small ferry boat being punted by a man in a red hat. It is not exactly like the normal ferry punts but does have passengers. Other boats show people fishing.

Today the scene is still normally of peace and calm, broken sometimes by dirt track riders on the Thames Path. Sadly, the cottages are now a heap of stones, the ornate bridge has gone although some large dressed stones which might have been the footings can be seen in the left bank. Through the still clear water can be seen some ironwork below the right bank which could have been where a landing stage was erected. When the great Abbey at Abingdon owned most of the land round here before the reformation, there was much coming and going along the river by boat and on foot to Oxford and back Present rights of way – footpaths and bridlepaths – bear testimony to this. One of them is a so-called Drover's Road and plans are being

The island below Nuneham Courtney was a tourist attraction and included a private ferry to the right bank near Pumney Farm. The large stone blocks in the bank are still *in situ* today. Photograph by Taunt *c.* 1880, from a private photograph album.

formulated to re-install it for walkers as per Roque's map of 1760.[24] It will leave Lower Radley by the track to Pumney Farm, skirt round it and pass by the new lakes formed by gravel pits. Next it should cross the Didcot–Oxford railway and follow on to Abingdon. Another bone of contention at present is the proposal to open up land to the north of the park between the Ferry Cottage and Lower Farm for extraction of gravel, with all the noise and inconvenience. Included would be a new bridge to give access to the right bank. This defeats the intention of the first earl to create a landscape of beauty. Much of the park now belongs to Oxford University.

Passing beneath the Nuneham railway bridge, the Thames has two weirs at the outskirts of Abingdon. The first is about a ½ mile below the bridge and had a ferry close by, where the towpath changed sides. It became known as the Ferry Weir.[25] Nothing is known about this ferry, it might have been one administered by the Thames Conservators solely to allow horses to change sides when the towing path was put in. A public footpath comes to this point from Abingdon Bridge. It is a place where many changes have taken place to the waterways, for it was in this vicinity that the Swift Ditch ran to Culham, thus cutting off a sharp bend towards Abingdon, and was sometimes the main stream. The stream called Back Water now performs this function, and basically it is the Swift Ditch under another name, although the main stream and the Thames Path both follow through Abingdon itself. The path is taken on to cross at the next weir to gain the left bank all the way to Clifton Hampden. The Abbey Stream branches off at the second weir. It was cut by the monks of the Abbey between 955 and 963 for 'the convenience and cleanliness' of the Abbey.

## ABINGDON CROSSINGS

The town of Abingdon-on-Thames is very old; on the site of the town centre was a late Iron Age oppidum or large enclosure, for the safety of animals, people and goods.[26] Previously it was an early to mid-Iron Age settlement. Major earthworks in the surroundings forming a defensive barrier show the place was of some significance, possibly a meeting place of tribes. The Abbey was first founded *c.* 675 and the town grew up around it, but only to the west.[27] On the east was Andersey Island and meadows stretching towards Culham, low-lying and often flooded. Leland in his peregrination states, 'of auncient tyme ther was no Bridge at Abbandune, but a Ferie'.[28] He goes on to say there were often mishaps at this ford or ferry. In 1316 the abbot – Richard de Clyve with his followers, monks and laymen persisted in crossing, contrary to advice.[29] The river was swollen with 'land water' and because their horses were kicking and plunging and were being managed badly and secondly because of the steersman's unwise management of the fragile craft they 'were all at one stroke drowned' in midstream.

By 1416 the town was sufficiently prosperous, not only because of the abbey but also from the wool trade, to warrant a bridge and causeway to be built in place of the ferry, or ford and ferry as there was ( and still is) an island in the middle of the stream ( Exp.170 490 977). Leland said the two stone bridges were built by 'John of St Helen's' under the auspices of the town's Fraternity of the Holy Cross, which also paid for some almshouses.[30] No toll was ever charged on the bridge. The part of it on the Abingdon side had seven four-centred arches and replaced a ferry and the bridge to the east originally had five arches. It was called Burford Bridge, which is a little confusing because the town of Burford is in a different direction. Apparently the name is a corruption of Borough Ford, the name of the ford leading to the borough from the east. Both bridges were opened in 1422 and were joined to the raised causeway running south towards Culham. The bridges have been strengthened and widened many times, including when the towing path was constructed for the improved navigation. The island in the middle became Nag's Head Island when the Nag's Head Inn was built on the road there. At the Dissolution, Abingdon Abbey was ranked as the sixth richest Abbey in England.[31] Most of it was destroyed for building materials. However, the town continued to prosper, largely because travellers to Gloucester and

The part of Abingdon bridge furthest from the town – known as Burford Bridge, running towards Culham. Postcard *c.*1910.

View of Abingdon taken from roughly the site of the other Abingdon ferry. The church of St Helen can be seen, with St Helen's wharf beside the river. The round building in the distance is the prison, close to Abingdon Bridge. On the right is Andersey Island. Photograph by Taunt *c.* 1880. From a private photograph album.

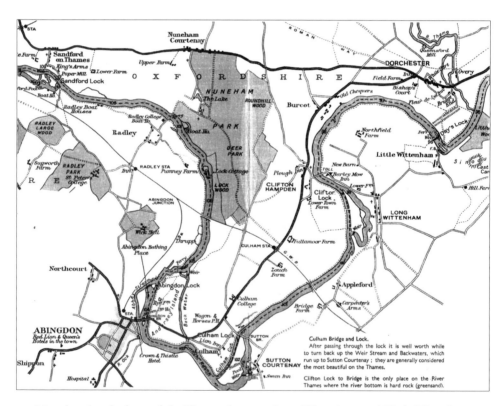

Map showing the loop of the Thames between Long Wittenham and Little Wittenham close to Dorchester. From *Stanford's New Map of the River Thames c.* 1900.

the West preferred to cross at Abingdon rather than Wallingford as before. Today the amount of traffic travelling along the causeway road and over the bridges is phenomenal.

About ½ mile below Abingdon Bridge was another ferry which was still working by row boat pulled on a chain in the early 1960s.[32] The site of it can still be seen on Wilsham Road which runs on the right bank of the Thames below St Helen's Wharf. Situated at the corner of Ferry Walk is a corrugated iron shed brightly painted in blue with a name board 'Ferry Boatyard'. Behind it is a compound with boats in various stages of repair, including one larger rowboat upturned and which might be the original ferry boat. Facing the river on the opposite side of Wilsham Road is a concrete wall with steps leading down to the water, matched by a ramp for foot passengers. The concrete wall is a replacement for an old brick wall, partially seen in a short stretch.

The ferry would have given a quick way to the Thames towpath travelling eastwards on foot; a continuation of a longer path across fields and passing beneath the railway to reach Clifton Hampden; or to join the main road A415 to Culham Bridge and Culham village. A speculation is made that the ferry was created to serve haywains crossing the river in summer to the large area of meadow land on Andersey Island, formed by the great bend in the river round Abingdon on three sides, and the manmade Back Water stream. The only permanent settlement on the island has been Rye Farm. The land had belonged to Abingdon Abbey before it was granted to King Offa of Mercia who died in 796, and then the supremacy of the English Kingdoms passed to Wessex. Offa had a hunting lodge on the island which much later was taken over by William I. The abbey regained the island in 1101. A ferry from the island to the town would have been a useful asset.

## CULHAM

Downstream from Abingdon the Thames is joined on the north or left bank by the Swift Ditch, which is crossed by the old Culham Bridge (Exp.170 501 957), and carries the Abingdon to Dorchester-on-Thames road. The bridge was built in 1422 at the same time as the Abingdon Bridges and the causeway with raised pavement to which it is linked, and was also paid for by the Fraternity of the Holy Cross.[33] Before the bridge this was the site of Culham Ford otherwise Culham Hythe, which was a more convenient landing place for goods bound for Abingdon than the town wharf itself. The ford dated at least from time immemorial (1087) and was important. When Charles I occupied Oxford in the Civil War, a skirmish took place at the bridge in January 1645. The bridge was partially destroyed by their opposition and the Royalists lost the day. The old bridge now stands alone just to the south of a new road bridge erected by Oxforshire County Council in 1928. A good view of it is obtained from the new footbridge made to take the Thames Path. Maintenance of the old bridge was the responsibility of Christ's Hospital, the body which succeeded the Fraternity.

Until 1807 there was a short road which branched off the main road by the Waggon and Horses Inn to reach a ferry over the Thames before the Culham Cut was made about 1811. The ferry was to Sutton Courtenay a large village in Berkshire. Widow Hewit was in charge of the ferry in 1793 and in 1798 Daniel Gibbons was doing the same job for 24s a month. In 1822 Gibbons was the lock-keeper of the new lock.[34] It was a very busy ferry as the Treacher papers reveal in 1801. 'Paid Mr Keep for a piece of haucer (hauser?) Cord for Cullam ferry Boat 4s.9d.' There are several similar entries; Keep was probably the ferryman. A turnpike road was built by Act of Parliament to join the main road with a road to the south via Sutton Courtenay. The

Act stipulated that a bridge was to be built in place of the ferry at or near it. In fact the ferry was just west of the present bridge. A right of way still cuts off a corner of the new road to arrive at that spot. Opened in 1807, the bridge, known as Sutton Bridge, was a private toll bridge until 1938 when it was bought jointly by Oxfordshire and Berkshire County Councils. There was a little toll cottage under the bridge lived in by the tollkeeper's family but it was damp in winter and often flooded.[35]

## CHAPTER TEN

# Clifton Hampden to Wallingford

And here are roads the river cuts in twain
With ne'er a ford where heavy wheels can run,
Nor bridge on which their course they can maintain,
And 'tis the ferry joins their broken threads in one.[1]

## APPLEFORD

Appleford (Exp.170 529 941) is a village with no access to the river, except by the railway bridge. It appears to have forsaken the Thames altogether, yet its name is derived from a ford. To put matters in perspective, the villagers celebrated the millennium in 2000 by changing the name to Appleford-on-Thames.[2] The manor was owned by the Abbey of Abingdon, which always set up a ford or ferry wherever possible on their lands. In this case the ford may have been very ancient, linking to a prehistoric way. A quick glance at the map shows a long straight footpath on the opposite bank, running parallel with the railway, from the Dorchester/Abingdon road to where it meets the river at a small copse. Opposite the copse are the meadows of Appleford Manor Farm and then the village and church on a knoll. The main road out of the village is in line with that footpath. The route through the town of Didcot running south can be followed on the map by roads and paths leading directly to the Downs, along which runs the prehistoric Ridgeway. The common belief in the village is that the ford was used to transport apples that grew in orchards on the northern slopes of the Downs, but where were they being taken to? An important hoard of pewter goods has been found at Appleford and this should give an indication of its antiquity.

## CLIFTON HAMPDEN

At Clifton Hampden was a natural fording place and ferry crossing from at least the fifteenth century (Exp.170 546 953). Not until Victorian times were they replaced by a bridge, the latest built over the Upper Thames until well into the twentieth century. The crossings are usually known as just Clifton, ford, ferry, or bridge. Hampden was added in Tudor times.[3] Until the Dissolution the village was associated with Dorchester Abbey, not very far away.

The natural shoals of rock just beneath the water surface were an impediment to navigation and were the reason why the first navigation commission, the Oxford-

Clifton Hampden. The supposed ferry place below the church to the east of the bridge built in 1867 to the design of G. G. Scott who also restored the church. From a private photograph album *c.* 1875.

Burcot Commission, had difficulty in accomplishing a satisfactory navigation. Burcot is the next village downstream. John Taylor, the Water Poet, describes the difficulties at Clifton in his poem 'Taylor on Thames Isis', his account of a journey he made in August 1631 rowing back to Staines from Oxford.[4] He had been part of a team of watermen taking a party of Commissioners by shallop on an inspection of the Thames on matters of improving navigation.

> At Clifton there are rocks, and sands, and flats,
> Which made us wade, and wet like drowned rats,
> The passage bare, the water often gone,
> And rocks smooth worne, doe pave it like free stone.

In winter, with more water running, the ferry took over the business from the ford. The earliest mention of ferrymen was in the early fourteenth century when John Broun performed the task and was succeeded by his sons, John and Richard, who also acted as Hithwards (wharfingers).[5] Around 1441 the ferry passed to some descendants, including Thomas Frenshe, alias King. Roger Roper of Watlington passed ownership of the ferry in 1493 to Exeter College, Oxford, who held other lands in the area, as well as the tithes. It was said in 1607 that the ferryman would sit in the inglenook at the Barley Mow watching for customers to come along.[6] It would have been a good vantage point because the ferry point was just a few yards downstream and went across diagonally to below the church which stands on a bluff. The ford stretched for about a mile upstream, westwards. In 1692/93 it was noted, 'At Clifton ffery is a great boat to carry horse and man over', and even in 1834 'Pedestrian' noted on his travels that the beauty of the scene was enhanced by the ferry 'continually passing to and fro' below the church.[7]

Robert Mylne in his report of 1802 noted that the shoals were still bad for navigation although some had been removed since his last survey ten years previously and only the hard ones remained.[8] Unfortunately, matters had not improved by 1826 when the Lord Mayor of London ventured on a ceremonial progress downriver from Oxford. His state barge was stuck on a rock outcrop at Clifton for several hours until sufficient water was let down through the weirs to allow it to be refloated.[9] By 1835 navigation had improved but it did not satisfy the villagers of Long Wittenham and Clifton Hampden who had been free to drive their cattle across the ford whenever they wished. It was obvious a bridge was necessary.

Henry Hucks Gibbs, a governor of the Bank of England, inherited the manor of Clifton Hampden and bought the ferry rights from his old college, Exeter, in 1861. Gibbs was willing to put up the money to build a bridge, and engaged the architect George Gilbert Scott to design it. An Act of Parliament was obtained at great expense in 1864.[10] The preamble stated that a bridge 'would be of both local and public advantage'. The Act permitted Gibbs to discontinue the ancient ford and build a bridge for conveying carriages, carts, horses, cattle and passengers across the Thames from a point where the ferry crossed from the left bank. Other works he was permitted to make included diverting and altering the towpath on the north bank, making an approach road and embankment through Clifton Hampden village and Long Wittenham, terminating at the north-east corner of the Barley Mow, and constructing an approach road and embankment to join the public highway from Clifton Hampden to Abingdon.

Provision was made for the arch over the towpath and navigation to be not less than thirty feet on the north side (in fact this arch was built narrower than the rest, partly because at that date the towpath was not much in use).[11] Navigation on the river was not to be obstructed in any way. It was to be a public, not a County Bridge. Tolls were allowed to be charged but were kept low to be used for maintenance only. Some people were given free passage, for instance the vicar of Long Wittenham and his family and persons engaged in towing on the river. From the day the bridge opened in 1867 nobody was allowed to use a ford or ferry within 200 yards of the bridge, except for towing horses.

Bridge at Clifton Hampden looking downstream. The Barley Mow is to the right behind the trees. From a postcard.

The toll house built on the right bank at Clifton Hampden. Postcard by Percy Simms of Chipping Norton, posted from Clifton Hampden, 28 July 1930.

After the bridge was opened the undertakers were empowered to stop up and discontinue the public thoroughfare called Ferry Road and the footpath from the east end of the Barley Mow to the ferry place on the south bank (this path is now part of the Thames Path which crosses over the bridge to change sides). Furthermore, the public thoroughfare known as Ferry Road was to be discontinued between an imaginary line from the north-east corner of a cottage garden in Clifton Hampden occupied by William Day and extending eastwards to a point where the wall of the parish church joins the blacksmiths shop occupied by William Bell. If at any time the bridge should become dangerous or need repair, the undertakers must provide a ferry.

Clifton Bridge was built in a medieval style in red bricks which were dug and made in kilns on Gibbs' land.[12] Local man Richard Casey was the builder and when the toll house on the south side close to the Barley Mow was completed with the toll gate, he occupied it as toll keeper. The narrow bridge today is controlled by traffic lights and is in continual use by vehicles and pedestrians, who take refuge in the triangular cutwaters provided. It is apparent from some documents that a bridge was planned a long time before it happened. In 1775 Gibbs' father exchanged some lands in Clifton for land near the ferry. The *Oxford Journal* in 1843 published a notice about closing the Church Path at Clifton Hampden and opening another through Gibbs' land.[13] The road through the little village connecting it with the main turnpike road was to be closed and another provided. The Barley Mow stands today at a very dangerous corner where the road from Long Wittenham takes an S-bend round to the left, skirting the garden of the inn to approach the bridge past the toll house. The front of the inn faces east and would have looked straight across to the ferry. Opposite, on a grass verge at the corner, is an old building which could have been a blacksmith's shop or a stable.

One of the most well-known inns on the river, the Barley Mow, has the date 1352 over a door and has the appearance of an olde-worlde pub on a calendar. The original building at the front was half timbered of cruck construction, the uprights being of wych-elm and filled with wattle and daub.[14] The large thatched roof was typical of the area and probably made of reeds cut from the river's edge, which formed one part of

The Barley Mow at Clifton Hampden. The road leading to the bridge is around the corner of the building as shown. Drawing from menu card issued by the inn, 2010.

the garden boundary. Inside, the parlour had a brick floor, a large stone fireplace and oak panelling that was around 400 years old. There have been many alterations over the centuries, including a large extension to the rear, but still the inn, despite being very busy, retains its country atmosphere. The thatch has caught fire several times, the last very seriously in 1975, when restoration cost £80,000. On that occasion the firemen had to tear down unburnt thatch to stop the fire from spreading. In 1997 the pub was restored again. Being so close to the ford and ferry, the pub must have been closely associated with the crossing. It was usual for the publican to operate the ferry as well. Certainly it would have provided food and shelter to all travellers in need of them.

In 1946 the joint County Councils of Oxfordshire and Berkshire bought the bridge from a private owner and made it toll-free.

## WITTENHAM FERRY

Little Wittenham is a small hamlet with church on the banks of the Thames (Exp.170 566 935) approached from Long Wittenham by a lane running due east. Here was a ford in ancient times overlooked by the twin hills known as Wittenham Clumps but the proper name is Sinodun Hills. Castle Hill, the larger of the two, is an Iron-Age hill fort measuring about 200 metres across its widest point.[15] Excavations have shown that preceding the Iron Age a late Bronze Age settlement occupied the site, a rare occurrence in the Upper Thames Valley. Archaeologists suggest the large enclosed area was used to keep animals and for storage, while the human settlement was mostly outside the defences, where a Roman masonry building has been identified and Roman artefacts found close to the surface.

The proximity of the church to the river shows the site to be of great antiquity, although the present church would have replaced an earlier one. It has, squeezed into a niche in the tower, a monument to Sir William Dunch who died in 1611 and his wife who was aunt to Oliver Cromwell.[16] The monument is saved from a much larger architectural affair. The Dunch family were influential in the Wallingford area for many generations as landowners and MPs until the male line died out in 1719. To the side of the tarmaced road outside the church is a well-made cobbled stone path which stretches a few yards then merges with the track, wide enough for vehicles, which leads down to the river. There is a Thames Conservancy lock-keeper's house and a footbridge to an island in the river. Several rights of way converge at this spot. One of them leads to Dorchester Abbey, seen about a mile away.

The ferry at Day's Lock was moved to behind where the photographer
was standing. In the distance the footbridge marks the spot where
the ancient crossing was. The towpath runs on the left hand side on
the left bank of the river. From a photograph album *c.*1880.

These are all factors pointing to the assumption that this, and not the ferry place
further upstream near Day's Lock, was the original ford, then ferry. Thacker says
nothing about this ferry except in passing to say that Leland mentioned it twice
around 1530 and suggests it may have been used only when the water was too
high for the ford. Operation of the ferry was in the hands of the local landowner, in
conjunction with the weir upstream. It is not known when the ferry place was moved
to Day's Lock at a point almost opposite the Dyke Hills. No right of way is marked
from the river bank there on the east, although the present right of way passes close.

   Papers from the Lamer Park Estate, near Wheathampstead in Hertfordshire, give
some history of Little Wittenham Ferry[17] (Thacker calls it Dorchester Ferry). A plan
dated 1838 shows the towing path on both sides of the river above the lock which
began building in 1788 as a pound lock. The weir was associated with it. There was
a toll bridge over a side stream, with no other way to it than the towing path. An
undated old indenture lists lands belonging to Edmund Dunch (a common Christian
name in that family) and along with properties in other places along the Thames,
including the ferry house, ferry and fishing at Eynsham in Oxfordshire, is the manor
of Little Wittenham in Berkshire which had free passage over the Thames. An
Abstract of Title prepared in 1839 seemingly to determine which county, Berkshire or
Oxfordshire, Little Wittenham was situated in, gives details of the manorial property.
At that time it was held in trust from the late Rt Hon. Robert, Earl of Cardigan and
the ferry was described as, 'all that messuage, or tenement or ferry House together
with all the outhouses and appurtenances belonging thereto commonly called or
known by the name of Wittenham Ferry situate in the island which lies in the River
Thames in Wittenham all in the parish of Dorchester in the County of Berkshire and
Oxford or one of them' The actual ferry was included, being over the river adjoining
the ferry house together with the ferry boats and the profits arising from the ferry.
Included also were parts of the river, its creeks and ditches and the fishery which was
about to be made. Surprisingly another clause refers to, 'all that new built messuage or
tenement or ferry house together with all outhouses etc.' There were two ferries!

A separate document dated 20 August 1828, made before the Earl died, is the lease between him and eleven of the Thames Commissioners of the properties on the Thames. The Commissioners were to take on the ferry house as described above, the lock and tolls gained from it, plus the fishing and ferry. All profits and advantages then in the tenure of Vincent Cherrill as tenant to the Earl were to be taken by the Commissioners, except the holdings held separately by Cherril. In October 1822 Cherrill had been earning 50s a month for taking care of Dorchester lock, but when the Commissioners took over he was asked to resign and was paid £6 18s for his weir tackle. The lock and weir were in a bad state when the Thames Conservancy took over in 1867.

A footbridge crosses now at the first ferry place to the island over a backwater and then over the mainstream down from Day's lock but there is no sign of a ferry. The one above the lock continued into the twentieth century but a crossing made over the lock is now used by the Thames Path to change sides. To continue along the path towards Shillingford, the way is to double back a few yards after descending the footbridge and then pass under the bridge next to the river, taking care not to slip on the steep bank although some studs have been inserted to prevent this happening. Several footpaths in the area afford a pleasant Sunday afternoon stroll for families. A former lock-keeper, Lynn David, noticed that some of these people took sticks from the hedgerows to play Pooh-sticks from the bridge.[18] As a fundraiser for the RNLI he decided to start a World Poohsticks Championship in aid of the fund although Little Wittenham was not the traditional Poohsticks place (Ashdown Forest). The championship started in 1984 and is still held in March each year, attracting contestants from around the world and benefiting RNLI by over £30,000 to date.

Traces of Roman artefacts found close to a clearly defined Roman Road indicate there was a crossing or ford across the Thames in the vicinity of Dorchester, which was a small Roman town. Some have suggested it was at the junction with the River Thame, where traces of a ford have been found.[19] But Dr Grundy and I. D. Margary both perceive it to be at Old Street Ford about ¾ mile south-east of Dorchester (Exp.170 587 933). Road alignments on the map strengthen this theory.

## KEEN EDGE FERRY

Only a few yards further downstream is the site of Keen Edge Ferry (Exp.170 590 932). This was a horse ferry set up by the Thames Commissioners about 1793, made necessary possibly because of a landowner's whim who did not wish the towing path to go through his land, or access to the river bank was difficult. The name is strange; originally it was 'hedge', not Edge.[20] Thacker, who found a similar place near Sunbury called Cane Hedge, considers it might have something to do with osiers or willow canes which had been planted as a hedge for the towing path. The type of marshy land in which they grow does border the main road at this point. As the ferry had ceased operation around 1953 and the projected replacement bridge was not built, the initial plan was for the Thames Path to continue on the left bank into Shillingford. That plan was abandoned and instead the ferry house was demolished, the adjacent small inlet filled in and a short public footpath made to join the very busy A4074 road. Walkers will need to take extreme caution because, on emerging through the roadside hedge by a milepost, there is no pavement. No warning signs are in place to inform drivers there might suddenly be pedestrians crossing the road. There are no parking places. The Path continues along the road and turns right through Shillingford village to reach the Thames bank again at Shillingford Bridge.

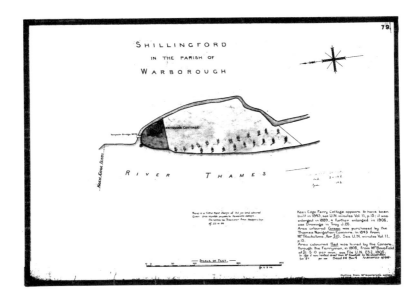

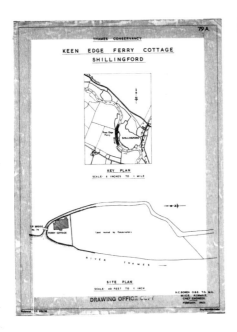

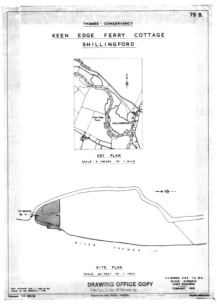

The site of Keen Edge Ferry near Shillingford as detailed in the Thames Conservancy file. Reproduced with kind permission of the Environment Agency.

Unusually, names of some ferry keepers have been handed down.[21] The first was William Lafford who worked until 1801 for 15s a month when it was raised to 20s. The Patrick family were at the ferry for a considerable time. In October 1822 James Patrick was being paid 24s. A single-storey ferry house was finally provided in 1843 and extra rooms were provided in 1889 and 1906. George Patrick had his wages reduced in 1854 from 32s to 20s a month. The Conservancy employed Mrs Hannah Patrick in 1866 at 40s and although in July 1870 she was declared incompetent, she remained in the post until October 1884. C. Clutterbuck took over in 1887 but, sadly, he and his wife both drowned on the night of 25/26 March 1892. Albert Wise was then appointed.

When Brian Eade's grandfather became ferryman at Keen Edge in 1925 there were two ferry boats.[22] A flat large punt was used to take livestock, including the towing horses, whilst the smaller punt transported people by rowing or punting across. Mr Eade had retired from the Royal Navy and served the Thames Conservancy for twenty-five years mainly as lock-keeper.

## SHILLINGFORD

Shillingford village grew up as a result of a ford over the Thames at the foot of Shillingford Hill on the right bank where the scarp slopes steeply to meet the river (Exp.170 596 920). The ford was replaced by a primitive bridge of sorts on the same trajectory. Thacker claimed to have found a reference to a bridge, with a way to it called the Bridgeway, in a Patent Roll of 1301.[23] This is a very early date for a bridge not on a main highway and although he knew 'the Patent Rolls have a way of being meticulously accurate', Thacker remained sceptical because he could not collaborate this information which he published in 1920.[24] Therefore he was delighted five years later to find in a Patent Roll of 1320 a reference indicating the Bridgeway was indeed the bridge at Shillingford, and in consequence he could date the original bridge to the year 957, thus making it the oldest of all the Thames bridges. Thacker wished to publish his findings in an Oxford newspaper.

It is likely the bridge was built by either the castle at Wallingford or Dorchester Abbey as it is equally distant from both, or even built jointly by them. The Victoria County History for Berkshire items that the profits of Shillingford Bridge belonged to Wallingford Castle and in 1300 were worth 12s 6d.[25] Is this the item that Thacker first found? By the fourteenth century it had become customary for the porter of the castle to receive a grant of these profits for life. Roger Hurst was the porter who received this grant in 1378.[26] After that are no more references to a bridge, it may have fallen or been taken down as a precautionary measure to secure the defence of Wallingford Castle, because from then on a ferry and a fishery are noted. They were usually let together. Around 1530 Roger Hacheman held the fishery and was appointed to the ferry and its boats at a rental of 33s 4d a year, in succession to William Yong. Fifteen years later Hacheman was still around as tenant of a little Ferry House beside the ferry. The present Shillingford Bridge Hotel may be the present incarnation of that Ferry House. In 1692 there was, 'a great boat to waft over Carts, Coaches, horse and man'.[27]

When he became Bishop of Salisbury in 1667, Seth Ward (1617–89) set about restoring the Cathedral.[28] He also founded the College of Matrons in 1682, possibly with help in design by Christopher Wren who was his friend of long standing. It was a hospital or almshouse for the benefit of widows of ten Anglican priests of the Diocese of Salisbury. To endow the College, Ward gave various lands in his possession which were augmented by other donations from time to time. The fee farm rents (rent charge) of Shillingford ferry were part of the endowment, given by Robert King of the Inner Temple by indenture of 1 February 1693. They yielded £3 13s 8d per year. This was to cause problems in later years.

William Cox died in 1745. Probate records describe him as ferryman of Shillingford in the parish of Warborough.[29] As the ferry was very dangerous when the river was in flood, some local gentry petitioned Parliament in 1763 to build a bridge. An Act for a new bridge and road to it was obtained in 1764 by Sir William Blackstone, who lived in Wallingford. It was built in timber on stone piers to replace the ferry. A loan of £7,700 had been obtained to buy out the ferry rights.[30] Yet in 1826 the bridge was already being demolished and the Bridge Trustees had started building a stone bridge, presumably as part of the turnpike. In the interregnum, 'a new and most commodious ferry boat will be provided for the purpose of conveying carriages and waggons [sic] horses and passengers across the river, and as proper men will be employed in the management of the ferry, no delay or inconvenience will be experienced'. The Trustees of the Shillingford, Wallingford, Reading Road and Shillingford Bridge, over the Thames at or near Shillingford Ferry Trust continued to pay the rents to the charity. But when their Act expired in 1874 and the bridge was taken over as a county bridge by the Counties of Oxfordshire and Berkshire, the rents became in arrears.[31] There were other disputes concerning repair of the bridge and roadway, settled eventually by the counties deciding the boundary between them should be halfway across the river bed.

Finally J. M. Davenport, Clerk of the Peace in Oxford, replied to Fitzherbert Macdonald, Sub Treasurer and Overseer of the Charity, stating that the County was under no responsibility for payment of the fee farm rent. The freehold of the bridge was not vested in the county, but in the owner of the soil (riparian owners). The Trust had ended with no tolls being charged, so 'your clients are in the same position as the Bondholders of a dis-turnpiked road'. 'Admitting that the bridge was substituted for a ferry and the rent being a charge on the ferry makes any claim upon the county

Shillingford Bridge ,which replaced the ferry a little further upstream to the left. The large field on the opposite side later became a cricket ground. The Shillingford Bridge Hotel now occupies the site of the Swan Hotel. From a photograph album *c.* 1880.

more remote.' However, the charity has continued to this day, albeit under a different constitution.

Recently, Oxfordshire County Council has announced two very welcome initiatives.[32] The speed limit on the road between Dorchester and Shillingford where it passes the exit of the Thames Path from Keen Edge is to be reduced to 40 mph. Secondly, as a result of negotiations with the landowner of North Farm on the south side of the river, an ancient footpath which has not been used since the eighteenth century is to be opened up and extended to provide a circular walk from Shillingford Bridge Hotel. The path used to lead to a ferry site which was stopped up when the second bridge was built in 1827. Therefore, it is deduced the original ferry was in a direct line with Warborough Road as it leaves Shillingford village where it forms a dog-leg to continue to the new road constructed to link with the bridge. Alternatively it could have been where the old towpath changed sides a little further upstream. There a footbridge and a hedge line runs westwards to join the old trackway which was the Roman road to Old Street Ford. It is hoped a similar project can be achieved on the other side of the Thames, but alas there are no plans to reinstate a ferry or bridge.

## BENSON

At Bensington – the name shortened by inhabitants to Benson from the sixteenth century – there was an embanked enclosure in prehistoric times called Medler's Bank.[33] It had a track running west to east along the bank and was crossed at right angles by three other highways and later a Roman road also crossed at this point. It seems the east to west track crossed the Thames at the point where the horse ferry crossed, at the same place where the original ford had been.[34] There is no sign of Medler's Bank now (possibly obliterated by Benson Airfield) and the ford is reputed to have been by what is now Rivermead recreation ground (Exp.170 612 916). The horse ferry was made necessary because the towing path from Wallingford had to cross, and this was where a cruiser station was set up. Benson was not only a crossing point in Saxon times, but the river was a boundary in 779 when Offa of Mercia beat Cynewulf of Wessex.[35] References have been made to a castle at Crowmarsh, which is the part of Benson parish that borders the Thames. No confirmation of the castle has yet been found.

In the middle of the street at Crowmarsh is the Swan Inn, now a private residence. It looked out to the river over a grassy patch, likely to have been a coal wharf. To the right at the end of a millstream is Crowmarsh Mill. Here there once was a ferry cottage, and perhaps another ferry, but the whole is now shut off to provide a very private residence. A few yards upstream where the millstream leaves the main river is a long fenced-off walkway across the weir to the lock house on an island. This is the right of way which replaced a ferry. Again, about 150 yards further upstream is another public footpath which leads straight to the river for no apparent reason. This may be another old crossing point.

## CROWMARSH FERRY

Benson ferry aka Crowmarsh (Exp.170 613 908) ferry was further downstream towards Crowmarsh Battle Farm.[36] Ferry cottage is a long, low building with its back to the road, the last house on the right-hand side. On the south side of the house is a stile with steps hidden in the hedge. The way to the ferry was through the garden, beside a hedge to the water's edge. On the opposite side a footpath still leads

The millstream (where the man is sitting), the river, now a weir, and lock at Benson. From a private photograph album *c.* 1880.

Benson Weir from the left bank on the upstream side. The walkway was the only access to the lock house to the right. A postcard from Wallingford 5 August 1905.

southwards from the former landing place. This was the quickest route to Wallingford. Now it is all stopped up on the Crowmarsh side and has been since 1920. G. D. Leslie RA came this way when he was writing his book; published in 1881.[37] He followed the towing path from Wallingford until he found this, 'pretty little ferry just below the weir. Near to it is a sheep-wash'.

This ferry was always important for the Thames authorities. In 1787 a surveyor was asked to report on the prospective line of the horse towing path and ferries from Pangbourne to the end at Benson.[38] A meeting was to be held on 24 August to determine sites at Benson for making the horse towing paths and ferries. Several expenses for Benson ferry are noted and works carried out by Robert Treacher in 1788. Mr Roles was paid £1 4s 4d for a ferry line; a chain was bought from Mr Phillips for £1 10s 6d; Henry Knap claimed 10s 7d for iron work of some sort. In September a padlock for the ferry cost 1s 8d and in December a new punt pole cost 1s 6d. Joseph Ashby was lock-keeper at Benson in 1793 but as he acted as ferryman as well, his salary was £15 12s per annum.[39] Mr Jones was the last ferryman at Crowmarsh Ferry. He enlisted in the Army in 1914 but unfortunately did not return from France and the ferry fell into disuse.[40]

The Thames Conservancy Board held a special meeting about this unsatisfactory state of affairs, on 2 February 1920 with Lord Desborough in the chair. It was pointed out this was not a navigation ferry, that was at the lock a little further upstream. This Crowmarsh Ferry was an ancient passage between two footpaths. The Conservators had no evidence as to the original grant; probably it was a legal or a franchise ferry. At that time ownership was vested in Lord Wittenham. The toll was regularly one halfpenny, but under the present ownership it had increased to one penny and toll tickets were issued on payment. In November 1914 a notice had been posted on the Oxfordshire side to the effect the ferry would be closed for the winter, but up to 1920 it had not been revived. The Conservators learnt of this in 1919 when local authorities approached Lord Wittenham who, without admitting liability, said he hoped to reopen the ferry in 1920 but was unable to find a man or accommodation for him. However, he did admit there was a ferryman's cottage and garden but he could not dispose of it. This was because it was occupied by a widow and her five children (Mrs Jones?) Then Lord Wittenham disclosed the takings averaged at 2s 6d a week, whereas the costs were £4 or £5. The ferry punt was at the bottom of the water and was in a bad state; 'They are difficult to get now'. The Board concluded that Lord Wittenham was committing an illegal act when he shut up the ferry.[41] He was empowered to offer the ferry to the parish council but they refused so it was closed for good.

However, the ferry at the lock continued for a while longer and in the 1930s Brian Eade's grandfather was both lock-keeper and ferryman.[42] Being a little deaf, some passengers complained he took no notice when they shouted. So he installed a bell but he later regretted this because no longer could he pretend he had not heard them! The ferry must have closed at the beginning of the Second World War. It is no longer needed because the weir walkway serves the Thames Path and other pedestrians.

# CHAPTER ELEVEN
# Wallingford to Gatehampton

## WALLINGFORD

Wallingford was one of the earliest and most important crossings on the Thames. The ford, although it did flood occasionally, was usually the most reliable on the river. It has been estimated that there was an early wooden bridge at the spot, defended by ramparts on the west bank.[1] William I, following his conquest at Hastings, was thwarted when he tried to cross the Thames at Southwark and marched on Wallingford, where he had friends. Soon afterwards the Normans built a large castle overlooking the river to defend the crossing. Some parts of it are still standing, in a public garden.

The timber bridge was replaced by one of stone, called the Great Bridge (Exp.171 610 894) possibly in the twelfth century. The earliest reference is in 1141. Thacker compares the design with that of London Bridge and speculated it might have been the work of the same architect.[2] There were nineteen arches included in the causeway and bridge. A Priory was nearby and a bridge chapel named the Mary Grace was at the town end. Over the centuries, the bridge has been widened, the arches strengthened and adjustments made to improve navigation. Stones from the Priory were used at times to patch up the bridge. It was found that the arches were too narrow to allow barges through, so Wallingford became a trans-shipment port, with warehouses on the wharves. By the sixteenth century or before, the bridge was vested in the Borough Corporation.[3] The Council minutes in 1756 record a winch provided for free use by bargemasters and the public. The town also bought a pont boat and chain at £7 for the benefit of bargemasters. The pont was a ferry worked by a rope or chain. A new one was provided twenty-seven years later. Perhaps the ferry aided trans-shipment or was necessary in times of flood. After a flood in 1809 destroyed four arches, the Council agreed to purchase ferry boats and hire men to take people, horses and carriages over the river at the expense of the Bridge Estate. They leased tolls for this temporary ferry but somehow the tolls were evaded.

The town had its own mint, but lost importance when Culham and Abingdon bridges were built in the fifteenth century, taking away traffic bound for Gloucester and the west. The many artefacts found at Wallingford ford and bridge illustrate how important the crossing was; some time-keeping instruments; a medieval pitcher; Saxon spearhead; medieval dagger; medieval water bottle; Iron-Age sword; medieval two-handled pot and numerous dirks and sheath knives. They are deposited in Reading Museum.

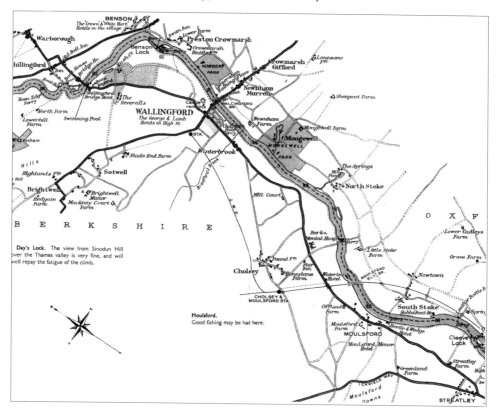

Wallingford is the chief town on this stretch of the river between Shillingford and Streatley. From *Stanford's New Map of the River Thames, c.* 1900.

Wallingford, showing part of the ancient bridge, wharf, boathouse and slipway. Salter's steamer *Cliveden* is awaiting passengers before proceeding downstream under the bridge. Postcard posted from the town in 1907.

## CHALMORE HOLE

At Chalmore Hole or Chamber's Hole (Exp.171 608 886) was an ancient ferry at the point where the Bradford's Brook enters the Thames. The brook forms the southern boundary of the parish of Wallingford. On the south side of the brook is Winterbrook which is part of the parish of Cholsey. Nobody knows the origin of the strange name but a lease exists during the time of Henry III in about 1265 concerning an acre of land in Chalmore.[4] The name does not appear on the modern map.

Under the Thames Commissioners when the horse towing path was set up, the ferry became an official ferry in 1787. It was supposed to carry the towing horses over the river from one bank to the other. However, Thacker found in the Treacher papers for 1811 that there were difficulties and horses were being walked back on the Berkshire side on the upward journey for quite a way to join the road and into the town of Wallingford, over the bridge, and back on the Oxfordshire side to reunite with their barge, a distance of three miles. The reason is unknown. The cost for each horse to cross was tuppence.

Robert Child of Wallingford was appointed ferryman at a wage of 3s 6d a week in 1778, the year John Wesley visited Wallingford. Other ferrymen identified were Richard Jones in October 1822 who earned 26s a month; James Jones was ferryman until his death in June 1829 when William Wilder took on the job. In 1830 a rood of land on the south side of the brook was purchased to build a ferry house, but it was not built until the new works were finished. Being susceptible to floods in that area, the house which was very small had five steps up to the front door which faced upstream. No trace of the house is evident today except a small fenced grass enclosure still in the ownership of the Thames authority.

Although suggestions had been made for a lock and weir at Chalmore Hole much earlier, it was not until 1837 that construction began.[5] Accounts for the period from 24 June until 30 December show there were two sorts of work, the lock and the weir,

Lock and weir at Chalmore Hole in a dilapidated condition pictured *c.* 1880. The first ferry house is shown clearly with a boathouse beyond, which was adjacent to the first ferry landing place. From a private photograph album.

1. Father Thames adorns the front cover of S. C. Hall's *The Book of the Thames* published in 1859.

2. Eisey footbridge near Cricklade carries a right of way over the infant Thames – a replacement bridge erected by the Environment Agency.

3. Ferry Cottage, Eaton Hastings, seen from the churchyard on 17 July 2008.

4. Duxford ford marked by stakes after February rain, 21 February 2009. The ford has a concrete base and could take vehicles if necessary, but this is not advisable.

5. Hart's Weir near Kelmscott at the site of the Anchor Inn. Some humps in the ground and this little storehouse and the pollarded willow are all that is left to remind of the former settlement. Looking north on 4 March 2010.

6. Paddles and rymers stacked up by the Thames Conservancy house at Rushy Weir near Buckland, Oxfordshire. 4 March 2010.

7. Rushy Weir: a steel walkway constructed over the weir to take the Thames Path. Formerly the ferry crossed just upstream of the weir.

8. Wallingford Bridge with St Peter's church, from Boydell's *Thames*.

9. Shillingford Bridge under repair, taken from the grounds of the hotel. 18 May 2010.

10. The Binsey poplars made famous by G. M. Hopkins in his poem of that name. They formed an avenue beside the Thames and were felled in 1879 when they were about 100 feet high. More have been planted since. Here is the modern version, 20 May 2010.

11. Horse Ferry between Goring on the left, and Streatley, from the hills above Goring. The road on the Streatley side which passed by the mill has travellers making their way to the ferry. From William Havell, *A Series of Picturesque Views of the River Thames*. Dedicated to the Commissioners of the Thames Navigation, 1818.

12. The secluded ferry cottage at Little Stoke, 19 May 2010.

13. Gatehampton Ferry Cottage, now used by fishing parties, 19 May 2010.

14. The Roebuck Hotel, which faces away from the Thames. Its future remains uncertain as of October 2010.

*Above left:* **15.** The Willow Walk at North Hinksey from the bridge over the Hinksey Stream showing a portion of the original surface of the path. A girl came 'then took her onward road' to Oxford, 21 May 2010.

*Above right:* **16.** Medmenham ferry. Monument erected to commemorate the successful court case fought in 1898 concerning the existence of a public right of way at the ferry, 15 April 2010.

**17.** Medmenham slipway. A traditional skiff, handmade by the owner, being taken from the river, 15 April 2010.

18. Ivy has grown into and split apart some Welsh slate slabs which bounded the path to the ferry at Temple Island. Others litter the ground. A form of fencing uncommon in southern England, it deserves to be restored. 14 April 2010.

19. Feeding the ducks at My Lady Ferry Cottage at Cliveden. The French windows are for the new kitchen. 15 April 2010.

20. Ferry Cottage opposite the church in North Hinksey near Oxford. A listed building, its outward appearance belies its ancient origins. 21 May 2010.

21. Hurley, an attractive path which was the way to the ferry. On the right is the boundary wall to the gardens and ruins of the former Priory. 14 April 2010.

**22.** The spring at Cliveden drawn by Samuel Ireland. The water table is now lower and this spot is a soggy patch in the lawn at the side of a boathouse. It is overlooked by Spring Cottage and the ferry place was a few yards behind the artist.

**23.** Datchet Ferry, looking towards Windsor Great Park. From Havell, *Picturesque Views of the Thames*.

**24.** Marlow. Looking across from the churchyard to the much enlarged Compleat Angler. The renowned suspension bridge is to the right. 14 April 2010.

**25.** The walkway for the Thames Path was cantilevered out from the Bourne End railway bridge to replace the ferries at Spade Oak and Bourne End. 13 April 2010.

**26.** The London Stone can hardly be seen from the river where it is stands in a corner of the children's playground at the Lammas Park at Staines.

each with different teams of workers. For the weir the team usually consisted of twelve men. In one week John Drake the foreman worked for six days and was paid £1 16s 6d for board and lodging. His under-foreman Thomas Coster for the same time earned £1 7s. Henry Egleton received £1 1s, but eight unnamed workmen worked for six days each at 15s. William Collet (a junior?) earned only 9s. However, Mrs Reading's bill for beer amounted to £1 6s!

The work, described as a 'summer or low-water lock and weir', was completed in March 1838. As part of the work an island near Wallingford which obstructed the navigation was blasted away. The lock was against the Crowmarsh or left bank and the weir stretched right across the river to the Chalmore side.[6] Stephen Wheeler was appointed temporary lock and weir-keeper and ferryman at 12s weekly. John Garratt took over in October 1839 at an initial salary of £39 per annum. As his duties diminished, so did his salary, being only £24 in 1854. At his death in June 1859 John Whiteman became in charge, followed by his son John Whiteman Jnr in 1866 at a salary of 52s a month and when he resigned in 1868 Edward Morris took over until he was sent to Cookham in September 1873 and John W. May succeeded.

By this time the lock and weir were hardly used and had fallen into disrepair. There was a fall of only 18 inches. The Conservancy proposed to demolish the lock and weir but faced opposition from the inhabitants of Wallingford, they were fearful of low water causing bad odours in the town.[7] The lock-keeper was told not to take tolls. Finally the lock and weir were removed in 1883 and the bed of the river deepened, but weir posts were left *in situ*, causing further problems to navigation.[8] The ferry continued, operated by J. Sparks until he retired in 1895, then followed by Charles Upstone.

During a large flood on 15 November 1894 the big ferry boat broke away from the moorings and was not replaced. Instead a row boat was used until 1953.[9] The Conservancy had tried to close down the ferry since 1938 but had to concede to popular demand, although it was no longer used to transfer towing horses. The projected Thames Path did not allow for a ferry and instead made a narrow path to Wallingford on the right bank, often cutting across gardens of houses which had had frontage to the river. The little ferry house burnt down and was replaced by a much larger one, resembling a boathouse, on a corresponding piece of land, including a large garden, on the north side of Bradford's Brook. It is also built up to avoid floods and was used to house an official of the Environment Agency, who still own it, but lease it out to tenants.

At the end of the road from Wallingford southwards through Winterbrook is a traffic roundabout where the bypass (A4130) turns left to cross the river by a modern bridge, Winterbrook Bridge. On the other side is Mongewell (Exp.171 607 882) which is listed as a lost village.[10] Here the ancient track of the Ridgeway runs in a straight line down from the hills, through the Grim's Ditch to reach the Thames as a public footpath a short distance upstream of the new bridge. On the Winterbrook side a track at a place called White Cross is in line with this footpath. Serving such an important cross country way there undoubtedly would be a ford or ferry. Now a recognised National Trail, the Ridgeway turns at Mongewell to run downstream parallel to the river on the left bank until it reaches Goring. The Thames Path runs along the right bank.

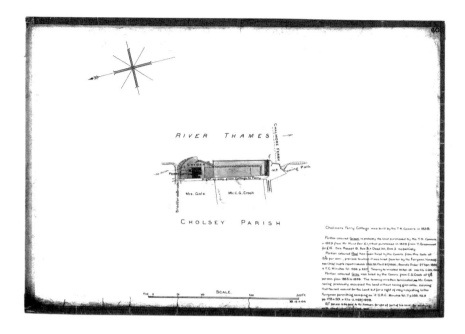

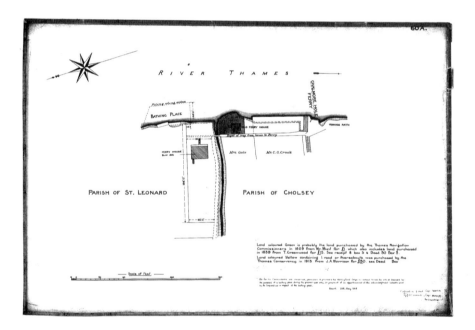

Thames Conservancy plan made in the 1930s of the two ferry houses at Chalmore Hole which give details of the acquisition of land. Reproduced with kind permission of the Environment Agency.

The larger ferry house built in 1915 from which the ferry operated. A large punt is moored in front and the ferryman is working another with a sweep. Reproduced with the kind permission of the Environment Agency.

## NORTH STOKE

North Stoke is a village lying next to the Thames on the left bank. At the end of the village street going north is a millstream with the mill and mill house now kept as private residences. The Ridgeway Path follows this street and a little beyond the mill a footpath branches off to lead to the river and the former ferry place (Exp.171 606 865). It is a wide path fenced on both sides, suggesting the ferry was used for hay and corn wains to get to the fields on the Berkshire side. Where it reaches the river the track opens out to a space which clearly was used as a wharf, with a small docking creek to the side. The towing path was on the opposite side until it reached Little Stoke ferry.

It is supposed that in this landscape criss-crossed by ancient trackways this ferry was an ancient institution. It was mentioned in a marriage settlement made on 25 March 1780 between the Marquis de la Pierre and Miss Dorothy Phelp who was heiress of her father, John Phelp of Hampton Wick.[11] During the Commonwealth a previous John Phelp had bought Hampton Court for £750, but it was restored to the Crown on the accession of Charles II when Phelps' purchase money was returned to him. After her father's death in 1760, Dorothy acquired considerable lands in Oxfordshire, Essex and London. They included a fishery and ferry at North Stoke, together with the ferry boat and all the ancillary properties of a riparian owner. They were all leased to tenants. In 1789 an agreement was made in court at Westminster concerning land at North Stoke leasing land and free fishing at North Stoke together with the ferry which was leased to Thomas Toovey and his wife Ann.[12] This document was for a covenant confirming the right of ferry.

Writing in 1894 as C. H. Cook, a lawyer John Bickerdyke, described the state of the river following the Thames Bill of 1894. His book, *Thames Rights and Thames Wrongs* purported to be 'a plea for the greater freedom and better management of the river and a protest against the neglect of the Conservancy and the extreme pretensions of some riparian owners'.[13] Cook referred to North Stoke as an ancient ferry and noted that its ferry boat still lay at the bottom of the deep pool opposite the church, so the ferry must already have ceased at that time.[14] He said that the road to the ferry was a public one, but 'Private' notices had been put up and the path to the old ferry closed, 'so far as notice boards can close it'.

## LITTLE STOKE FERRY

Cook was also concerned about public access to Little Stoke ferry (Exp.171 602 854) a mile further downstream. He said the tenant of Little Stoke House had attempted to interfere with the public right to use the path to the ferry. There followed litigation in the Chancery Division of the High Court between the tenant and Henley Highway Board. The outcome was that the public had a right to use the road. It is still a public road today and so is the lane on the opposite side, usually known as Papists' Way.

Actually, Edward Thomas when exploring the area prior to writing his book *The Icknield Way* published in 1913 was told slightly different information.[15] He describes arriving at Little Stoke and walking down the short wide path lined by elm trees to the ferry where he was rowed across to Cholsey by a boy who told him the road on that side was called Asylum Road because it led to the huge red-brick asylum on the main Reading–Wallingford road. It was only after the way had crossed over that road was it called Papist Way. Thomas was puzzled by this appellation, but the reason went back a long way. During the sixteenth, seventeenth and eighteenth centuries the Roman Catholics in England were persecuted. The Hildesley/Ilsley family were Catholics who lived at Little Stoke Manor and were the hub of many recusant groups who lived close to the Thames. To travel by trackways and the river would be a fairly safe means of meeting up for worship.

The ferry at Little Stoke existed before the Commissioners adapted it for a horse ferry. A small Anglo-Saxon monastery was situated at Cholsey, a village over a mile from the river on the Berkshire side. A church existed in the late tenth century and the Manor Farm had a large barn dating from the late twelfth or early thirteenth century, allegedly the largest in Europe, which belonged to Reading Abbey.[16] Rights held by the abbot included free fishing and the ferry or passage across the river in Cholsey parish, mentioned in 1633. Obviously a busy ferry, its trade increased when Cholsey became much bigger in the nineteenth century, and even more when the Moulsford Lunatic Asylum was built in 1870 and enlarged in 1878.[17] There were 700 inmates in 1923. Later called Fairmile Hospital, it closed in 2000 and ten years later it stands derelict. The ferry became obsolete and the new Winterbrook Bridge took the traffic.

Apart from the manor, Little Stoke is a mere settlement on the Oxfordshire side of the river. The name Heslitesford has been identified with this place. Set back from the river is Little Stoke House and opposite is Ferry Cottage, a Grade II listed building in red brick which may have once been two cottages.[18] There is a date stone for 1759, although the brick end stacks seem added and suggest an earlier date. When contemplating setting up the horse towing path, the Commission recorded in 1787 that the Little Stoke ferryman lived in the parish of Checkenden, opposite Moulsford ferry, and he may agree to take horses over.[19] In the event, the towpath did terminate

Little Stoke/Cholsey Ferry with the ferryman waiting with the horse punt and the smaller one for passengers beside it. On the opposite side, Fairmile Hospital is regarded as a blot on the landscape. The ferry road in its last stretch before the river is almost impassable at present. Taunt photograph *c.* 1890. Reproduced by permission of English Heritage.

at this ferry to change sides. A Taunt photograph of 1890 shows the horse punt moored with a smaller passenger punt beside it.[20] An advertisement for a sale by auction appeared in *The Times* on 7 July 1841. It was for a dwelling house, Little Stoke House, described as 'suitable for the residence of a family of respectability'. It was to be sold together with two tenements, brick-built and tiled called the Ferry House, with garden adjoining, and the ferry, then let at £14 a year. Fishing rights, osier and reed beds were included. Two days before the auction, due on 30 July, the property was sold to a private buyer, the price not disclosed.

## SOUTH STOKE FERRY/MOULSFORD

From the main road southwards, A329, at Moulsford a pub sign for the Beetle and Wedge points left to the river and what was the landing place for the ferry from Moulsford across obliquely to South Stoke (Exp.171 592 836). The strange pub name is one used in carpentry. The beetle is a mallet for driving in a wedge, used for splitting wood. The nearby church has a wooden bell-turret, a shingled broach spire and timber porch. Again, Reading Abbey had an interest in the ferry and in a dispute with Eynsham Abbey, the Abbot of Reading claimed the ferry to Moulsford Mill belonged to his manor of Cholsey.[21] The ferry, an important one, always passed with the inn in the Moulsford Manor Estate. In the nineteenth century the estate was in the hands of the Morrell family, the brewers, of Oxford. In the 1930s it was split up.

The Thames Commissioners chose this ferry as another crossing point for a horse ferry. There were well-made ferry lanes to the river's edge on both sides and when the Thames Path was made the Moulsford one became part of the official path, and was made to join the main road before returning to the river further on. Likewise the Ridgeway on the Oxfordshire side had to pass through Little Stoke southwards to Goring.

Many writers have extolled the beauties of the Thames and broadcast the amenities of the Beetle and Wedge, including Jerome K. Jerome, though it is H. G. Wells who gives us a good insight into how the inn was run in *The History of Mr Polly*, first published in 1910. After surviving the conflagration at Fishbourne when his business was destroyed, Mr Polly 'cleared out' and hit the road. Finally he arrived at The Potwell Inn (a thinly disguised Beetle and Wedge) beside the Thames, where he found his 'shangri-la,' apart from the criminal assaults of the landlady's nephew. Here he was offered the job of ferryman, but that was low down on the list of jobs he was expected to do. The list amounted to 101 jobs which Wells proceeded to enumerate. He gave up when he got to seventy, resulting in the longest sentence in the book. Without any training, on the first day Mr Polly was sent across to pick up a gent from the steps on the opposite side. He found a punt and a pole and managed to reach the man. Then he cruised with him for about 20 minutes and, after hitting him with the pole twice, he finally landed him in a hay meadow forty yards downstream. Wednesday was a slack day for the ferry with only one or two people crossing. Thursday was the busiest, apart from Sunday, when it was early closing in the town. People would then come to the inn to have tea and 'omlets'.

Old photographs of the Beetle and Wedge and the ferry landing show it to be busy and prosperous, as it remains today. Situated in the courtyard facing the river is a substantial square brick house, possibly early nineteenth century, called Ferryman's

The Beetle and Wedge Hotel at Moulsford with the square Ferryman's Cottage next door. Ferry to South Stoke left from the waterfront. Postcard from Goring 22 July 1934.

At Moulsford a girl poses in the horse punt. A passenger punt and a rowing boat also await passengers. The landing place at South Stoke is seen across the river. Postcard courtesy of Ken Townsend.

Cottage. This is unlikely, given it is too late and too big. A few yards away in Ferry Lane is a timber-framed house with painted brick infill.[22] This is the original Ferry Cottage which is listed Grade II by English Heritage, who describe it as a jettied house of the seventeenth century. It now has a tile roof, which has signs of previously been thatched. The central brick ridge stack could indicate an earlier date for the building, but the interior was not inspected.

## LEATHERNE BOTTEL FERRY

Below South Stoke, about half way between there and Goring/Streatley, is a former inn, now restaurant, named the Leatherne Bottel (Exp.171 601829). A ferry is marked on *Stanford's New Map of the Thames* (1900) at that spot and also on a sketch map by Thacker in 1920. No further information has been found about this ferry, but the Leatherne Bottel was well known and operated their own private ferry to draw customers from the towpath which was on the opposite side in Berkshire. Apart from its hospitality, the inn was famous for a medicinal spring which attracted pilgrims from afar to partake of the water in the seventeenth and eighteenth centuries.[23] It was supposed to cure skin diseases, eye complaints and corns. Gradually the water business declined and pilgrims chose to visit for other reasons.

## GORING & STREATLEY

A little further down is Cleeve Lock, well known to boaters on the Thames. It is close to Goring and has always been associated with that town. Here is one of the most beautiful stretches of the Thames, from Cleeve Lock to where the river turns eastwards before Brunel's Basildon railway bridge. This is the Goring Gap with steep beech-hung cliffs on the right bank, and more gentle slopes down from the foothills of the Chilterns on the left. In prehistoric times this is where the tracks of the Ridgeway and the Ickneild Way joined to cross the river at a shallow ford a little down from Goring church (Exp.171 595 805). The river formed the frontier between Wessex and Mercia, there being hostility between them which continued between Streatley in Berkshire and Goring in Oxfordshire until the twentieth century. Artefacts from all periods from the Stone Age to the early modern age have been found at the crossing. The Romans built a raised causeway, supplemented by a ferry.

In 1181 the Normans established an Augustinian Priory at Goring. It was granted Streatley mill, fishing rights and the ferry. One of the earliest records for the ferry is in the accounts for one John de Baucomb in the 1380s.[24] When he travelled to London in spring 1382 he paid for a ferry passage 'at Goryng'; likewise in 1385 when he arrived in London on 25 November and again in Easter term 1388 after he had met up with a relative. It is not known from whence he came. After the Dissolution, Henry VIII granted on 12 March 1537 to John Stoner, a serjeant-at-arms, 'a house and the site of the suppressed priory of Gorynge … with certain lands, a weir called Gorynge Were and the fishing thereof, a windmill there and the ferry over the Thames there', other lands, plus 'the cartload of fire wood yearly out of the wood of the Earl of Derby at Gorynge which the late prioress had.[25] Clear annual value, £5 8s 4d, rent 11s.'

Sadly, in 1674 a terrible disaster occurred somewhere near the ferry. Returning to Streatley after attending the Goring Feast in a boat, the boatman got too near the weir, or flash lock.[26] He lost control and about sixty people were drowned – men, women and children. There was one survivor as he told his tale to a chapman, who got it printed. Some neighbours considered the victims got their true deserts for going to Goring in the first place.

Mrs Elizabeth Burd of Castle Street, Reading was an exceedingly rich widow.[27] She died on 31 July 1748 aged fifty-nine and the inventory produced for probate reveals a large property portfolio. Even the cash in hand amounted to more than £500. Mrs Burd must have been a money lender, for the list of loans and mortgages owed to her covers several pages but her own debts as listed are insubstantial. Much of the property was associated with the brewing industry, for her first husband Robert Noake, who died in 1720, was of a brewing family. Robert Burd, her second husband was a Doctor of Medicine and died in 1742. At Streatley Mrs Burd owned a messuage, eyot, fishery and the ferry. Together with half an acre, these brought her £500 a year. Further downstream at Tilehurst she owned a messuage called The Roebuck and three closes of land in Pangbourne Lane in the occupation of Francis Warwick and for which she was paid £155 18s per annum.

The ferry landing place on the Goring side was at the end of Ferry Lane and the wide open space there indicates it may also have been a hythe or wharf. This was the place adapted by the Thames Commissioners for a horse ferry. On the Streatley side the ferry was beside Streatley Mill. Were there two ferries? A document in the Powys-Lybbe family archive dated 8 June 1654 concerns a messuage, watermill and mill house, called the Eights and includes a ferry belonging to the Manor of Goring.[28] If this is Goring ferry, and the other was Streatley ferry, owned originally by the Manor of Streatley, then this one would have been next to Goring Mill, at the same place as the springings of the present bridge or vice versa (Exp.171 595 807). If so, it would explain why the best seventeen- and eighteenth-century buildings in Streatley line the High Street which goes straight uphill from the present bridge. The church is just off the High Street, but more significantly the Swan Inn, now Hotel, on the bank by the crossing, has a seventeenth-century core and a former stable block with an early

Goring/Streatley. A wide-angle view of Goring taken from the Streatley bank *c.* 1895. It shows the first toll bridge with gate and toll bar. On the left bank is the ubiquitous Lombardy poplar. From a private photograph album.

Similar view of the toll bridge taken from Goring towards Streatley with the church to the right. From a private photograph album *c.* 1895

sixteenth-century cruck frame. Considering the reputed animosity between the two villages it seems highly likely each had their own ferry.

With increased prosperity, the Commissioners considered erecting a bridge.[29] In 1810 they canvassed subscriptions for a carriage bridge but the scheme was abandoned and not revived until 1837 when an Act was obtained to build a timber toll bridge. Money was raised on mortgage to build the bridge and to buy out the then ferryman, Moses Saunders, who had established a business in 1830 specialising in repair and construction of Thames locks and weirs at the Swan boathouse.[30] Later the firm became boat builders. However, the ferry had to be kept in readiness in case there was a problem with the bridge. Eventually the ferry toll board was re-erected in the Morrell Room at Streatley.

In 1840 the Great Western Railway opened a station at Goring, and from then on the area became a Mecca for writers and artists. It was already known to some.[31] The philosopher John Stuart Mill (1806–73) and three companions, including his lifelong friend Edwin Chadwick (1800–90), undertook a walking tour centred on the Thames Valley between 3 and 15 July 1828. On the fourth day they arrived at Goring and crossed by ferry to Streatley, 'which is a very neat village', and stayed at the crossroads at the top of the main street. Mill's account of the tour, with positive descriptions of all the places visited is delightful. It was not published during his lifetime.

A painting labelled 'Goring Mill and Weir' in Victoria Art Gallery in Bath by Charles Napier Hemy (1841–1917) actually shows Streatley Mill with a smartly dressed ferryman with a shortened punt having just landed a lady and little girl by the mill. The oil painting dates from about 1881. This mill was completely destroyed by fire in 1926. The shortened punt was artistic licence, for the same artist made a correct study of a Thames punt in a watercolour dated about 1878.[32] The Streatley paintings are some of his early work, for he moved to Falmouth and concentrated on maritime paintings. Benjamin Williams Leader (1831–1923) painted in oils, 'A Lock on the Thames Streatley' in 1898.[33] A lovely evocative scene, it could be Cleeve Lock, not Streatley, which is usually called Goring Lock. Leader had stayed in 1872 with his fellow artist friend Samuel Phillips Jackson (1830–1904), who lived at Streatley, and made many sketches then which he later worked up as oil paintings in his maturity.

The Streatley ferry continued to operate after the bridge was built as the bridge had heavier tolls. It was also known for people to wade across the river and it would have been easy for those on horseback or even in a small carriage.[34] Although the timber bridge was considered unsafe in 1910, the war and lack of funds prevented the building of a new one until a concrete bridge was erected in 1923 and the tolls extinguished. Now it is not adequate for the amount of traffic it has to take.

## GATEHAMPTON/BASILDON

Gatehampton (Exp.171 609 796) was one of the lost villages of Oxfordshire.[35] In 1251 a charter describes the village as having a fulling mill, a tenter ground for drying cloth and a fishery, plus houses for the workers. By 1279 it had declined, but the death knell fell in 1402 when the manor was acquired by the ruthless Rede family of Boarstall in Buckinghamshire, which itself had lost its former importance. Beresford alleged the Redes specialised in buying up manors already in decay and being sold cheaply. Then they would turn the lands into pasture. In 1515 they evicted fourteen people from Gatehampton. The river here had been crossed by a primitive trackway to Basildon on the Berkshire side, and used by the Romans, but with a decreased population and not being on a through road it had gone out of use.

Seeking ways of improving navigation, the Thames Commissioners considered in 1787 reviving the ferry.[36] Because of very steep cliffs on the Oxfordshire side bordering the river, the horse towing path needed to change to the Basildon side at this point. Not until August 1810 was a ferry boat ordered and ferryman Charles Emmett appointed in September. Thacker gives names of subsequent ferrymen. In October 1822 James Hall was receiving 24s per month; Thomas Costiff held the post in 1854 at 52s a week along with having charge of Cleeve and Goring locks. Costiff's wage had been reduced from 83s, and in 1862 he resigned from the ferry and the locks. Under the Conservancy John Sheppard in October 1866 was paid £2 a month, but he was injured and retired in February 1875. His successor Williams was discharged in the September in favour of Henry Belcher. He occupied a wooden hut on the Gatehampton bank and when it became in a bad state it was rebuilt for him for £25 but he drowned in February 1879 and G. Piggott took over until he died in 1880. C. Bossom took charge of the ferry, but was pensioned in August 1894 when his son T. Bossom succeeded him. Both father and son died in spring 1897. T. Collier, grandfather of Gordon Collier who lives in Wantage, then became ferryman and held the job for a long time.[37]

Foot passengers did not make much use of Gatehampton/Basildon ferry; there was no need, except perhaps for workers on the country estates and picnickers in summer. However, two ferry boats were provided, one for foot passengers, the other, larger, for transporting the towing horses.[38] The Act allowed for horses to be charged between

Gatehampton/Basildon ferry and ferryman captured on camera by Taunt in 1892. The Horse punt is moored by the entrance to the little backwater. Building materials are piled up at the site prior to the ferry cottage being rebuilt higher up the bank and enlarged. Reproduced by permission of English Heritage.

one penny and threepence a time. The big boat had to be 22½ feet long and 4½ feet wide with a ramp at each end for easy loading and unloading. G. D. Leslie noticed that punting the large punt was easier than expected and calculated this could not have been a natural hard bottom to push against, so it must have been given an artificial bottom to help propulsion of the heavy boats. In fact there is a good hard gravel bottom covering several hundred yards.

In 1879 the Conservators ordered that the ferry was to be used only by persons engaged in the navigation of the river. Mr Sworder, then owner of Gatehampton Manor received compensation for foot passengers put over by Conservancy men, so there were protests and petitions signed. In 1884, Charles Morrison, owner of Basildon Park and land on both sides of the river, wanted to obtain use of the ferry for himself and his household to the exclusion of the public; this was refused. Thacker points out these ferries were instituted solely for the benefit of the navigation under restrictive covenants with the riparian owners. 'They are not immemorial links in a public highway'.[39]

The land at the ferry point is subject to flooding and in 1891 the ferryman's little cottage had to be rebuilt further up the bank to its present position. It was completed in 1893 and extended later by the addition of a bathroom. Between 1907 and 1949 seven licences were issued by the Conservators for boat houses on the creek behind the cottage. They gradually fell out of use and eventually collapsed. As a result of Conservator's policy the ferry was closed in 1954. G. C. Carter, the last ferryman left the house on 28 December 1954. Gilbert Spencer, brother of artist Stanley, wrote to *The Times* from Upper Basildon on 16 August 1955 bemoaning the loss of the ferry. He said it 'was a haven of beauty and rest, where one could have tea and then go on to Goring or Whitchurch in lovely surroundings.' Now the only way to gain the Oxfordshire bank was the railway bridge and the risk of being fined.

Posed photograph produced for a postcard *c.* 1910. Held like this the punt poles would not have got the ladies very far – see the man in the right corner for how it should be done! Courtesy Ken Townsend.

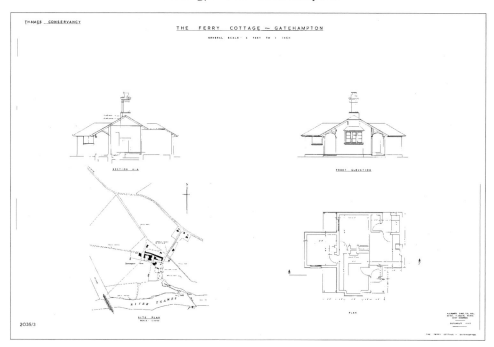

Plans produced by the chief engineer of the Thames Conservancy in December 1960 when a bathroom was added to the Ferry Cottage at Gatehampton. Reproduced with the kind permission of the Environment Agency.

When the ferry cottage was sold at auction in July 1961, the purchasers were the Sandon Trust in Liverpool. They sold it again to the Nicholas family who lived at Gatehampton Manor, and eventually it has become the property of John Farr and his wife Tina who now live at the manor and are the riparian owners of half the river. On the Basildon side, the estate having become the property of the National Trust, the Environment Agency are now riparian owners. The Thames Path, after passing beneath the railway bridge makes a diversion away from the river to respect the private property of Gatehampton Manor.

# CHAPTER TWELVE
# Whitchurch to Sonning

## WHITCHURCH

Whitchurch-on-Thames is well-known for its picturesque toll bridge, one of only two in private hands on the river. The first one here (Exp.171 635 767) was built in oak by Act of Parliament in 1792.[1] The Act allowed for the removal, to aid navigation, of a shallow a few yards above the bridge site which had been the ancient ford. This was used as a crossing by a branch of the Ridgeway, and as a result the small town of Pangbourne grew up on the south bank in Berkshire and the village of Whitchurch in Oxfordshire on the north side. A very busy ferry was later run in conjunction with the ford.

Robert Elliot was described as the ferryman when he died in 1745.[2] From Pangbourne the way to the ferry was down a pathway to the side of the George Inn in the main street, later called Ferry Lane.[3] On landing by the mill on the Whitchurch side the passenger would walk in the mill grounds to the bridge over the mill race, and into Mill Lane.

In 1792 the ferry was owned by Revd John Lichfield of Goring and his wife Hannah, but it was held in trust for Hannah Dunce, wife of Joseph Dunce of Reading.[4] If she died the property would pass to Hannah Litchfield. These people proposed to build a bridge at their own expense and to keep it in repair and as a consequence they would give up their rights in the ferry if they received compensation. Together with seven other people they formed a company, The Company of Proprietors of Whitchurch Bridge (shortened to The Whitchurch Bridge Company). The preamble to the Act explained the reason for the bridge to be, 'of great utility and advantage to the public'. When erected it would be, 'fit and proper for the passage of travellers, cattle and carriages'. The right of Revd Lichfield and his wife to run the ferry would cease, and the Act stated that in consideration the Company would pay £350 in recompense. In the meantime they were allowed to hold, use and enjoy the ferry and receive profits from it in such and the same manner as if the Act had not been made. 'A toll of a halfpenny for every passenger would be charged', and in case the bridge became impassable or unsafe, a ferry must be provided until the bridge works were completed and the tolls from that ferry were to be paid to the Company.

Work started on the bridge in June 1792 to the design of John Treacher and was opened in November 1792 at a cost of £2,400. There were twenty wooden piers. At the Whitchurch end was a substantial toll house, now a listed building. Payment was collected at the front door which faced the toll gate. In 1966 a new front door was made to the side, up steps and a kiosk erected in the middle of the widened road. The first toll-keeper was Mrs Waters, widow of James Waters, who was lock-

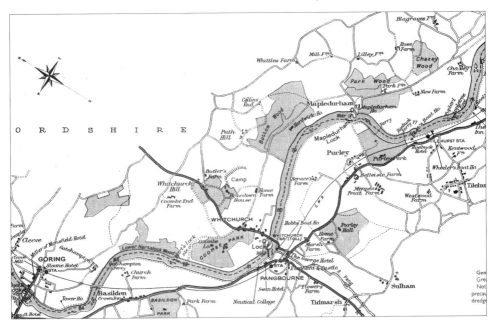

The Thames between Goring and Tilehurst with Whitchurch Toll bridge a feature. From *Stanford's New Map of the River Thames, c.* 1900.

Whitchurch/Pangbourne. The ferry plied from the mill at Whitchurch to Pangbourne before the toll bridge was built and continued afterwards if the bridge became impassable. From the Halls' *Book of the Thames* 1859.

keeper at Whitchurch Lock.[5] She succeeded him there and also ran the ferry. On her appointment as bridge-keeper she became an employee of the Company, earning £16 a year until her death in 1820. The horse towing path remained on the Pangbourne bank, but because the path cut across the path to the ferry the Thames Commissioners had to pay a rent.[6] In 1795 the charge to them was £2 10s 2¼d paid by Henry Allnutt the administrator of the Commission.

The Ferry Boat, a public house in Whitchurch, was formerly called the Ferry House. It has a long history, but no connection with the ferry. A document of 1749 concerns a mortgage on property in Whitchurch which included the way to the Ferry House.[7] Another document dated March 1806 concerns the sale of the property by John Stephen, a brewer of Reading for £400. The purchaser intended to pull down the pub and its outhouses and build another on the same site. As it is not near the ferry, the name merely indicates it was at the place where the access to the ferry left the High Street.

A new wooden bridge was built in 1852 with fewer piers and a less elaborate balustrade on either side. This was replaced in 1902 by the present metal structure with lattice balustrades.[8] Now it is time for another bridge. Scheduled for 2011 it has been postponed and work will now start in October 2012 for completion in April 2013. During the procedure the Company has decided to provide a temporary footbridge for the convenience of foot passengers and cyclists. The original Act called for a ferry in such circumstances, but the Proprietors chose the more expensive option of a bridge because it would lessen inconvenience for the bridge users. They do not declare how the 3,000 vehicles, which at present use the bridge each day, are going to fare. The present bridge is Grade II listed and its metal balustrades will be restored and re-erected.

## MAPLEDURHAM FERRY

Domesday lists the settlement at Mapledurham, (Exp.171 667 768) the mill and the manor house. The scene beside the Thames is of the chocolate-box type. To quote Pevsner, it is, 'a small village, still feudal in spirit and dominated by the manor house'. The Blount family who are descended from the Normans bought the manor in 1490 and have lived there ever since.[9] They were recusants and as a prominent family in that movement there would have been a lot of coming and going in secret on the river and of necessity a private ferry to the opposite bank at Purley on Thames. Today there is no access to the river at all, not even to have a look from afar. On the right bank there is only a glimpse through the trees from the Thames Path just as it is diverted inland away from the river until it reaches Roebuck. In 1930 it was possible to cross the river over Mapledurham (actually Purley) Lock, as Harper said, 'greatly, no doubt, to the chagrin of the Blounts' – who have won![10]

When the Thames Conservancy was set up under the Thames Navigation Act of 1866, provision was made to take over all the private appurtenances on the river, the locks and weirs, for which tolls were being paid to the owners. It was of great public importance that the stream, bed and banks of the river were preserved. The Act stated that any private owners should apply for compensation within three months of its passing.[11] If there was any difference of opinion concerning the provision, then an independent arbitrator be consulted. Michael Henry Blount (1789–1874) did not apply in respect of his properties within the three months. He had been taking tolls for the lock and weir and keeping them in repair as necessary. The Conservators took possession of his property under the Act and Blount objected. The arbitrator judged the sum of £500 was due. The Conservators claimed they no longer held sufficient

Pangbourne. The weir a little further upstream from the Whitchurch toll bridge. The bridge seen in the far distance may be the Brunel railway bridge at Basildon. From a private photograph album.

Mapledurham. The mill and church as depicted in the Halls' *Book of the Thames* in 1859. The ferry crossed between Mapledurham and Purley on the right bank.

'ring-fenced' money to pay, and Blount took his case to court. The defendants claimed they would not be able to pay, perhaps for a century. The judge ruled that no man's property should be forcibly taken from him and that he should be made to pay therefore for works of public good, was intolerable. He considered the Conservators could find the money somewhere in their coffers and also should pay the costs of the case.

The pound lock at Mapledurham was built in 1777 against the Purley bank.[12] About the same time it was necessary to extend the horse towing path upstream from Tilehurst. The Commissioners were thwarted by a Mr Worlidge who claimed he was exempt from selling or letting his land in Purley Meadow for a towing path. They talked about a form of compulsory purchase but he was obdurate. In 1780 Worlidge was too ill to negotiate and still the debate went on, not helped by complaints from bargemasters. 'Inconvenient it is to take off the horses at Mr Worlidge's field, and go thro'a Lane round his House. It occasions a delay of half-an-hour, besides the additional labour'. The Commissioners settled the matter in 1794 by establishing a double ferry to avoid passing through Purley Farm. One was below the Roebuck and the other a third of a mile above, near Purley church. Both were made to take towing horses across the river and back. Benjamin Cottrell, a towing contractor between Kennet Mouth and Gatehampton still complained of, 'the danger and delay of setting the Horses over at Two new ferries'. The danger was from the rapidity of the stream and the time taken, which he claimed was a half hour longer even than going round Purley House as before and the flashes from the weirs were often lost.

Alexander Geddes was lock-keeper at Mapledurham in 1798.[13] In 1801 he wanted more money & it was considered whether he could look after the two Purley ferries as well, but they were too far away. However, he did get an increase from 24s to 47s a month but resigned in 1805. His son James took over, and when he died in June 1816 his widow Cecily took his place. By October 1822 she was earning 70s a month and looked after the Purley ferries as well. William Sheppard was appointed when Cecily resigned in May 1828 and he experienced a reduction in wages to 24s a month although he was allowed to keep the revenue from pleasure boats in 1854. Somehow he managed to upset Mr Michael Charles Blount who forbade him to 'land on his property to obtain supplies', possibly because of the impending court case. The Conservators were going to transfer Sheppard to Hambledon but changed their minds, much to Blount's annoyance. Sheppard retired as lock-keeper and supervisor of the ferries in April 1882 at the age of seventy-nine after fifty-four years service.

Lock at Mapledurham photographed in 1904 showing the Conservancy gate and bridge over a side stream to the left, possibly the mill stream. From a photograph album.

## ROEBUCK FERRY

One person at a time then became responsible for both Purley ferries. In 1798 he was A. M. Storer who earned 32s a month and his successor, George Reynolds earned the same amount in August 1799. He was dismissed twelve years later, to be replaced by George Holdgate. The association of these ferries with the Warrick family began in 1820 when George arrived, and then in 1854 Alfred went to the Roebuck ferry. In April 1869 he was reported as insane, but through local intervention he was allowed to stay, as he was half owner of the Roebuck ferry house. Later the Conservancy bought his share for £7. The Berkshire Health Authority condemned the cottage in February 1876 and a new one was ordered for £50, but obviously not built because the old one was still being complained of in July 1878. J. Collins who had taken over the ferries in February 1873 died aged seventy-three in 1895, succeeded by his son Oliver, who resigned in October 1900. The ferryman then was Richard Jones.

Officially the two Purley ferries were Upper and Lower. Of the upper there is no sign at all, the Thamesside marina and the large housing estate of Purley Park have completely changed the area. As the ferries were created solely for the towing path, there was no path to them. The lower ferry (Exp.171 671 753) soon became known as the Roebuck from being close to the inn on the main road, A329. 'This quaint little inn' as G. D. Leslie described it in 1881 had remained practically unchanged since the time when Mrs Burd owned it: now it was to be changed. Between 1881 and 1883 a large, commodious hotel in red brick was built, designed by architect G. W. Webb for fishermen guests. At the west end a small portion of the original seventeenth-century inn is incorporated. Now it stands empty and boarded up and has been for some years, although there is some activity. Perhaps potential owners have heard about the ghost which haunts the hotel, an old admiral who tried to rescue his dog in a fire and is still looking for him.

The path to the ferry, part of the Thames Path, descends very steeply to the Bristol–Paddington railway which it crosses by a footbridge, then drops down again to the ferry place where the hotel put up a pub sign to attract people on the river to their hostelry. At the water's edge the public footpath continues to the right as the Thames Path, but to the left it leads to the ferry house. The compound is surrounded by a high chain fence and the gate padlocked. Bushes obscure the view of the house built sometime after 1876 to replace what was merely a wooden shack. The permanent house, seen in old photographs is of typical Thames Conservancy design, single storey, pyramid-shaped with a central chimney.[14] Boats were available for hire and teas served in the early twentieth century. Getting furniture and provisions to this spot must have been very difficult, were they brought by boat? The Roebuck also hired out rowing boats, but when John Bickerdyke turned up in 1894 expecting to cross by ferry or even by private boat he was refused.[15] None of the employees were allowed to take him or even go with him for fear of losing their licence.

On the agenda at the last meeting of the old Thames Conservancy Board on 9 March 1931 was a proposal from Reading Corporation that they should take over as public open spaces land belonging to the Conservancy no longer used by them.[16] They referred to parts of the towing path between Sonning lock and Caversham Bridge, and some of the islands not then in Conservancy ownership. Included specifically was Roebuck ferry house and garden. The Board agreed in principle but asked for the ferry house property to be excluded, (did they wish to sell it?). Some of the islands they thought might be needed in the future. They had no objection to two new bridges, one being over the mouth of the River Kennet. Lord Desborough, the chairman, ended the meeting by proposing that once again they should give seeds and offer prizes for best-kept gardens at locks, weirs and ferries. This was agreed.

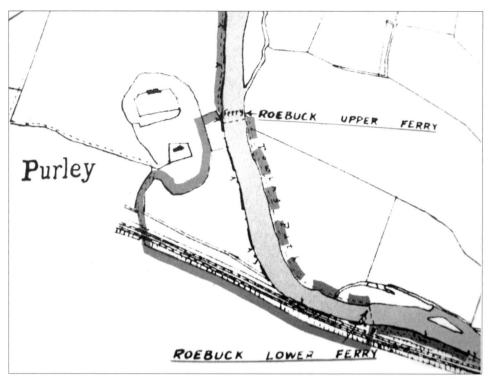

The two Purley ferries were created to avoid the towpath passing through Purley Farm. When the Thames Path was created they were both abolished and a new path formed which crosses twice over the railway. From a book of maps, 1947, courtesy of Gloucestershire Archives.

The Roebuck Hotel near Tilehurst Station. A steep path descends to the former towing path and ferry landing place. From a postcard sent from Reading in 1908.

## CAVERSHAM

Reading was a Romano-British settlement which grew up near the confluence, to the east, of the River Thames with the River Kennet. Actually the town shunned the Thames on its north side, apart from wharves built along the waterfront. The main way to the north was across the Thames to Caversham, formerly called East Throp, in Oxfordshire. A ford was not mentioned in Domesday but two may have existed at opposite ends of the village, because it grew in two parts, Upper and Lower Caversham, with farmland in between. After the Conquest the manor of Caversham was allowed to Walter Giffard whose descendants continued to hold it for a considerable time. Around 1162, a Walter Giffard, 2nd Earl of Buckingham founded Notley Abbey in Buckinghamshire for Augustinian Friars. A ferry was established near the church in Caversham used possibly when the ford was impassable. In 1329 John Waley was drowned when fording near Caversham Rectory, that is, near the church.[17]

The earliest date Thacker found for a bridge was 1231 when the chapel of St Anne on the bridge was mentioned in the Close Rolls (Exp171 711 745). The bridge was built of timber at a point where several islands were situated in the river.[18] In the same year Henry III gave orders to the keeper of the Royal Forest of Windsor to deliver one good oak to Andrew, the Sergeant of Caversham to make a boat for ferrying the poor people over the Water of Caversham. Apparently they could not pay to traverse the bridge. Later the canons of Notley Abbey, to whom the bridge and ferry had been passed by the Giffard family, were given several oaks to build a ferryboat to carry pilgrims to the shrine of Our Lady of Caversham close to the Church of St Peter. This chapel may have possessed its own ferry. The holy well of St Anne also drew visitors from afar because of its healing powers. During the reign of Edward II (1307–27) Caversham ferry was held by the Earl of Gloucester and Hertford for 'service of half a Knight's fee'.[19] In 1479 James Hide was given a lease of the ferry. The people of Reading complained in about 1480 to Edward IV, who had taken possession of the manor in 1377, about negligence of the abbot to repair, 'a parte of Causham bridge with a chapel there-upon of the holy gost'. Henry VII in 1493 leased to Notley Abbey

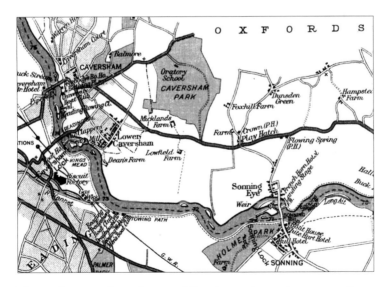

Thames between Caversham and Sonning as it was in *c.* 1900. From *Stanford's New Map of the River Thames.*

and Convent lands and properties in Caversham including the ferry passage and the ferry barge for sixty years at £20 per annum. All this land reverted to the Crown at the Dissolution of the Monasteries.

Richard Smythe and Richard Justice were appointed keepers of the manor in June 1510 and the ferry was included. In 1542 Francis Knollys, one of the Gentleman Pensioners, was granted the ferry and ferry barge of Caversham. In addition he was granted all the watermills, the mill barge, the lock and the weirs and waters from the lock down to the mills.[20] The ferry is also mentioned in a deed of covenant dated 26 April 1631 about an annuity of £56 to be paid from the manor and mills to one Edward Manning to be held in trust for one Mary Emerson.[21] The bridge was damaged during the Civil Wars and repaired. Both counties, Oxfordshire and Berkshire were responsible for it. As a result, when a new bridge was built in 1830 the north end differed from the south, 'the Oxford half an old fashioned stone and brick structure; the Berkshire half a sort of makeshift wood and iron skeleton'.

Arches for the Oxfordshire half can be seen in a lovely photograph of 1869 by Canon Grimwade when the iron replacement bridge was being built.[22] A very crowded large ferry punt is approaching the Berkshire bank carrying a horse and trap, a milk float, several foot passengers and a group of workers. It is propelled from the back by a sweep and from the front by a punt pole. In the background on the north bank is a three storied white building which may be an inn or hotel or even the ferryman's house. At the time the ferryman was 'Old Man Piper' and this tale fits the description of his house.[23] On 29 January 1869 his house was moved *en masse*, by an American technique, to a new site 8 feet away to allow for the new bridge. Legend says that during the operation his family and furniture remained inside and nothing was harmed, no windows were even broken. The house weighed 150 tons and the whole process took three hours. A short right of way round the house to the river still exists. It was used to drive cattle down to be conveyed by the large punt to the Friday market in Reading. On an island in the river reached from the middle of the bridge across a walkway is a restaurant and bar. The name of the island is Piper's Island to commemorate the venerable old ferryman.

One of his predecessors in 1812 had caused complaints to be made to the Thames Commissioners.[24] Bargemasters maintained that ferry boats were being kept locked, particularly at Caversham. Often it was necessary to walk 2 miles to get the key while the boat and the horses were kept waiting. The Commission replied that the ferry boat at Caversham was only ¼ mile from the ferryman's house and other stations were less. The craft were kept locked up to prevent fishermen borrowing them and leaving them on the wrong side of the river! Charles Benwell who was lock-keeper cum ferryman in 1854 received no wages because of falling profits caused by competition from railways.[25] Instead he was to keep for himself tolls he took from pleasure craft and to live in the lock house rent free.

When the Borough of Reading sought in 1911 to enlarge their boundaries to encompass Caversham, the Select Committee of the House of Commons required that the Borough should carry out improvements to Caversham Bridge within three years and also they should provide a footbridge over the Thames near the present Clappers Bridge.[26] The ratepayers decided however that they needed a new road bridge at the Clappers and the Caversham Bridge be widened. But as that bridge was in an unsatisfactory condition it was decided to remove it and erect another more suitable for the traffic of the day and alter the towing path.[27] The new bridge at Caversham had to wait until 1924–26 and Reading Bridge at George Street until 1922–23.

Caversham, although a sprawling suburb today, has some old nooks and corners which indicate its historic importance. At the end of Bridge Street is a junction of roads which form the hub of the village. There, facing the bridge are some medieval

The strange bridge at Caversham built in 1830 by two counties. The Oxfordshire or north half was built in stone and the Berkshire south side in wood and iron. From the Halls' *Book of the Thames*.

Caversham Bridge was rebuilt and enlarged about 1869 in iron, like a railway bridge. The eel bucks can be seen upstream. From a private photograph album.

Eel bucks at the end of Buck Side, Caversham. The timber-framed house can be just seen through the trees on the right. Caversham church where there was another ferry is in the distance. From a private photograph album *c.* 1890.

timber framed houses in a row. One larger one is end-on to the road and has been of some significance. Turning left on to Church Road A4074 after a few yards is a crossroads. To the right is St Anne's Road which leads directly uphill to St Anne's Well on the corner with Priest Hill. To the left is a short stretch of road leading to the river down a very old track called Buck Side. Between the bank and an eyot in the river opposite was a set of eel-bucks, which were possibly noted as present in 1632. They were demolished in about 1915. On the right of the narrow lane is a large timber-framed house which seems too grand for an owner or keeper of bucks. It is suggested this was the site, being very close to the bridge, of an original ford, the one for pilgrims as the way leads directly from the spot to St Anne's Well.

## KENNET MOUTH

Of all the interesting and lovely ferry places on the Upper Thames, the one at Kennet Mouth is the least attractive (Exp.159 730 738), being the most industrialised and shut-in. Two railway bridges, the skeleton of an old gasometer, some new ones, and a large supermarket make up the drab scene where the canalised River Kennet joins the River Thames. The original towing path followed the south bank of the river, and the Thames Path now uses the same course. When the Kennet & Avon Canal was opened in its entirety, without ceremony, in 1810, a ferry boat was ordered for crossing the new cut at the mouth of the Kennet, made in 1802. The first mile of that river was made navigable and administered by the powerful Reading Abbey the large premises of which bordered the river. As there was no floodplain, many wharves were built from the twelfth century at the riverside up to High Bridge in the centre of Reading. By the Act of 1750 the Thames Commissioners took on the first mile of the Kennet including Blake's Lock.[28] Subsequently the stretch was administered by whichever authority had charge of the Thames Navigation. At present it is governed by the Environment Agency from its Reading office.

Thacker researched names of some early ferrymen.[29] The first to be appointed in September 1810 was Peter Breach at 20s per month, who was found later to be not 'above board' in dealings with the Thames Commission over some bucks, as his family had also done before him. Breach was to collect tuppence for each horse conveyed by ferry. James White took over the ferry in 1812 at 15s per week. He was to be in charge also of Blake's Lock and Withy Eyot. By 1823 the ferry was being worked by a chain. The wage was 'raised' in June 1841 when apparently the ferryman ceased to be in charge of the eyot or lock and his sole responsibility was the ferry, which must have been busy then. His status was enhanced in July 1843 when the Commission declared his house was 'a wretched hovel' and built a new one for £70. William Johnson, based at Blake's Lock, was also given the ferry to look after in 1854 at a wage reduced from £4 2s to £2 10s but he was dismissed in February 1859. Widow 'Brandson' took over the ferry in October 1866 under the Conservancy. Possibly her husband was one Brunsden from nearby Sonning. She earned 10s a week until discharged in September 1869. John Holmes was dismissed in September 1874 for illegal fishing after he had been in the post since November 1869. Someone called Rockall was reported dead in March 1885 so R. Humphreys from Cookham Upper Ferry took his place. Three men acted as ferrymen and lock-keepers in quick succession from April 1890 until October 1891 when J. E. Russell became in charge.

The Great Western Railway had built a bridge at Kennet Mouth for their main line from Paddington to Bristol in 1840. When it was widened in 1890 they suggested a towpath bridge should replace the ferry and be built immediately alongside the railway bridge on the Thames side. It was almost complete in February 1892 when the railway bought up the ferry house and other property from the Thames Conservancy. Built to take towing horses the bridge, known as the Horseshoe Bridge had slats to prevent slipping and it is said had marks from horseshoes.[30] Since becoming the crossing for the Thames Path and following a consultation in 2005 it has been redecked and is now 'user-friendly' with the lattice sides painted in blue. Both the GWR and Horseshoe Bridges are listed. The Southern Railway bridge from Reading to Waterloo is only a few yards away.

## SONNING

Sonning-on-Thames (Exp.159 755 756) was described as an old-world village, perhaps it is still, provided a visit is made at 5 a.m. on a bright summer's morning. To a stranger, the first impression is one of water, everywhere. Between Reading and Sonning is a vast area of lakes formed by gravel pits which on the north bank are separated from the river by a narrow bank of land. There is a lock, a weir, a mill and inlets which all have their own watercourse, besides the main navigation stream of the Thames. Three small bridges cross these streams and the main stream is crossed by a splendid brick bridge of eleven graduated semi-circular arches with the widest at the centre. A causeway connects all four bridges. It is not apparent whether the causeway crossed the minor streams or whether there were primitive timber bridges; it is unlikely a ferry would have been available for each of these crossings.

A very early document, undated but post conquest, outlines the extent of the Bishop of Salisbury's Palace on the banks of the Thames. It comprised of the area now known as Holme Park and extended south to 'the parcel of Elias the ferryman'.[31] The only vestige of this huge estate is a large Tudor brick wall in the churchyard. Thacker suggests Sonning was another place where a ferry co-existed with an adjacent bridge.[32] The earliest reference he found to a ferry was 1785 when John Pither was in charge and worked it by rope but a chain substituted it in 1823. The following year a new windlass and rollers were provided for the ferry. Heavy Thames barges found difficulty in manoeuvring through Sonning Bridge and regularly would run down the ferry boat.[33] In May 1825 an item in the accounts records the cost of 9s for men to raise the 'Sunning [*sic*] ferry boat that was sunk and for beer etc'.

At that time one Cannon was responsible for the ferry and the lock but his wages were reduced to 10s when George Edwards was brought in to look to the ferry at £2 a month.[34] A ferry house was built and in 1834 ferryman Brunsden was told he would be redundant when the new horse towing path was complete. After August 1835 the path, which previously ran on the right bank, was changed to the left bank. This may mark the end of the ferry.

Sonning Bridge, as we know it today was built in 1773 in Berkshire. The other three are Oxfordshire County bridges. Some people have claimed there was a Saxon bridge over the main stream built of timber. Many times repairs were done and several times the bridge was reported as being in decay and in 1605 was practically rebuilt. However, it does survive today. Not so the other three bridges which were built as follows: Mill bridge, an old wooden structure 188 feet long over the mill stream; New Bridge, a brick and timber structure over a branch of the river, 139 feet in length; and Hall's Bridge, a wooden structure over a back channel leading from the weir and 111 feet long.[35] The average width of all three was 15 feet. In August 1902 the Roads and Bridges Committee of Oxfordshire County Council reported they had inspected these bridges and found them getting weaker and unfit for the heavy traffic passing over them. Therefore, the County Surveyor recommended that rather than spend money on repairs, radical alterations should be made, making them virtually new bridges at an estimated cost of £8,000. There was opposition from some County Councillors who wanted to preserve the beauty of the Thames and maintained that iron girder bridges would destroy that beauty. Others said no sub-committee or county Surveyor should be allowed a free hand.

Sonning Bridge over the main stream of the Thames, built in 1773. A ferry punt lies in readiness below and was probably used for transporting farm animals as the bridge is narrow. From a private photograph album.

The controversy automatically sparked off letters to *The Times*.[36] On 11 September 1902 there were three. One from W. Holman Hunt (1827–1910) the Pre-Raphaelite artist who spent his summers at Sonning in a house designed for his retirement by his wife and daughter. He was most concerned that the rebuilding and widening of the three bridges would cause the main bridge to follow the same fate. He objected to 'tasteful' lattice-work sides and the strengthening of them to 'support the demands of heavily-laden traction-engines'. He enclosed a letter from an acknowledged expert on bridges who rather 'sat on the fence' by pointing out that the cheapest option of materials was not necessarily always the best option. Personally he preferred a masonry or brick arch, but girder construction could be beautiful too. G. D. Leslie, (1835–1921) artist and author of *Our River* and son of CR Leslie, artist and biographer of Constable also was worried about the beauty of the river. To him, 'this piece of cheap vandalism is to be perpetrated solely for the benefit and accommodation of those who own and use traction engines'. He believed new bridges should be built away from established towns and villages in places where the aspect would not be ruined and suggested Little Stoke where the lunatic asylum had already marred the landscape. This was not to be.

The first announcement in August gave as a reason for new bridges at Sonning the report Oxford County Council had received in February 1892 when they were told the bridges would not for long withstand frequent heavy traffic or serious floods. The bridges were an important means of communication between the Oxfordshire and Berkshire sides of the river, the nearest bridges being Caversham about three miles west and Henley about 5 miles east. 'The traffic over the bridges is considerable and includes constant heavy traffic'. One hundred and twenty years later and the situation is much worse rather than better. Only one other bridge is built, Reading Bridge about 2 miles away. The three bridges did get rebuilt as specified, and one is now replaced again by a concrete bridge. Sonning Bridge is unchanged and all are controlled by traffic lights. Traction engines are a thing of the past but the traffic, particularly at peak times is horrendous. The noise and fumes are constant, and there is no chance to explore the village because there are no car parks. The church is kept locked.

# CHAPTER THIRTEEN
# Wargrave to Marlow

From Sonning the Thames takes a sinuous course northwards and passes through a flat, sparsely populated landscape to Shiplake where there is a steep bank up to the church. After Shiplake Railway Bridge, the small town of Wargrave is on the right side. Its name is derived from 'weregreave' meaning grove, an area of woodland, and weir. The Thames at this point consists of numerous side streams and backwater, some of which may be former courses of the river. The town was mentioned in Domesday. Henry I granted the Norman church here to Reading Abbey when it was founded. It remained in their possession until 1536 when the Abbey was dissolved. Historically Wargrave grew up on the banks of the Thames near the church which was by a mill and overlooked a large green, Mill Green. The Manor House was nearby and so was the ferry, approached along Ferry Lane from Church Street which is one of four streets which meet at the Crossroads in the High Street.

## FIRST WARGRAVE FERRY

In the thirteenth century the settlement moved from by the church to the main road and a linear village was set up in burgage plots with back lanes. Ferry Lane was one, running parallel to the river and at the end turning at 90 degrees left to descend to the river's edge where today the landing place is a public slipway (Exp.159 784 788). Some very old houses are on this narrow lane. Thamesford is listed as sixteenth/seventeenth century but could be much older.[1] Rather big for a cottage, probably originally single-storied, it looked out to the river where as the name suggests, a ford existed. Timber framed, it is L-shaped with a two-bay crosswing, with some bays, previously probably of wattle and daub, now with roughcast infill, and some of brick noggin. Some windows have leaded casements from the eighteenth century. Although the roof now has old tiles, the steepness of it suggests it was thatched, most likely with reeds. The only obvious modern alteration is a twentieth century front door. Almost opposite is a little timber house set in an orchard and facing the river with its back to the lane. Possibly dating to Victorian times, it is a strong contestant to have been a ferry cottage. A letter dated 25 February 1789 may provide a clue to this theory.[2] The actual named Ferry Cottage is at the bend in the lane and faces down to the slipway. It is white (usual colour for a ferry house), tall and narrow with steps up to the door, to avoid flooding. On the opposite corner is a similar house, L-shaped to occupy the whole corner. That also is up steps and despite alterations, is reminiscent of a ferry inn, like the Flowerpot at Aston Ferry. A reference in a footnote in VCH Berkshire Vol. 3 to a fishery and ferry with appurtenances in Wargrave in the seventeenth century is

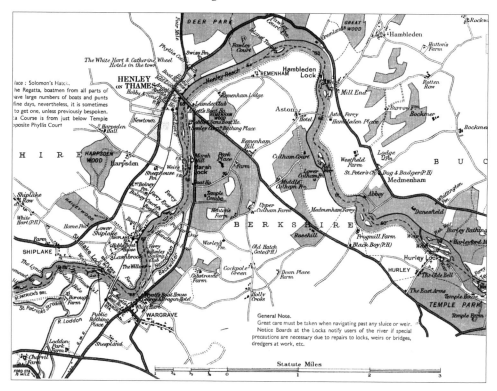

The Thames takes a big loop to the north between Wargrave and Temple to avoid high ground. From *Stanford's New Map of the River Thames, c. 1900.*

the only known early written source for this ferry.[3] In the second edition of his book *Thames Rights and Thames Wrongs* published in 1895 C. H. Cook lists this ferry as 'ceased'.

## SECOND WARGRAVE FERRY

Thacker confesses he was confused by the notes he made for Wargrave ferry, and seems to have totally missed there were two. Information he gathered was for the later George and Dragon ferry (Exp.159 786 789), which plied from the riverbank in front of the inn, the last house at the Henley end of Wargrave High Street. On the left of the inn is a wide track leading between walls down to the river. From it is an entrance to the large house next to the inn, Ferry House, built in the nineteenth century to a neo Tudor design in brick with gables and mock timber framing. It is suggested this was an original ferry house which was greatly extended about 1889 when the George and Dragon was also extended by architect George W. Webb. The house in 2010 is undergoing restoration, involving the retention and restoration of the Wargrave end; demolition of the middle or servants' section and building two new three-storey town houses. The track down to the river is still a right of way which suggests it was the original site of this ferry.

It is not known when the George and Dragon took on the running of the ferry from the premises but there was a wharf operating from there since at least 1847 and Wyatt's boatyard next door downstream, now occupied by modern flats. In the winter of 1878 a terrible accident occurred.[4] The Thames froze over and became a favourite place for skating. A Captain Markham insisted the ferryman should take him and his sister over that they may join in. The ferryman was reluctant but took his young daughter to help. The boat sank and the adults made it back to shore, but the little girl was drowned. Her ghost still walks the path beside the river in front of the inn, now gastro-pub.

Six years later ferryman W. Stevens was reported as dead.[5] Was he the little girl's father? He was succeeded in July 1884 by G.Couzens who by November 1884 was also dead, followed by Henry Bright who was not afflicted by a supposed curse, for he merely retired. In January 1886 Henry Tibble was ferryman until transferred to Spade Oak in the November. Henry Bryant was in charge from January 1887 until the July when Thacker found the ferry recorded as being private. Perhaps the Thames Conservancy vested it in the inn instead of running it themselves as Mrs Wyatt of the boatyard was also the publican. The ferry was used a lot during regatta weeks, but perhaps not much at other times.

One of the most notable features of the George and Dragon is its inn sign.[6] Sign painters regard themselves as artists although the public consider it a craft. This sign was painted by two Royal Academicians, G. D. Leslie and J. E. Hodgson in 1875. The former took on the job and painted the usual depiction of St George fighting the dragon. Hodgson asked to have a go on the other side and because he had to return to London, completed it in two hours. He portrays St George, having defeated the monster, quaffing his tankard of ale in celebration and nonchalance. Many visitors, including Jerome K. Jerome in 1889, and the Pennells who remarked on the respectability of Wargrave, have commented on the sign. Although repainted and restored several times, the paintings, now badly cracked and discoloured are still preserved behind glass on the front of the building. Bright copies now hang on a high post at the edge of the road. The Pennells stayed at the inn and noticed the evening stillness everywhere, broken 'by the one-armed ferryman of Wargrave in a punt coaching a beginner'.[7] Was this Henry Bryant?

A difficult case concerning the right of way to the ferry on land belonging to the George and Dragon was brought to Wargrave Civil Parish in 1902 and dragged on for sixty-six years.[8] At first a report was made by the Highways & Bridges Committee of

Wargrave/Shiplake Ferry at the George and Dragon Inn. The rowing boats are pulled up on the bank which later became a garden. The Willows boathouse and yard is to the left. From a postcard *c.* 1920s.

Berkshire County Council following an enquiry about an alleged obstruction of the public right of way. The report stated, 'In a place such as Wargrave which is much frequented by visitors for the purpose of using the river, every means of access to the river is important'. The following year an attempt was made to solve the problem when some freeholders offered to make a path but they would not admit a right of way to the public over the existing wharf. Nothing happened and the public continued to use the ferry place and would also congregate to watch activity at the wharf and on regatta days.

Then on 28 March 1933 a letter was sent by the Clerk to Wargrave Parish Council to H. & G. Simonds, the brewers at Reading, because the brewers wanted to plant a garden on the wharf frontage adjoining the ancient [*sic*] ferry. It referred back to the 1902 discussion when the problem was caused by the owners of the inn building an extension which encroached on the right of way to the ferry. The proposed alternative way to the ferry was not an adequate compensation to the public and the Parish Council could not agree because it implied the wharf would be in exclusive private ownership. A site meeting was arranged. The owner of Wargrave Court sent apologies as he could not be present, but expressed his opinion that the frontage to the river was not worthy of the village and compared it unfavourably with other places on the river. The brewery claimed the wharf as their property in April 1933.

The Clerk to Wargrave PC wrote to Wokingham Rural District Council quoting a report made in 1898. 'There was formerly an uninterrupted right of way leading out of the road passing through the centre of Wargrave to the Thames on the south side of the old boundary wall of the George and Dragon Hotel. This has been and is now partially obstructed and has been made impassable for vehicular traffic owing to the extension of building of the George and Dragon; enlarging of stables and the placing of a fence and gate at the entrance from Wargrave main road. If the wooden fence and outside staircase on the side of the stables were removed, a vehicle with one horse could pass'. The public are entitled to the right of way on and over the wharf and adjoining ferry slip and are entitled to free access to the ferry and slip with horses and carriages. The Council considered it doubtful if litigation would result in a right of way 15 feet wide, and requested Berkshire CC should not become involved.

In all there are ninety-three items in the bundle concerning this case, neither side willing to give way. It emerged that there was also an access over the wharf to a sheep-wash beside the ferry. As the wharf and ferry became little used as circumstances changed, the brewery did put down gravel, made steps and planted a lawn surrounded by a rope with a notice, 'KEEP OFF THE GRASS'. Later a licence was given to the public to use it. Finally, in May 1962, an agreement was made that a new public right of way would be created to the north of the hotel and a notice put up to indicate this. Then Val Wyatt of the Willows next door came forward to say that for many years there had been a seat where the grass area now was for passengers waiting for the ferry and he had old photographs to prove it. Today it is very restful to sit and look out to the river from this little garden.

To celebrate the Silver Jubilee of George V in 1935 an anonymous local person in Wargrave offered to give £500 to provide a footbridge from Wargrave to Shiplake to replace the ferry.[9] A cantilever bridge from the existing railway bridge was suggested. Then the possibility of a steel girder and wire rope suspension bridge was explored, as at Thames Ditton. By 1937 there were objections from thirteen riparian owners and above all from the sailing club. Wargrave Parish Council wrote to the Ministry of Health. 'There is a ferry service at Wargrave which conveys the public across the Thames to the Oxfordshire side on which are the towpath and right of way across a field to Shiplake. This ferry has been worked for very many years by a local boat proprietor and the public pay for journeys to and fro'. The purpose of the letter was to

The George and Dragon ferry when the place was full of activity. The big horse punt is pulled up to the slipway. From a postcard *c.* 1908.

Shiplake Lock, not far from the Lashbrook/Wargrave ferry landing, photographed *c.* 1951 by Eric de Maré. He was an architectural historian and photographer who specialised in unusual aspects of rivers and canals. His book *Time on the Thames* did much to boost our pride in the river. Reproduced by permission of English Heritage find out if the Parish Council could provide a more efficient and cheaper ferry service themselves. The Ministry's advice was for them to contact Berkshire CC. as only they could provide a ferry according to the Acquistion of Ferries Act of 1919. A report in *The Times* on 20 November 1937 announced that Berkshire CC could not accede to Wargrave's request on legal grounds; cost had nothing to do with the decision.[10]

## LASHBROOK FERRY

Continuing northwards on the A321 to Henley, a short distance from the George and Dragon is Willow Lane, branching off to the left. This is a long private lane serving some secluded houses but has a right of way until the houses end and a short path, once wide, now narrow and neglected leads to the river's edge. Here, through a broken gate is the landing place for Lashbrook ferry, (Exp.159 779 798) which was occasioned when the horse towing path was being set up and the owner of Bolney Court nearly a mile away on the Oxfordshire side refused to allow the towing path through his grounds. The ferry ran obliquely across to the left to meet a public footpath at Lashbrook, called Lys Brk on Rocque's map of 1762. As the towing path needed to be on the left bank the ferry carried the horses over to the right bank where a new towing path took them to the return ferry at Bolney. The present Thames Path avoids the problem by skirting Shiplake altogether until it rejoins the river beyond Bolney.

A new horse punt was provided for this ferry in 1909, costing £70.[11] The operation of the transfer was extremely inconvenient for all concerned, resulting in loss of time for the bargemasters, as each ferry took ½ hour to work. Also it was dangerous as sometimes the horses slipped overboard.[12] On one occasion during the Lord Mayor's view in 1775 a horse slipped on the soft mud and could not be rescued for ½ hour until the other horses were fastened to him and pulled him out by the head. One Sanders was ferryman in 1793. Thomas Thorp was in charge here and at Bolney from December 1855 until August 1858, being paid 20s a month.

Local people would use Lashbrook ferry to reach Shiplake railway station before Wantage got its own station. There was a ferryman's house which is shown as inundated with flood water in a 1925 photograph. The ferryman is seen handing his furniture out through the window for it to be taken away by boat. There are new houses built on the land now. The towpath still is a right of way on the Berkshire side until it reaches Bolney Eyot but is only moderately kept up. In October 2010 the way was blocked by a large ash tree which had blown across the path. On the opposite bank with large gardens down to the river are executive houses, some dating from Edwardian times. Here we have the answer to the obstreporousness of the Bolney Court owner. He was looking to the future when his descendants could sell this desirable property for residential use. If a horse towing path was next to the river the land value would have been considerably less. Perhaps due to the present recession some of these houses appear to be empty.

## BOLNEY FERRY

Bolney Ferry, (Exp.171 778 809) a.k.a. Beggar's Hole or Harpsden Ferry is associated with Lashbrook ferry for the changeover of the horse towing path. It may have already been an ancient ferry which was adapted by the Commissioners. Bolney Court is situated on a gravel terrace 1½ miles south of Henley and lies in the parish of Harpsden which is inland but like some other parishes has a river frontage. A Roman road from Dorchester on Thames via Nettlebed crossed the Thames near Henley and would have been easily accessible from Bolney, then named 'Bull's Hythe'. Roman remains have been found in the area. Lands at Bolney were subject to tithes paid to Abingdon Abbey.[13] The hythe or early landing place declined in importance in the Middle Ages when nearby Henley grew and became a trans-shipment point.

A rope ferry existed in 1775 when the ferry was probably at the same spot as marked on a map of 1900, leaving the left bank just north of Bolney Court and passing the tip of Ferry Eyot to reach the further shore where a footpath descends from the main road. George Jackson was ferryman in 1793 followed by John Jackson in 1798, both at a salary of 26s a month.[14] After 1813 the Hooney family of Marsh Mill upstream seem to be responsible for Bolney and Lashbrook ferries. An entry in the Commission's minutes for 1835 records their intention of repairing the ferryman's shed to give protection from the weather. A new house was being built for him in December 1838. When the Conservancy took over in 1866 the ferryman was earning £2 a month.

Hennerton backwater branches off from the main river at the George and Dragon and runs as a narrow stream on the right bank until it joins the Thames again at Bolney Ferry. A ford crossed the backwater to Ferry Eyot and this was replaced in the eighteenth century by Johnson's Bridge, although there may have been earlier bridges.[15] Hennerton House on the opposite side of the road was built in 1817 by C. F. Johnson and partly as a result of the Inclosure Awards both he and his successor William Rhodes came to own land on both sides of the backwater and therefore claimed the stream which was later given the name Hennerton. Rhodes in April 1868 asked the Conservators to remove 'the old house at Beggar's Hole Ferry'.[16] 'It was a great eyesore and had not been used for years.' Back came the reply that if he paid £2 he could buy it and remove it himself, which he did.

Making ferrymen double-up on ferries led to difficulties. Sometimes travellers were not able to summon a ferry to carry them across. This happened to the Victorian Joseph Ashby-Sterry, (1838–1917) who called himself 'The Lazy Minstrel'. In his poem *Bolney Ferry* published in 1886 he describes the experience of a poet travelling by foot downstream from Wargrave to Henley.

> Alas! There's neither punt nor wherry
> To take him over Bolney Ferry.
> He gazes to the left and right-
> No craft is anywhere in sight,
> Except the horse-boat he espied
> Secure upon the other side,
> No skiff he finds to stem the swirl,
> No ferryman, nor boy, nor girl!
> He sits and sings there 'Hey down derry:'
> But can't get over Bolney ferry!

Then a girl who was sketching comes to ferry him, bringing her bull dog Jerry. The verse ends by him toasting the girl in Mrs Williams' sherry. The Lazy Minstrel was very fond of young girls. When the Pennells arrived at the same spot as described in their book of 1891 they were reminded of Sterry, but as they had their own boat, they did not need the ferry. However, two people who arrived in 1938 were disappointed at Bolney.[17] 'We saw the expected ferry-boat opposite, but no amount of hailing would produce a ferryman. We waited five minutes, then in concert we hailed, but nothing availed, and we decided that the whole population on the opposite shore was still abed.' So they had to make a wide detour to Shiplake where they decided not to cross anyway.

The site of Bolney ferry is found at the point where the backwater finally rejoins the river. Nothing remains of the ferry there but the scene is beautiful. Beyond a hedge to the right is a very private garden and house buried among bushes which is Bolney Ferry Boathouse. The roadway to it is lined by trees and on the right hand side the boundary wall with Bolney Court is old, built of stone and in the past has been whitewashed. The roadway is so very wide it reminds of the drovers' roads. At intervals along it are old gas lamp posts. Was this ferry used to take cattle to Smithfield? It could have been a shortcut. The ferry operated until the mid-twentieth century.

## MARSH LOCK CROSSING

Below Bolney the Thames Path takes a very unusual diversion from the river bank at Marsh Lock (Exp.171 775 815). Here the river is wide and has an island towards the Berkshire bank. On both sides there were two mills operated from a large weir and causing a blockage to the towpath. A pound lock was built in 1773 between the island and the Berkshire bank.[18] To reach it and to provide for the towpath a wooden walkway was built out to the island and then back to the Oxfordshire side, forming a flattened semicircle into the river. The lower half downstream was the first to be built about 1843. This is a most impressive construction, the only one of its kind on the Thames. To reach it by car, from the main Reading–Henley take the next turning past Tesco, and a car park is at the end of Mill Lane. A ferry would have been dangerous to run so close to the weir but Thacker was told by local inhabitants there had been a way to cross on foot.[19] It was along a horsebridge, over the lock and on to the road through from the mill yard. He was not able to verify this. Certainly it was not a public right of way.

A walk from the car park northwards on the Path through Marsh Meadows is very pleasant. On the way the River and Rowing Museum which opened in 1998 is set back from the river. It is a purpose-built museum which concentrates on rowing, as expected at Henley. They have changing exhibitions, activities for adults and children, an educational programme and a decent café. Upstairs are the permanent collections which include displays on watermen, Thames Conservancy, regattas, *Wind in the*

Marsh Lock near Henley. The river crossing from the Henley towing path is by a wooden walkway to the lock island, then back again by a similar walkway. From a private photograph album, *c.* 1895.

*Willows* and river police. The only item connected with Thames ferries is a prehistoric dug-out canoe recovered from the river. They suggest it was a ferry boat but this is doubtful, it is too narrow.

## HENLEY

Henley is famous not only for the regatta, but for the view of it from the river. The bridge, church and the Angel Hotel are recognisable far and wide (Exp.171 763 826). Although it is said that the Romans crossed at Henley in pursuit of the British, this cannot be verified. There must have been some means of getting across the river because it is such an important crossing, so busy now it is not advisable to stop.[20] When King John visited the town at the beginning of his reign in 1199 there was a ferry.[21] The first bridge, St Anne's Bridge, with a chapel was built in 1232 but did not have enough income to ensure its continued maintenance.and in 1754 was declared unsafe. The Corporation closed it and bought a ferry boat from Maidenhead for £46 6s and this operated for thirty years. In 1774 what was left of the bridge was carried away by floods and an Act was passed to build a new bridge in 1781. One clause in the Act stated that no ferries could operate within 1½ miles of the new bridge, which opened in 1786. It is a listed structure, still in use today. A public slipway is on Wharf Lane which branches off from Thames Side and the incessant traffic. It could have been the ferry landing place.

## ASTON/HAMBLEDEN FERRY

The towing path crossed Henley Bridge and continued on the right bank to avoid the grounds of Fawley Court, until the river bends to run southwards again to reach Hambleden Lock, weir and mill. The Thames Path follows the same route until it comes to the public slipway at the site of Aston ferry, where it turns right to follow the lane to the Flowerpot Inn at the crossroads in the hamlet of Aston (Exp.171 786 845). The original horse towing path crossed to the Buckinghamshire bank at Hambleden Place. In 1785 there was a rope ferry controlled by the lock-keeper at Hurley Lock nearly 3½ miles downstream.[22] Sometime later the rope was replaced by a chain which ran along the riverbed, and the ferryman had to hoist it up to pull on it. Between 1793 and 1798 John Gould of Hurley lock had charge of this ferry but was succeeded in 1800 by young family member William and then by Robert Moore, who also operated Medmenham ferry, for a very short time. In October 1822 responsibility for Aston /Hambleden ferry had again fallen into the hands of the Hurley lock-keeper, Carter.

By March 1854 Henry Hobbs was ferryman at a wage of 18s a month, reduced from 24s. The ferry was still held by the Hobbs family when the Conservators took over in 1866 but in October 1870 H. J. Hobbs resigned. It seems there was not a ferry house, for when S. Somers took over he was given an extra 2s to pay rent. Perhaps his home was elsewhere and he stayed at the inn. His son G. Summers [*sic*] was appointed after he died in January 1876. One Levi Collins came from Gatehampton in 1879 and was too ill to work in December 1888. His son Robert succeeded him only to resign in July 1893 when James Hawkes became his successor and may have still been working when Thacker wrote his book in 1920.

A pontoon bridge was built across the Thames near Aston in the early 1900s as an army exercise when some army and some private cars were driven across.[23] The exercise followed one which took place a little further downstream near Medmenham ferry in

Aston/Hambleden Ferry. A favourite spot for river bathing *c.* 1958. Reproduced with permission from **a website.**

1870.[24] On that occasion it was men, waggons and horses who had crossed. When the Conservancy decided to close the ferries in the 1950s Aston/Hambleden was included. However, there was a protest in the form of a protest swim.[25] It had proved an ideal spot for free river swimming. The protestors were not successful, but had a good time!

Culham Court was in the process of being built in 1770 for a lawyer, Richard Michell, who had married a sugar plantation heiress. The Act obtained that year for a new horse towing path included a clause forbidding any towing paths, landing places or bridges to be built on the estate. No 'boat or float' was to be moored within 200 yards of any island or land belonging to the estate.[26] This then is the reason why the towing path changed sides at Aston ferry and back again at Medmenham ferry, a distance of nearly two miles. Subsequent owners were more sympathetic and land on both sides of the river was given to the National Trust. In the early twentieth century Sir William Henry Barber and Lady Barber lived at Culham Court. He had made a fortune developing Birmingham's suburbs. On his death in 1927 Lady Barber set up a trust in his memory to build the Barber Institute of Fine Art and at her own death bequeathed their collections to the university in trust.

## MEDMENHAM FERRY

Medmenham Abbey is well known as the meeting place of the eighteenth-century Hellfire Club, but in fact it was founded as a genuine abbey by the Saxons. King John in 1201 confirmed it to the Cistercians and dedicated the abbey to the Virgin Mary.[27] At first it came under the aegis of Woburn Abbey in Bedfordshire but later was transferred to Bisham Abbey just downstream. At the Dissolution, Medmenham was granted to Robert Moore, succeeded by the Duffield family who held it until 1779. The ferry and ferry rights were always included with the estate and had been since time immemorial (Exp.171 806 837).

The title to the property rested on several legal documents. On 27 May 1713 an agreement was made between Francis Duffield Esq. of Medmenham, Jonathan Sayer of Henley, gentleman and Francis Sayer of Medmenham, yeoman.[28] J. Sayer was to pay 10s to Duffield and thus obtain possession of the mansion house known as the Abbey of Medmenham then held by Duffield. It included farm land etc. and 'all that passage over the river of Thames called Medmenham Ferry and all the 2 acres of arable land called The Hale in the Great Town Field'. In a lease for one year dated 2 June 1740 between Duffield, Henry Cruwys Esq. and Elizabeth Mills of Medmenham, Cruwys was to pay 5s for the Abbey and the wharves and the ferry.[29] From the 1740s Duffield rented Medmenham Abbey itself to Sir Francis Dashwood MP (1708–81) who proceeded to make alterations for it to become a mock abbey. In about 1745 he founded the 'Franciscans of Medmenham' and it became the scene of orgies and debauchery, as rumoured. A release of estates in Buckinghamshire of 10 January 1778 allowed for property to be sold in trust.[30] Francis Duffield had borrowed large sums of money and is making lands over to John Morton of Danesfield, (a neighbouring estate). The lands included the right of ferry over the Thames at Medmenham 'as the same now is and heretofore had been used or enjoyed by Francis Duffield and his ancestors'. Supposedly he also gained riparian rights; £5,000 was mentioned. By a lease and release of 10/11 June 1779 John Morton and Sambrooke Freeman of Fawley Court (another neighbouring estate) and Duffield accepted 5s from Elbro Woodruff for the abbey.[31] Included in the sale was the ferry, an eyot and osier beds of 27 perches lying in the Thames and other eyots. The Duffields had now severed all connections with the Medmenham Abbey estate.

The owners in the nineteenth century were the Scott-Murray family who added some buildings to the estate. A terrace of four ferry cottages was built on the east side of Ferry Lane in the early nineteenth century.[32] They are of flint with brick dressings and shared chimneys and now listed Grade II. The abbey building was in poor condition and in 1862 it was 'divided into several tenements for labourers'.[33] The timber-framed wing on the west was detached to become the Ferry Boat Inn.[34] It achieved a notable reputation for 'a ready and hearty welcome always awaits the visitor' and was much frequented by artists. Henry William Caslon (1815–74) lived there as a retired guest until he took a lease on Rose Cottage where he died.[35] Caslon was the last in the line of the family of the Caslon Type foundry of Chiswell Street, London EC. As he had poor health he had not been able to 'enhance the fortunes of his family'. He is buried in Medmenham churchyard.

Some information concerning the ferry is gleaned from a court case which took place over three days in May 1898.[36] The Medmenham Abbey estate was sold in 1895/96 and divided into two parts. The soap manufacturer Robert William Hudson (1856–1937) became one owner and Hudson Kearley (1856–1934) later Lord Devonport founder of International Stores, the other. He was Liberal MP for Devonport, Plymouth and lived at Wittington. Hudson took the abbey at the bottom of Ferry Lane on the left and rebuilt much of it in white chalk and adding buildings. He actually lived at Danesfield. The court case was to establish whether there was a public highway and ferry on the north of the river at Medmenham across to the Frogmill on the south side and from there a public path and through the farm to the main road at the Black Boy Public House. Mr Justice Day gave judgement for the plaintiff (Mr Kearley) in the first action and for the defendant (Mr Hudson) in the second, which was a case of trespass.

When the cases were taken to the Court of Appeal in March 1899 more details came to light.[37] The ferry had worked from in front of the Ferry Boat Inn. The innkeeper worked it and received the profits. An old man of seventy-seven who had been called as witness said the road to the ferry on the north had always been used

Medmenham Abbey shown on an early print *c.* 1772. Note the path leading to the river. Copper engraving by J. Newton from Francis Grose's *Antiquities of England & Wales*.

Medmenham/Frogmill Ferry showing the Abbey on the right and the hotel on the left. Postcard courtesy of Ken Townsend.

by Her Majesty's subjects without interference, together with horses and carriages. Likewise, the way on the other side, where passengers landed in a meadow, was subject to flooding. There was no made-up roadway there but a right of way to the mill and Frogmill Farm had been used as of customary right. From the farm it was a proper trackway. Another statement was mysterious; they said the Conservancy had set up another ferry to serve the horse towing path about 250 yards upstream but it had been discontinued in 1851. All the old photographs show the horse ferry in front of the inn. Indeed there is still a right of way from about that point on the Berkshire bank which runs southwards to join the main road at Culham Court Lodge. Perhaps the Commissioners had difficulty in setting up the ferry at Medmenham and did it themselves, but the Conservancy were successful in persuading the Medmenham owners to amalgamate with them for economy's sake. There was a large boat for carts, carriages and saddle horses, and a smaller punt for foot passengers. The fare was 1*d* for them, 3*d* for a saddle horse and 6*d* for a cart or carriage. The case against Mr Hudson showed that he was the owner of the ancient ferry and was entitled by franchise to collect tolls. He was bound by law to keep the ferry running and was not allowed to bar people from using the lane or the ferry, and by obstructing the way he had committed an offence. He replied the ferry had been set up by the Conservators who no longer needed it, but this was not the case with an ancient ferry. The real reason (unstated in court) was that Hudson had bought land on both sides of the river and wanted to keep it private. The verdict was that the judgement of Mr Justice Day was re-affirmed and the appeals of both actions were dismissed with costs. The right of way was secured.

The place of the ferry landing at Medmenham is now a public slipway and the land to the right of it must be common land. A monument was set up there in 1936 to commemorate the successful lawsuit. It is rather like a war memorial with a pantiled roof and a putto pointing towards the defunct ferry. The inscription reads: 'This monument was erected to commemorate the successful action fought by Hudson Ewbank Kearley, 1st Viscount Devonport which resulted in the Court of Appeal deciding on the 28 March 1899 that Medmenham Ferry is public.' The questions arise, why was this monument erected so long after the event? Was it to perpetuate the memory of Kearley who was not one of the most popular of men? The monument was designed by Sir Edwin Cooper and the sculptor was C. L. J. Dorman. It is inscribed with the motto '*Fit via vi*' (Determination finds a way).

As to whether the whole thing was worth it, well the ferry continued in service until about 1957 when, in spite of tolls charged being six times those of Conservators ferries, it became unviable and occasioned a letter to *The Times*. The roads to the ferry on both banks remain as rights of way. But the whole area round the abbey and down to the river is very private with a high wall around the perimeter and clearly there has been some encroachment on to the roadway. A house called Ferry Nab is closest to the wall and has occupied the same layout since 1925. An archaeological watching brief carried out in 2004 suggested the layout reflected the rebuilding on the site of the demolished hotel.[38] Although a Roman villa was known to exist at Hambleden, the only finds recorded at Ferry Nab were a chalk built wall and floor, undated but possibly medieval.

## HURLEY

One of the footpaths from Frogmill Farm leads by a well-made path directly to Hurley (Exp.172 825 842). This is a lovely village, steeped in history, with nowadays a complicated system of waterways, weirs, locks and islands. There was an important

Medmenham Ferry being worked on a chain by two ferrymen, not in uniform. Postcard *c.* 1910, courtesy of Ken Townsend.

Medmenham ferry punt and other river craft moored in front of the hotel. Postcard by Taunt. Courtesy of Ken Townsend.

ford in the fifth century to Harleyford on the north bank. It was defended on the Buckinghamshire side by earthworks still to be seen recently in the grounds of Danesfield House where there is an Iron Age hill-fort, and Harleyford Manor. A battle with the Danes was fought in AD 870. A Benedictine Priory, a cell to Westminster Abbey, was founded beside the river in 1086. The priory church and other monastic buildings are still extant and some are incorporated in modern buildings. The ford was replaced by a ferry.

An inventory of the priory at its Dissolution in 1536 does not include the ferry as one of its possessions. The monastic buildings were bought in 1544 by John Lovelace and one of his descendants built Lady Place, a large Elizabethan mansion overlooking the river by the ferry. There was a tradition in Hurley that somewhere in the vicinity of the ferry a great treasure in the form of a golden calf was buried.[39] Many searches for it were made in vain. Then some electricians digging a cable to serve the Old Bell Inn in 1946 unearthed a pot full of dirty – but not corroded – coins. The source suggests they were gold and could have borne the image of a calf. Unfortunately, this could not be checked, 'because they rapidly disappeared'. Two map references show that the ferry may have continued for longer than expected. A road map of 1698 (which marks Lady Place as Hurley Place) shows the ferry connecting the Reading Road to Hurley. Thomas Gardner's map of 1719 of the route from London to Bath notes turnings to Hurley Town and Hurley Ferry.[40] In the way of things the ferry was discontinued when the pound lock was constructed in 1773. The attractive path to the former ferry site and lock is still a right of way and has a footbridge to cross the lock stream.

Hurley Lock. An early Taunt photograph of 1885 showing the lock in poor condition and a thatched shed for the lock-keeper at the side. Reproduced by Permission of English Heritage.

# TEMPLE FERRY

Temple is part of the parish of Bisham (Exp.172 839 842). There are two islands in the river, Lock Island and Temple Island. Mills were built on the latter, which was reached by a private ferry or footbridge. The Commissioners set up their own ferry upstream of the islands to allow the horse towing path to change sides. No references have yet been found to suggest the existence of an earlier ferry. Nor is there much information about the horse ferry. In 1785 it was worked with a rope.[41] A new ferry boat to be built of sound oak was ordered in August 1803 to cost £50. The new pound lock was made in 1773 and in October 1822 the lock-keeper's wages were £3 a month, but he also had to look to the ferry. It is not known if this was a permanent arrangement.

The prosperity of the area increased enormously when Thomas Williams (1737–1802) came from Anglesey to set up copper works on Temple Island in 1788. He began his career as a lawyer, specialising in disputes over country estates.[42] When high grade copper ore was discovered in Parys Mountain on Anglesey Williams was able to exploit it. Gradually he came to dominate the copper industry in Britain, apart from the flourishing Cornish trade, for which Boulton and Watt had contributed a good deal by their expertise in machinery and investment. Matthew Boulton and Williams hated each other but maintained respect. Matthew Boulton described Williams as 'The Copper King – the despotic sovereign of the copper trade'. Apparently the mills Williams took over at Temple, Bisham and Wraysbury were owned by him personally and were not part of his copper companies.

Williams engaged Samuel Wyatt in 1790 to build Temple House for him overlooking the island. Mrs Lybbe Powys, a lady who specialised it seems in visiting country houses and making subtle comments, remarked in 1796 that the house and gardens were lavish – poor taste? She added that the only pictures on show were ones of Williams himself. The way to the ferry upsteam led through the estate by a public right of way by a high wall on the left, then through a brick-lined tunnel just wide enough to take one horse and man. The roof arch had been supported by cast iron brackets, of which a few still survive, but concrete slabs now support the roof. On emerging from the tunnel the boundary was marked on the left side by a fence made of slate slabs with an arched top with a hole, as used on Welsh slate roofs. They are now sadly fallen in many places and deserve to be reinstated. Samuel Wyatt's younger brother was an agent at the Penryn slate quarry on the mainland side of the Menai Straits opposite Williams' copper mines on Anglesey. He pioneered the use of slate for some unconventional purposes, including fencing.

When the copper trade began to lessen at the end of the eighteenth century, Williams retired in 1799 and died of asthma in Bath in 1802. He left the businesses and estates to be divided among his two sons, Owen and John. Soon afterwards the empire was split up. The mills became paper mills and later made paperboard. Temple House was demolished in 1910 and in 1974 planning permission was given to demolish the mills, although some mill cottages were kept. Today the whole area is fenced off and controlled by security gates. There is no way at all to get to Temple Island and no way to even look at it. Superior housing blocks are now built there and on the site of Temple House.

In 1953 the ferry closed, due to lack of manpower. However, the ferry way has been extended to go a long way round back to it where there is now a new footbridge to carry the Thames Path at the same spot.[43] Designed and built by Messrs. Sarum Hardwood Structures in 1989 it is a single span of 82 metres made of West African hardwood supported by two concrete piers paid for by Thames Water and Buckinghamshire CC together with other public and private donations, it is an elegant addition to the river scene, unlike the modern housing development. At the lock, still in constant use, the lock-keeper's family serve refreshments in the garden.

# BISHAM FERRY

Bisham, (pronounced Biss-am), at the end of Temple Lane from Temple is made up of an abbey, a church, both seen prominently on the right bank just below Marlow Bridge, and a small compact village. The abbey began as a preceptory built by the Knights Templar in the twelfth century. In 1337 it became an Augustinian priory until 200 years later it was refounded as a Benedictine Abbey. That was short-lived as the abbey, along with many others, was dissolved and mostly demolished in 1540. Naturally it would have possessed a ferry as the river is very wide at this point. The church is isolated at the end of the village and to the north of the churchyard there is a right of way about twenty yards wide running down to the river from Town End, an old seventeenth century vernacular timber framed farmhouse. At the waters' edge there could be a slipway and as the bank is walled, a wharf in former times.

There is nothing to confirm this was a ferry place but it looks right (Exp.172 848 854). Particularly, with such a wide easy access it could have been used as a drover's road, or an alternative crossing to Marlow for cattle if the bridge there was not suitable. The abbey passed into the Hoby family who built a Tudor mansion using materials from the former Abbey. From 1963 it has been developed as the National Sports Centre.

## CHAPTER FOURTEEN

# Marlow to Maidenhead

## MARLOW

At Marlow in Buckinghamshire there was a bridge over the Thames to Bisham on the Berkshire side as early as 1309. As it was associated with the Knights Templar establishment at Bisham and may have replaced a ferry, but of this nothing is known.[1] In around 1530 it was described by Leland as being built of timber. When partially damaged by Parliamentary forces in 1642 the bridge was quickly repaired. Thacker could not discover exactly at which spot this bridge was erected, but suggested it was on the line of the present bridge, being at the end of the main street. However, a new site was chosen for the second bridge which needfully replaced the first one in about 1789 (Exp.172 859 862). This one was erected in timber from the end of St Peter's Street (formerly named Duck Lane) across to land belonging to the old inn, The Compleat Angler. Not being a county bridge and with a monastic origin, it was paid for by subscription.

By 1828 the bridge was in a poor state, possibly because it was built from materials salvaged from the previous bridge, and planning began for a new one. Until it could be built, a temporary ferry was set up close to the riverside end of St Peter's Street, which is only a few yards away on the other side of the churchyard from the present crossing (Exp.172 852 862). Marlow has always been a busy, but attractive town and fashionable. The artist Frederick Walker (1840–75) painted in watercolour 'Marlow Ferry' showing a rowboat leaving the slipway with a single passenger, watched by swans and with the ubiquitous Lombardy poplar in the background.[2] This suggests the ferry continued to run from this spot even after the bridge was replaced by a suspension bridge on the original site in 1835. At the same time a new church was being built beside the bridge and one of the Commissioners' wharves alongside was used as a makeshift church (Exp.172 851 861). The Commissioners were asked to 'continue their towing path' from the new bridge and in front of the churchyard to the second bridge.[3] This towing path was shown on a map of 1847 but no sign of it has survived. The Thames Path has to make a circuitous way, called by locals 'Seven Corner Alley' back to the river opposite Lock Island downstream, the same route as used by the horse towing path. At number 1 St Peter's Street is a distinctive three-storied seventeenth-century house called 'Marlow Ferry', listed Grade II.[4] Was it so named because the ferryman lived there or because it stood by the ferry?

'The Compleat Angler' Hotel is synonymous with Marlow and has stood at the river crossing for centuries. In 1600 it was recorded as a small inn with six letting rooms. Renamed later after Isaak Walton's book published in 1653, it still retains a

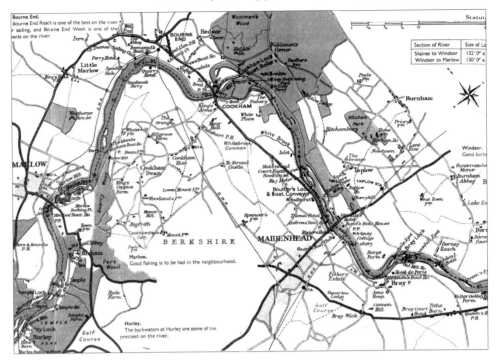

The Thames takes another loop northwards from Marlow to avoid the high ground of Winter Hill and Cookham Common. It resumes an easterly course at Bray. From *Stanford's New Map of the River Thames c.* 1900.

The Compleat Angler Hotel at Marlow has expanded considerably since the Halls visited prior to the publication of their book *The Book of the Thames* in 1859.

fishing atmosphere but would also have served travellers at the crossing. Percy Shelley explored the Thames in his boat 'The Vaga' when he lived in Marlow for a short time.[5]

## RIVERSIDE FERRY

Below Marlow a ferry existed called Riverside at a point where the Thames, after turning northwards to skirt Winter Hill has two quite substantial islands.[6] The ferry was marked on a map of 1900 just short of the higher island (Exp.172 870 869) and seems to be on a parish boundary. Not a conservancy ferry, it apparently had no specific purpose, except perhaps to transport passengers during a regatta, or to take picnicers to the beauty spots of Quarry Woods and Winter Hill. It closed early in the twentieth century.

## SPADE OAK FERRY

Spade Oak Ferry (Exp.172 883 873) is not an ancient ferry, so Thacker claims, although it is said the ferry was controlled by a Benedictine Nunnery, founded before 1218, at Little Marlow, Bourne End.[7] Required by the Commissioners as a crossing point for the horse towing path, the ferry was first mooted in 1789, but was not implemented.[8] In 1814 the City of London urged it be set up 'to encourage and enable persons to use their own horses in towing'. Contrary influences were at work because it was not until April 1822 that a boat was finally provided. Apparently one Mr Rose, a farmer of Spade Oak, 'exercised an exclusive Right to tow the barges to near Marlow, and even makes a charge for towing up such path, when the Bargemaster has towed his Barge up with his own Horses, or with men'. John Rennie also mentioned this strange uncompromising arrangement. By 1825 there may have been a ferry house. The ferry landing on the Berkshire bank was sited on the former wharf belonging to Mr Rose.

John Cutter was ferryman at Spade Oak in March 1854 with a wage of 30s a month, a figure he was still receiving in 1866. When he died in 1875 his place was taken by James Collins for whom a new house was provided in 1883. In December that year Collins was transferred to Abingdon. His successor was Robert Lloyd who died in November 1886. Then Henry Tibble from Wargrave ferry was at Spade Oak until his resignation in September 1891. There followed in quick succession H. Edmonds, J. Sparks and W. H. Round, in May 1893. A new punt (for passengers) was bought for the ferry in 1909 at a cost of £15.[9]

Why it was necessary to change the horse towing path from one side to the other is not obvious, unless it was to avoid the built up area and wharves through Bourne End. It then continued on the Berkshire side until it reached Cookham Bridge. There was an influx of population in the late nineteenth and early twentieth centuries into Bourne End, prompted by the branch line railway. Writers and artists settled here, including artist Frederick Walker RA who lodged at the ferry house in May 1871, a month notable for its grim weather. However, he made many paintings of the Thames in the area. Besides Marlow Ferry, 'Rainy Day at Bisham' in watercolour and body colour is in the V&A Museum. Walker's life at Cookham where his family lived is chronicled by his friend G. D. Leslie in *Our River*. He is buried at Cookham. Whilst she was living at Old Thatch, next door to the Spade Oak Hotel, previously Ye Ferry Hotel, and before that the Rose and Crown, the children's author Enid Blyton wrote about fourteen books. Many of them use places in the locality but it is doubtful if the ferry caught her attention.

Spade Oak Ferry. During the time of floods in the 1930s Townsends were called upon to bring the coffin of Mr Lysip across the river to Bourne End for burial. Those paddling were Eric Norman with Rob and Les Townsend, guided by their father Ernest and the undertaker. Courtesy of Ken Townsend.

Spade Oak Ferry House is in the background and a purpose-built Thames Conservancy (TC) punt is being operated by a TC ferryman in uniform. Courtesy of Ken Townsend.

Before the ferry closed in 1956 the Conservancy were using a dinghy and a punt on a chain.[10] The ferry house on the opposite bank from Bourne End can still be seen with the typical Thames Conservancy white ticket office in the garden, although its position may have been moved. There is a public footpath leading to the house, the last single storey white house in the row. The last road turning on the left on leaving Bourne End for Marlow is the access road to Spade Oak wharf, from where the ferry plied across the river. Beyond is a useful car park, then past Spade Oak Farm is a little level crossing over the railway from Bourne End to Marlow. Now the wharf is a greensward between the railway and the river and was bought for the public. At the ferry place are children feeding ducks.

To replace the ferry and to create the Thames Path, the existing towing path was extended from Spade Oak by a wide clinker path, through former wharves and boatyards and now marinas and sailing clubs to Bourne End Railway bridge. When first built in 1857 it was of timber construction and a menace to navigation but rebuilt in iron in 1895. A cantilevered footbridge to take the Thames Path was attached to the upstream side in 1994/95. The path now continues by following the course of the original towing path to Cookham Bridge.

## TOWNSEND'S FERRY

Townsend's Boatyard close to the railway bridge ran a very successful private ferry for nearly seventy years during the time when pleasure boating on the river was in its heyday (Exp.172 888 873). The boatbuilding business was started by Ken Townsend's grandfather in 1884.[11] Until it closed in 1962 to become Bourne End Marina it was a truly family business and they lived in a red brick house next door to the boatyard. It was situated at the bottom of Wharf Lane. Behind the site is a small area with numerous little brooks running through it, part of the grounds of the nunnery. Here Robert Haden Tebb, (c. 1862–1945) a London architect, surveyor and property developer came along and saw the potential to build an exclusive estate for Londoners to 'take temporary refuge here from London life'. To this end Tebb negotiated an agreement in 1896 with Mrs Louisa Townsend to allow access through the boatyard from his land for his tenants to use their own canoes, punts and other small craft on the river.

During the Second World War an affiliated branch of the Home Guard was set up to guard the Thames; the UTP – Upper Thames Patrol. Personnel were taken from lock-keepers and others who worked on the river and had a fleet of their own small craft. They were based in an upstairs room at Townsend's boatyard. Townsends had a contract for building lifeboats for navy ships.

As a young man Ken Townsend helped with the ferry at busy times. On one bank holiday they carried 3,500 people over the river each way.[12] They would be visiting the Quarry, a café and bar on the other side and the large recreation area of Cock Marsh, now an ASSI. The fare in 1937 was one ha'penny. A very large punt would be used which needed at least two strong men to use a pole about ten feet in length. The river is wide, but it was possible to cross with four shoves or even with three if the punters were very strong. In the middle of the river the depth was usually 12–14 feet deep and at the sides about 8 feet. Therefore a strong shove in the shallow parts would provide enough momentum to glide over the deeper part.

At Cookham there are four major streams allied to the River Thames. They were crossed by four different ferries in order to provide a towing path.[13] One ferry connected Cookham village with the parish of Wooburn on the Buckinghamshire side. This was discontinued when the first bridge was built in 1840. But instead it was

Townsend's Boatyard at Bourne End with a horse punt moored. The firm owned many craft of all shapes and sizes. They built boats as well as running a ferry and hiring out pleasure boats. Courtesy of Ken Townsend.

Townsend's were especially busy at the times of Bourne End Regatta, one of which took place in 1906. It was usual for men to stand while being punted across. Courtesy of Ken Townsend.

Townsend's Ferry carried thousands of people on Bank Holiday 1937. The ferries for Spade Oak and Townsends were eventually replaced by the walkway for the Thames Path which was attached to the railway bridge seen in the distance. Courtesy of Ken Townsend.

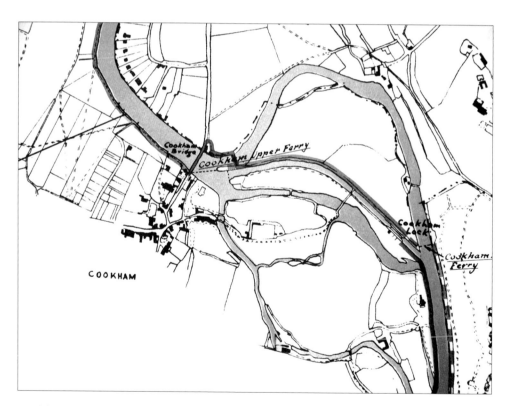

Cookham. Plan showing the bridge and the three other ferries which were abolished when the towing paths closed and the Thames Path created. From a book of maps, 1947, courtesy of Gloucestershire Archives.

replaced by the Upper Ferry from the same spot opposite the church to the head of Lock Island. The Middle Ferry operated across the tail of the weir stream at Hedsor and carried the towing horses to the left bank. The Lower Ferry was best known as My Lady Ferry which carried them back again to the right bank.

Thacker tended to presume the first mentioned was the oldest, being the predecessor of Cookham Bridge, although he could find only one old deposition for it in 1633 and that only alluded to the ferry. In fact there are many references, including Court Rolls, to Babham ferry at Cookham, as it was on the main route from London to Oxford and the west before Maidenhead Bridge was built.[14] This old road came from the east and passing Burnham Abbey, kept to the high ground until it reached what is now the Cliveden Estate, where it descended on a gradual slope to the river at or near My Lady Ferry or alternatively Hedsor Ferry or ford, or even between the two.[15] Then it crossed Cookham Moor by a raised causeway and came to Bisham ferry. The Babham family lived at Babham End where their manor house was bought in 1794 by Admiral Sir George Young. He built Formosa Place at the site where there may also have been an inn. The house, although enlarged, still exists, right by My Lady Ferry.

## MY LADY FERRY

An explanation of the unusual name of the ferry is not generally known, except that the field on the Cookham side at the landing place is called Lady Mead (Exp.172 907 848). It is suggested that somewhere in the vicinity there was a holy well. The springs near the landing place at Cliveden seem not to have a name. Stanley Spencer declared 'you can't walk by the river at Cliveden Reach and not believe in God'.[16] Furthermore, an ancient stone on the Cookham side marks the Great Whitten Hare Warren which existed until the beginning of the twentieth century.[17] Here the warrener in medieval times held games at the stone on the Feast of the Assumption, 15 August, which was also the pagan feast day of the mother goddess, Diana. One of her emblems is the hare which appears on the face of her moon and is depicted on a medieval floor tile in Cookham Church.

The ferry lapsed after the London–Bath road came into being, but in 1789 the Commission were contemplating using the crossing.[18] However, it was not established until 1808 as part of the horse towing path. The horses changed sides here as the hanging woods of Cliveden came too close to the river on the left bank and were unstable. This reach needed a wide path because up to eight horses were used in towing here. In 1825 the purchase of a new boat was considered. This was probably in use when the charge of two pence per horse was fixed in November 1828. It was then stipulated that, 'no persons or horses other than those actually and immediately concerned in the navigation to be under any pretence permitted to pass over the ferry'. This did not become an issue anymore when a passenger ferry was established alongside the horse ferry, nearer to the ferry cottage slightly upstream. Both ferry landings, and one on the opposite side can still be detected. One Barfoot was ferry keeper in December 1833, but following complaints about him he was dismissed in August 1836. Thomas Staniford did the job for £2 a month until he died in September 1870. Charles Curtis his successor received an extra 2s a week, 'until the ferry house is built'. He transferred to Upper Ferry in 1885.

Unusually, although the ferrymen worked for and were paid first by the Commission, then by the Conservancy, the ferry cottage was built by and owned by the Cliveden Estate. It was designed by the architect George Devey (1820–86), who built other artisans' cottages on the estate, in 1861. They all have a cottagey, cosy look. This one at My Lady Ferry has a single storey with a porch, main living room and two small bedrooms. The front windows are about shoulder height, it is said to prevent strangers on the towpath from staring in. Improvements were made in July 1915 when an agreement was made to supply piped water from the Cliveden main to the cottage via a one inch iron pipe into a 20-gallon tank.[19] It was to be for domestic use only, not for the garden or visitors. Major Waldorf Astor MP was to be reimbursed for the cost of £8 12s 6d. Clause 6 of the agreement reiterated one made in 1878 which forbade the sale of refreshments of any kind at the cottage. Nevertheless, perhaps owing to public demand as the area had for long past been a place of festivities, the Astors relented and by an agreement of 8 January 1917 the occupant of the cottage was entitled to sell to visitors and people on the towing path and the river, tea, coffee, cocoa, mineral waters, milk, bread, butter, biscuits, cake, or other similar refreshments, being not of an alcoholic or intoxicating nature. Provisos were that the occupant must be in the employment of the Conservators as ferryman; no other sales to take place; and no sign or placard to be put up without the consent of Major Astor. He was at liberty to discontinue the agreement at any time by giving one week's notice to the Conservancy in London.

The Astors gave Cliveden estate to the National Trust in 1942. Both Ferry Cottage and its neighbour New Cottage were included and are now let out as holiday cottages. A stay in them is delightful with only the sounds of the river and birdsong for company. This ferry closed in 1956 and was the last of the Conservancy ferries to do so. The cost of keeping it up in 1953 was £495 with revenue of £24.[20] Only the original towpath from the weir by Middle Ferry which terminates just beyond the ferry place, is a right of way on the estate. In spring 2010 it was closed due to its being unsafe. From Cookham the Thames Path joins the riverbank opposite the cottage and keeps to the right bank past Boulter's Lock to Maidenhead Bridge.

The large passenger ferry at My Lady Ferry being punted across in the 1920s. The tables are laid for tea in the cottage garden. Courtesy of Ken Townsend.

In 1926, the Thames Conservancy ran a project to photograph all their ferrymen and lock-keepers and their houses. Here is Mr J. T. Brooks, ferryman at My Lady Ferry. Reproduced with the kind permission of the Environment Agency.

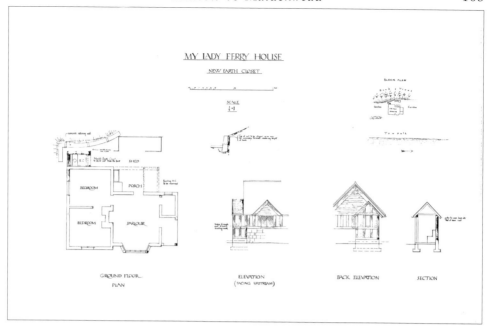

Plan made for an earth closet to be fixed at My Lady Ferry Cottage. Today it is a store cupboard connected to the second bedroom. The National Trust has made a large kitchen and a bathroom where the back porch is marked on the plan. Reproduced with the kind permission of the Environment Agency.

The ferry service at My Lady Ferry continued by rowing boat until 1956, although working at a loss. Both the Ferry Cottage and New Cottage shown on the left are administered by the National Trust as holiday lets. From a postcard *c.* 1950s.

## COOKHAM FERRY

Another ancient stone called the Tarry Stone stood at the ferry landing place at Cookham, opposite the church (Exp.172898 856). It was by an enclosure called Dodson's or Dobson's Close which became the property of the Commission and it was from here that the ferry ran across to the left bank.[21] Later it served for the springings of the bridge and for the horse towing path which went on the new alignment of the ferry to the Lock Island. James King in 1772 was engaged by the Commissioners to waft (ferry) barge horses from Dobson's Close to the Shawsies in Wooburn parish for a year at £20.[22] On 25 April 1796 Joseph Wyatt, a young man from Cookham, returning after visiting a village on the Buckinghamshire side to fix his wedding day, decided to wade across fully clothed and was drowned. A ferryman's house was built in Dobson's Close about the same time the bridge was built.

In 1837 it was decided the ferry was a 'great inconvenience and risk' and as the GWR were shortly to reach nearby Maidenhead it was desirous to have a bridge instead. An Act was obtained in May 1838 to build a bridge at or near the ferry by the Proprietors of the Cookham Bridge Company.[23] There were 200 shares at £25 each. The Company was empowered to charge tolls, and a toll house was set up on the bridge. They were to allow compensation and satisfaction to the owners or the persons interested in the ancient ferry called Cookham ferry. It was felt necessary not only to replace the ferry but to improve the roads on either side of it. The turnpike from High Wycombe to the horse ferry at Wooburn and the road leading from Cookham village north to the ferry were so narrow that carriages could not pass each other and the curves in the roads were inconvenient and circuitous. It was laid down that the Bridge Company should purchase the ferry along with any rights. They were to, 'keep and use boats for carrying and conveying persons, horses or other beasts, cattle and carriages over the ferry until the bridge was erected. It was not lawful for any other person to operate a ferry and only the Company could collect ferry tolls. If, after it was completed the bridge became dangerous, in the case of accident or damage, then the Company must provide a ferry instead. It should be deemed a public bridge. I. K. Brunel was approached to design and build the bridge but declined.[24] In the end George Treacher was accepted at his estimate of £2,000 plus contingencies of £3,000 for a timber bridge. Added to that was the compensation of £2,275 to Mr Poulton the ferry owner. At the time there was one ferry barge with chains and rollers for carrying cattle and one ferry punt with poles to carry passengers. To enable the ferry to continue as per the Act they rented the ferry to John Beasley at £2 4s 3d a month until the bridge was completed in 1840. The bridge was replaced in 1867 by one of iron.

## COOKHAM UPPER FERRY

As it was necessary to keep the horse towing path, another ferry was set up by the Commission to take the towing horses. This was the one known as Upper Ferry (Exp.172 899 856), as described above, and which continued until the 1950s. In 1854 the Commission proposed to dispense with the services of Edward Godden and let his house.[25] He, however, was still there in 1866 when he worked as both lock-keeper and ferryman, but was replaced at the ferry by his son in the following January. In October 1867 they were swapped round until Edward was pensioned in September 1879. Then G. Collins from Marlow succeeded until he was drowned in August 1881. Several changes in personnel were made, including another drowning, until the arrival of J. Brooks who often ferried Thacker and had partial charge of the weir.

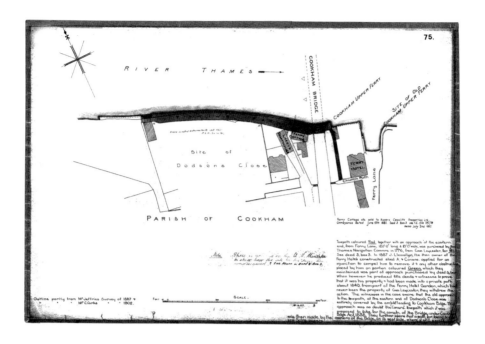

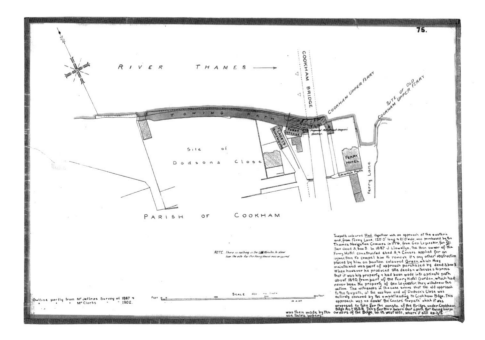

Cookham. Plan based on the Thames Conservancy surveys of 1887 and 1902. Shows the site of Dodson's Close and the old and new Upper Ferry landing places on the Cookham, right bank of the river. Reproduced with the kind permission of the Environment Agency.

Cookham. The Upper Ferry depicted in Tombleson's *The Thames* c. 1830 before the bridge was built. Artistic licence has been taken with the location of the church which is not quite so near the river.

The horse punt moored just upstream of the first Cookham Bridge c. 1866 before it was replaced in 1867. Reproduced with the kind permission of the Environment Agency.

The cost of maintaining this ferry in 1953 was £512 as opposed to the income of £24. It closed soon afterwards. The Ferry Cottage at Dobson's Close was offered for sale in *The Times* on 27 September 1961. It had two reception rooms, two bedrooms, kitchenette, mains water and electricity and drainage and included 65 feet of towpath frontage. Offered with vacant possession, it was up for sale again on 16 May 1962.

## HEDSOR WHARF & MIDDLE FERRY

Hedsor wharf, like the one at Burcot noted above, was an important trans-shipment point from earliest times. A Roman road crossed by a ford and remains of a Roman bridge has been found. A pile dwelling was excavated at the wharf in 1895. It was said there was a road in medieval times which was in a direct line from Marlow through Bourne End to the priory at Hedsor. This priory cannot be confirmed although there is a Victorian edifice with that name. Negotiating the double bend of the river was difficult, so a pound lock and a new cut were constructed and opened in November 1830, resulting in Hedsor wharf being cut off from the navigation. This upset some people, including Lord of the Manor, Lord Boston, who was deprived of his towing path profits and to whom the construction of two weirs was an anathema.

The Middle Ferry (Exp.172 806 857) was used merely to take the barge horses over this defunct part of the navigation and then to skirt the river through the Cliveden estate until My Lady Ferry was reached. One Dyson had charge of the ferry in April 1885. It closed many years ago.

## BOULTER'S LOCK

At Boulter's Lock (Exp.172 902 825) on the outskirts of Maidenhead is an area of great antiquity which was a hive of activity. Here the old parishes' boundaries of Bray, Cookham and Taplow met. Now there are two main eyots in the river, Ray Mill Island and Boulter's Island. In the seventeenth century there were many more which have been swept away in the cause of navigation. There were watermills at Ray Island, which can still be seen and more mills at Taplow on the left bank. The name Boulter probably derives from the mills as it is a milling term. The Ray family was associated with the island and mill since 1346.

Cookham Upper Ferry which replaced the original one and crossed to connect with the Middle Ferry. From a postcard of the 1950s.

Lock Ferry, Cookham. 3051.

Cookham Middle Ferry a.k.a. Lock Ferry. Also on the Cliveden Estate with a ferry house similar to the other two at My Lady Ferry. The ferry punt is moored alongside. Courtesy of Ken Townsend.

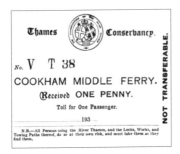

Cookham Middle Ferry apparently was still in service in the 1930s. Similar tickets were issued for the Upper and Lower Ferries. Courtesy of Ken Townsend.

Recent archaeological investigations using geophysics at Taplow Court reveal it was a settlement by the Thames in Anglo-Saxon times.[26] There is a burial mound with possibly an early church nearby, Iron Age earthworks, an enclosure dating to Roman times or earlier and an early baptismal pond. The very steep escarpment is wooded, mostly with yew and falls directly to the narrow bank of the river. In the river some fine Bronze Age artefacts have been found; spearheads and a bronze scythe. Evidence of a henge monument on the site has been obliterated. It is thought that here was a very ancient crossing of the river which was revered as sacred and used for religious rites.[27] Usually such crossings had the noted features near them plus other Christian symbols such as a holy well, tree or shrine and were consecrated to St Ann. By the old church, which was above the river, were an old oak and a holy well. St Ann's shrine was probably near the pub which would serve travellers and provide 'libations to the gods for a safe crossing', accidents would occur at this wide and dangerous passage. Due to the vagaries of the river and frequent flooding there would have been several spots which served as landing places. This crossing was the predecessor to Maidenhead Bridge, built to serve the Great West Road to Bath and Bristol, (A4).

Lands at Taplow are listed in some eighteenth century documents as part of the Bradwell Grove Estate in Oxfordshire.[28] The first dates from 1673, another in a marriage settlement of 1720; in a Grant of Annuity in 1771, and a lease for a year in 1776; all of which included the 'barge and barging ferry and passage over the river Thames' and mentioned the islands, most of which seem to have had mills on them. The right of free fishing and to a ferry across the Thames occurs among the liberties of Taplow Manor during the eighteenth and nineteenth centuries.

Those familiar with the Pre-Raphaelite painting *Boulter's Lock, Sunday afternoon 1882-97* will know what a busy place it was, especially on Ascot Sunday.[29] All manner of craft jostled to get a place and a close look at the painting, by Edward John Gregory (1850–1909), will reveal many accidents waiting to happen. It is a fascinating example of subtle humour! The original painting is in Liverpool Museum. Gregory spent seven years painting the scene and during this time the lock-keeper was William H. Turner who came to this lock from Cleeve Lock in 1882.[30] The following April he saved the life of a young boy at the lock, the first of many such acts of bravery. He was described by Krause in 1889 as 'one of the most popular lock-keepers on the river'. Thacker called him, 'the great imperturbable, unquestionable Turner of Boulter's'. Turner, an ex-navy man, a gunnery and cutlass instructor, left the lock in 1905 when he retired.

On the wall of the north chapel in Cookham church is a splendid monument in white marble relief by Flaxman in 1814. It commemorates Sir Isaac Pocock (1751–1810), brother of Nicholas Pocock, the Bristol marine artist.[31] Sir Isaac had a career in the navy and served as captain in the American War of Independence. After his retirement he and his wife returned to live in Cookham, her birthplace. There he built Ray Lodge near Maidenhead Bridge. He worked hard for the benefit of Cookham and was instrumental in saving the common lands from enclosure. While out punting on the Thames near Boulter's on 8 October 1810 with his niece he suffered a heart attack and died. The plaque depicts his death, with a ferryman in the background. Although the death did not occur on the ferry, the craft is a punt and the stance of the punter shows clearly that the model was a bona fide ferryman.

To visit the area round Boulter's Lock is very rewarding. There is still plenty to watch, not so many craft as in Victorian times but the boats going through are big, carrying corporate parties and others slightly smaller, described by some as 'gin palaces'. The little bridge leads to Ray Mill Island which is a public garden full of wildlife. A hotel is lively but mill buildings have been converted to residential use. All around is water.

Boulter's Lock. William Turner and family outside the lock house before it was altered and the lock lengthened. He retired as lock-keeper in 1905 and this postcard may have been issued to mark the occasion.

The tomb of Sir Isaac Pocock in Cookham church depicting his death when out punting near Boulter's Lock. The pose of the punter is that of a ferryman. 14 April 2010.

## MAIDENHEAD BRIDGE

Maidenhead Bridge (Exp.172 901 813) was first built about 1297 in timber. It was intended to replace the ferry to the north at Taplow. The only significance of Maidenhead at that time was as a depot for goods and there were many wharves or hithes at the riverfront, hence the name 'Maydenhith'. The road from London to the west was diverted to cross the bridge, and Maidenhead town grew up to the west. As the traffic was heavy and the bridge not strong, it had to be repaired regularly. Between 1337 and 1428 fourteen different grants of pontage were made.[32] Each time the bridge was closed a ferry was provided.

Tolls were taken at the bridge on behalf of the Corporation of Maidenhead by bridge keepers who probably paid a franchise each year in advance.[33] In 1655 an allowance had to be paid back because of the small takings, 'by reason of the plague in the City' (London). In 1657 there was an order 'for repairing the Towne Bridge and Boate'. Charges had to be made for a ferry in 1679, 1732 and 1751 because of 'the bridge being in great decay'. The present stone bridge was built between 1772–77 with a causeway and seven (now six) semicircular arches over the river itself. The M4 motorway now takes all the heavy traffic away from the town.

Maidenhead Bridge. The scene looking downstream from the bridge showing hay barges, punts and rowing boats. From the Halls' *Book of the Thames*, 1859.

# CHAPTER FIFTEEN
# Bray to Staines

## BRAY FERRY

Bray in Berkshire has a large church which stands almost on the river bank and close to it was a ferry landing place down a different turning, Ferry Road. At the end of the road is a wide slipway where the ferry ran to the opposite bank across a very wide river. (Exp.160 903 797) To the left is the Waterside Inn, now an upmarket restaurant, but was once the George Inn which served the ferry and those who came to spend time on the river. Thacker picked up the information that there had been a ford here, followed by a ferry on the same trajectory but he searched in vain for confirmation.[1] He thought to find evidence of a monastic origin but missed Merton Priory on the Buckinghamshire side, a moated site at Amerden Bank. A ford called Bray Ridle or Pighe was mentioned in 1360. As the manor belonged to the Crown from time immemorial, it must be presumed the records are buried in vaults somewhere, or even destroyed.

There is no corresponding ferry place at Amerden on the opposite bank although that is the side where the towing path ran, and is now utilised by the Thames Path. Thacker discovered the Commissioners had trouble with a local farmer, an Irishman called Murrough O'Brien, who later became Lord Inchiquin, over the horse towing path, so in 1790 they stationed a ferryboat off Amerden Farm to take the horses past O'Brien's property and land them on their eyot, possibly at or near Bray Lock.[2]

Ferry Road leads from the High Street to the river and on the right is a row of cottages called Ferry End. They were not built until 1904, by a developer. At the bottom of the road was the Ferry Cottage, built sometime after 1883 by Charles Mickley the younger.[3] The Mickley family were associated with the Thames at Bray for two generations and were responsible for erecting the 'Ryepeck' an iron-shod pole for securing punts, shown on a map of 1875. C. E. Hughes (Whacker Hughes) took a lease on Ferry Cottage in 1910 for use in a boat building business and probably ran the ferry in conjunction. The house was sold and the ferry landing stage taken away in 1973. From photographs of the time it seems the Thames Conservancy men were employed in the 1950s at the ferry using rowing boats.

The watercolour artist Peter de Wint (1784–1849) was known for his paintings and sketches of the Thames. He was particularly attracted by the stretch of river at Bray and some studies are in the Tate Collection. He also had some drawings engraved for a book, *Thames Scenery*, published in 1818, which included *Osier Island near Cookham* and *Bray*.[4]

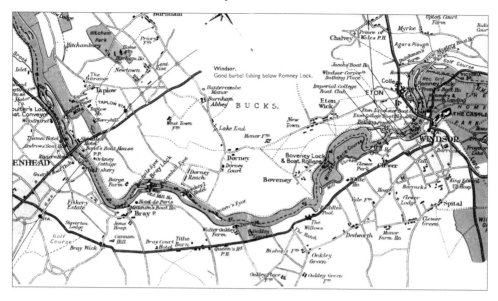

The Thames between Maidenhead and Windsor. From *Stanford's New Map of the River Thames*, c. 1900.

Bray. The waterfront with the boathouse and ferry landing on the right. The ferry ran to Amerden on the opposite bank. From a postcard of about 1909, courtesy of Ken Townsend

## MONKEY ISLAND

From the village of Bray, Old Mill Lane runs south, crosses over the M4 and after a mile, where the road ends and a bridle path carries on, is a short road on the left which leads to a car park. This is the only access to Monkey Island (Exp.160 914 791) except by water. Connecting the car park with the island and the hotel is a miniature suspension footbridge erected in 1949 to replace the ferry. (It shows very clearly how a suspension bridge works). The island was called Monk's Eyot, as it was used by the monks for fishing from 1197.[5] It was bought by the 3rd Duke of Marlborough in 1735 or so. He built a fishing pavilion and banqueting house at a cost of £8,000. The pavilion is octagonal and around the coving and on the ceiling of the ground floor room are painted murals of monkeys all in eighteenth-century dress engaged in occupations familiar to the Duke's guests such as shooting and fishing. High up in one corner is a lady monkey standing punting a gentleman monkey. An inn preceded the hotel now established on the island. It was said the daughters of the innkeeper were proficient punters and the younger ones always managed the ferry.[6] Thus the island gained its nickname of Monkey Island, or did the artist use monkeys as a pun on Monks Eyot? The ferry was over the narrower channel on the right bank of the river. The other channel, by dredging, became the navigable channel in about 1775, so the towing path followed on that side, as the Thames Path does too.

Monkey Island, near Bray, where guests would cross by small ferry to disport themselves at the summer retreat, later a hotel. From the Halls' *Book of the Thames.*

Monkey Island. A drawing of the ferry taken from the mural showing the innkeeper's daughter punting a guest. From a brochure issued by Monkey Island Hotel. 2010.

Robert Gibbings the writer in his book *Till I end my Song* reveals that his son and daughter were at one time the managers of Monkey Island and he makes the observation that the Conservancy gates on the towing path were painted a sort of grey and each had a number on it. No doubt their boats were in the same colour.

## SURLEY FERRY

Further down the towing path, before the river takes a slight deviation towards Boveney on the left bank, was Surley Hall.[7] It is impossible to tell from the modern map where it stood or where was the inn mentioned by Thacker. The whole area has now changed beyond all recognition, with caravan parks, marinas, hotels and des res. Apparently there was an inn which belonged to the Duchess of Sutherland and the innkeeper in January 1886 obtained permission to set up a ferry which worked on a chain, provided the boat was kept on the hotel bank. The Duchess closed the inn in 1899 and it was entirely demolished in 1901. Nearby Dedworth was then a small hamlet and is now a vast housing estate.

## NEW WINDSOR / ETON

When William the Conqueror came to build his new castle at what became New Windsor, the village and parish of Clewer in which the prominence was situated overlooking the Thames, was already well established. Most of the communications necessary for the building and management of the great castle would have been by the River Thames, a fairly easy journey about 20 miles from London (Exp.160 967 772). The earliest mention of a bridge connecting New Windsor on the Berkshire bank with Eton in Buckinghamshire on the north bank was in 1172, although a bridge of sorts was likely to have existed before that. Frequent grants of oak trees for its repair were made from the Royal Forest of Windsor, as in 1242. Similar grants of pontage were made between 1314 and 1461. A new bridge was applied for by the citizens in 1775 but nothing happened and a ferry service had to be provided by law.[8] Mr Collins, a local carpenter, was appointed to run the ferry and provide a boat fit for purpose.[9] Tolls were charged and the whole operation proved expensive, but was still in operation when the present bridge was erected in 1822–24 in cast iron with granite piers. It was closed to vehicles in 1970 and is used today only for pedestrians. Traffic has to follow a long roundabout diversion via Datchet.

Eton College was founded in 1440 by Henry VI and has accumulated land ever since. There were no enclosures in the town. At some stage a ferry was established, possibly by the college from their land at the Brocas, a meadow bordering the Thames, across to Windsor. The Thames Commission made an agreement for the horse towing path to be made through the Brocas, for which they paid rent.[10] On 23 May 1772, a report was made about 'mischief done to the towing path at the Brocas'. The Commission were obliged to erect a fence to separate off the towing path. Some images exist which show this ferry. One is a pretty aquatint, dated 1825 by Robert Havell the younger, showing a robust-looking rowboat about to depart the Windsor bank for Eton at the Brocas.[11] Its method of propulsion is not clear. An early photograph of about 1880 in the collection of the RIBA shows two long ferry punts, not so big as those up-river, with a family seated as passengers and a ferryman with punt pole. The other punt is moored at the landing stage.

Windsor Castle on an eighteenth-century print, provenance unknown. It is looking south from a point on the left bank upstream from the Windsor-Eton Bridge shown in the distance.

## RIVERSIDE FERRY

On the modern map a ferry is marked just downstream from Riverside railway station at Windsor (Exp.160 968 779). It is level with the park-and-ride car park, which is separated from the river path by the railway line. The Thames Path uses this nice shady walk. In October 2010 there was no sign at all of the ferry, which crossed to Eton, passing the tip of an eyot which reached as far as the college. Did the Eton boys no longer use this ferry, preferring to swim instead?

## DATCHET FERRY

The shortest way to London from Windsor Castle was across the great park to a ferry over the Thames to Datchet (Exp.160 985 779) which was already an old settlement before the castle was built (Exp.160 985 768). In 1249 Henry III ordered a great oak from Windsor forest to be delivered to the Datchet ferryman, John le Passur, for a ferry boat.[12] A great barge was provided for the ferry in 1278 paid for by Edward I. When, in 1335, Edward III gave the Manor of Datchet to Sir John de Molyns, the ferry was included. Later when de Molyns fell from favour his lands, including those at Datchet, were seized by the Crown. His family managed to recover most of them but the king kept the ferry. Margaret, Sir John's daughter-in-law, petitioned to have it restored because the dispossession had been illegal, but the then King, Richard III was determined not to forego such a valuable asset. The ferry remained in the Crown possession for centuries and would be let out to trusty servants. Richard Marlborough held the lease in 1501 and it was probably to him that Henry VII paid 3s 4d each time for his queen, Elizabeth, to pass over on 6 July and 13 November the following year.[13]

Christopher Rochester and John Rookes became the lessees in 1509 and seem to have held it until 1536.[14] Many references to the Court passing over the ferry appear in Court Rolls and royal household accounts. Princess Mary, elder daughter of Henry VIII spent her childhood at Ditton and would pass over the ferry to visit her father at Windsor for Christmas.[15] In 1517 he paid for two crossings by Mary and her entourage. Henry VIII led a grand cavalcade of the Order of the Garter from London to Windsor by river on 27 May 1519. Queen Catherine of Aragon watched it at Colnbrook, then rode to Datchet with her retinue and crossed by the ferry while the king continued via 'Slow' (Slough) to Windsor.[16] Princess Mary Tudor crossed Datchet ferry in August and in September 1522.[17] She was the sister of Henry VIII who took his whole retinue across with him on 30 April 1529 when 20s was paid to the ferryman.[18] A strange transaction took place in 1543 whereby Edmond Pygeon was granted the ferry and the land and property which went with it for life, for no fee; perhaps because in 1535 the ferry had made only £10 profit.[19] Subsequently, Edmond took his son Nicholas into partnership by permission of Elizabeth I (who came to the throne in 1558). In turn Nicholas took Morris Hale into partnership, still with no fee paid. The term 'no fee' did not mean no money was paid, it was a special 'fee farm' lease whereby a rent was paid when demanded. Over a hundred years later, in 1678 one Hale was still ferryman because a complaint was made that he had delayed the King's messenger at the ferry. Even today, that is an offence.

Windsor parish register records that in 1594 six gentlemen were buried who had drowned in an accident at the ferry.[20] In 1631 Charles I granted Datchet Manor to his surveyor-general, Sir William Harboard who promptly sold it to William Wheeler.[21] Queen Anne ascended the throne in 1702 and in 1706 decided to build a bridge in timber at the site of the ferry at her own expense and stipulated that it would be free from tolls. The ferry was discontinued; it was in her possession, as Colonel Andrew Wheeler, a descendant of William Wheeler, had sold it before 1700 to her predecessor

Datchet Ferry featured in a print from 1686. The flat punt, almost like a raft, was operated by two men pulling on a rope or chain. It carried horses and riders. From Wikimedia Commons.

William III who wanted to enlarge the castle grounds. A total of £7, 831 4s 8d was paid for the ferry and some land by the Treasury. In order to build the bridge sufficient 'non-Navy timber' was cut from Windsor forest and Queen Anne cut across some land acquired by King William near the ferry to make a carriage drive for her new bridge. This was Datchet Lane, which according to some watercolours by Paul Sandby, was very wide. Unfortunately, the bridge proved costly to maintain, needing constant repairs and reconstructions, resulting in its closure in 1794, being 'absolutely dangerous for carriages to pass over'.

The ferry was reinstated by George III free of tolls but he refused to pay for a new bridge, saying it was now the responsibility of the local authorities. Matters were now at an impasse. Negotiations had begun in August 1793 to revive the ferry following a presentation by the inhabitants of Datchet and Windsor for a new ferry boat.[22] A contract was entered into with Robert Patrick to provide and maintain a ferry and the expenses claim for four years from April 1795 amounted to £759 18s 6d, which included £98 9s for a ferry boat. However, the boat proved too small for the purpose and a larger one was petitioned for in November 1799 to the Lords of the Treasury. The total bill for the period from that date until 1808 when preparations for a new bridge were under way, with all taxes etc. included, was £3,679 8s 3d. Much discussion took place as to the best course of action to take. It was decided that as the bridge was on the turnpike road to Windsor the Turnpike Trust should build the new bridge and be given a sum of money by the Treasury.

It transpired that a new turnpike road was in consideration at the time and so no agreements were made until a new Act was obtained in June 1801 Then plans and estimates were to be drawn up pronto. An iron bridge was to be built on the new line of road instead of rebuilding the old bridge. It was proposed the expenses of maintenance would be met by a small toll on the bridge. However, the Turnpike trustees agreed this was not satisfactory as it was contrary to the wishes of the petitioners for a free bridge as they had from 'time immemorial enjoyed and always understood and intended'. They were no further forward. The County of Buckinghamshire at their Quarter Sessions put forward the solution that money which had been allowed annually for upkeep of the ferry, about £500, should be transferred from the ferry to pay off the loan on the bridge and 'His Majesty will be exonerated from any further burthen in maintaining the ancient ferry'.[23] The County of Berkshire would also be expected to provide a share of the costs. The new bridge was finally opened for traffic on 16 December 1811.

In 1836, the bridge again needed to be rebuilt and a squabble ensued between Buckinghamshire and Berkshire. The former rebuilt in timber, the latter in iron with an uncomfortable join in the middle where the county boundary was. Once again the ferry was brought back into use and this is verified by a document in Buckinghamshire Quarter Sessions archive of 27 June 1836. Eleven gentlemen of Datchet presented a petition to Sir John Dashwood King Bt, Chairman to the Board of Magistrates at Aylesbury (distantly related to Sir Francis Dashwood) asking for the working hours of the ferry be extended.[24] They considered 10 p.m. was too early and had approached Mr Raingers on the matter and had been informed his agreement with the Magistrates was for him to close at that time. Furthermore he said the price allowed him was inadequate for the duties he was engaged to perform, and certainly would not allow for an extension after 10 p.m. The petition was presented to the magistrates in September 1836, but it was unlikely a satisfactory result was gained.

Few regrets were expressed when the bridge was demolished by order of Queen Victoria in 1851. She was keen on the new fashionable railways and looked favourably on the request of two railway companies to bring their lines to Windsor and highly advantageous terms were settled by all parties.[25] The London & South Western

Railway paid £60,000 and GWR paid £25,000. HM Commissioners of Woods and Forests together with the Corporation of Windsor under the Act were able to use the money to improve roads in the area and this involved discontinuing the bridge and diverting traffic over twin new bridges, above and below the old bridge. The Victoria Bridge to the north takes the present B470 to Datchet at the bottom of the High Street at the point where the ferry, then the old bridge, crossed the river and where it joined the present B3021 which continues south and skirts the river, avoiding the town, to cross back again at Albert Bridge. The advantage to Victoria and Albert was that they were able to close public access through the park and develop the area by the river as a beautiful private meadow. At the ferry spot a pair of brick cottages, designed as one, was built beside the river, possibly to replace the two 'sheds' built for workmen in 1770.[26] Typical royal estate houses, they are listed Grade II. Otherwise, there is no sign at all on either side of the river that here for centuries was a very important crossing place.

After passing Datchet the Thames takes a big meander to the north which is separated from the main river by New Cut, thus forming Ham Island. The boundary of Windsor Great Park with the Thames ends at Albert Bridge. Then the river flows alongside the large parish of Wyrardisbury, aka Wraysbury, on the left bank and Old Windsor on the right. As the river is here very wide there were several ferries in this stretch, four were marked on a 1900 map plus the ancient ferry at Ankerwyke, as far as the London Stone near Staines. Available sources at present do not distinguish clearly between these ferries, and Thacker ignores them, apart from a mention in passing of Ankerwyke ferry. Perhaps they were all private ferries.

## WRAYSBURY FERRIES

There were two manors: Wraysbury and Remenham. Both seemed to own a ferry which included fishing rights.[27] Ankerwyke Priory owned an estate which went with the Manor of Wraysbury. The ferry furthest upstream is possibly the oldest and went by the name of Old Windsor Ferry (Exp.160 992 745). In Anglo-Saxon times the place was a residence of kings until superseded by New Windsor in the twelfth century. A ferry and wharf would have been necessary. From their palace at Old Windsor the Saxon kings, their horses and retinue crossed by ferry to Wraysbury for hunting. The large area around Wraysbury was a royal hunting chase, now largely covered by reservoirs. The ferry place on the Wraysbury side was approached by what is now Old Ferry Drive, passing the very old three-storied house, King John's Hunting Lodge, a name it was given in Victorian times: before that it was merely a farmhouse. Whether it was what it purports to be is debatable but as there is an aisled hall, open to the roof, it is assumed to be at least early medieval, if not earlier. The ferry crossing was nearby; where an old public right of way from the church emerges from woodland to cross the drive and lead on down a narrow footpath to the river. This footpath is now much narrower than it used to be and is made obvious by a continuous yellow line. At the riverside it opens out without a fence to a slipway and boatyard which are on private ground. In October 2010 some notices posted on trees announced there was to be an enquiry into rights of way. Local information reveals the boatyard was Weldons (or Wilders) who operated the ferry from there. One of the opulent riverside houses is Old Ferry House, where Mr and Mrs Arnold lived in the bothy. Did they work the ferry?

On the opposite side of the river the church at Old Windsor is kept locked, but the footpath round the churchyard leads to the river and the ferry place close by, where the Thames Path is joined. From here steps on the Wraysbury side are seen and by

Datchet. Victoria Bridge, which together with Albert Bridge superseded the ferry in the 1850s. From the Halls' *Book of the Thames*, 1859

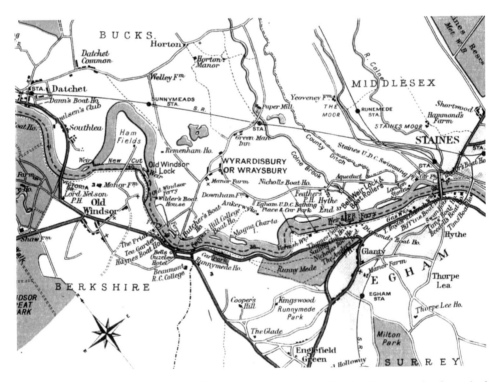

The Thames from Datchet, near Windsor, to Staines where the London Stone marks the end of the Upper Thames. From *Stanford's New Map of the River Thames*, c. 1900.

Wraysbury was a popular destination for rowing parties. Now the public are discouraged from venturing anywhere near the river. Postcard courtesy of Ken Townsend.

scraping around in undergrowth corresponding steps are found on the right bank here. In 1921 Mr Reffell of Wraysbury wrote to Old Windsor Parish Council (was he the ferryman?) saying it would help him if they could provide steps or a landing stage on the bank.[28] For some unspecified reason the Council 'had no power to help'.

Further downstream a short distance is a ferry place reached by a suburban road from the middle of Wraysbury (Exp.160 994 744). At the river end of it is still a short public footpath to the water's edge, otherwise there is no public access to the river anywhere in Wraysbury until Ankerwyke. This ferry crossed to a place in the new part of Old Windsor called the Priory. There was a tea gardens and Haynes boat house in 1900. This may have been the New Ferry.

## THE BELLS OF OUSELEY

The same suburban road, Ouseley Road, from Wraysbury runs in a straight line to the river (Exp.160 992 736) and continues still with same name on the other side. Undoubtedly this is a good case for a ferry. Indeed it was quite an important one, to a very old inn, The Bells of Ouseley which dates back to about 1300 or before, and in its time served bargemen and others on the river, highwaymen, travellers by road when it was a coaching inn and all and sundry; even Queen Victoria passed that way. How it got the name is a mystery but Oxfordians believe it came from when Osney Abbey in Oxford was dissolved and its bells, except for Great Tom which was installed in Tom Tower at Christ Church College, were shipped to London. The barge sank somewhere near the inn and the bells were never recovered. An idea of how busy was the inn is gained from a watercolour by Thomas Rowlandson (1756–1827) in Egham

Museum.[29] An illustration of 1906 shows the ferry which had a chain ramp to take horses, cattle and vehicles.

A dispute about a public right at the inn was fought in 1922 when Mr Butcher the ferryman received a letter ordering him to stop using the landing stage.[30] The Parish Council of Old Windsor maintained he was within his rights and urged him to continue the ferry. He was happy for private boats to land on his property opposite the Bells of Ouseley at any time. The Parish Council asked the Rural District Council to take legal action against MR X who had sent the letter. They wished to protect the public legal rights and the public landing stage. Nothing happened. The Thames Conservancy gave permission for the landing stage and dredged the river to give better access. The dispute continued and, in 1929, the Parish Council agreed to a notice put up which read 'Ferry to Wraysbury, Horton and Colnbrook'. They also allowed a wider landing stage to take prams and cycles. In 1934 the residents put up a fence along the towpath. In 1936 the inn burnt down and was rebuilt on the same site. The Hotel was hit by a flying bomb in 1944. The owner and his wife were killed and some others seriously injured.

Ankerwyke Priory ran its own private ferry across the river to the land on the opposite side at the foot of Cooper's Hill called Runnymede. It is not known where exactly the ferry points were, but probably on the Wraysbury side from the end of the ancient path which ran past the church diagonally to the river. On the right bank is a right of way which corresponds to this. Both areas on each side of the river are now marked on the modern map as access areas, meaning that the public has access. The priory, which was associated with Bisham Abbey was dissolved in 1537 when supposedly the ferry came to an end. In 1539 Thomas Edwards and William Danby took the weirs, formerly the property of the priory, but not seemingly the ferry.[31] Magna Carta Island is much written about.

## HYTHE END FERRY

The River Colne Brook forms the eastern boundary of Wraysbury parish and from earliest times mills were set up on its banks. Its outflow to the Thames is at Hythe End (Exp.160 019 720) just a few yards away from the bridge which carries the M25 over the Thames. At this spot was an important wharf or hythe and a ferry. Higher up the river the road from Wraysbury to Staines was carried over the Colne Brook by a ford. From that road today just before the motorway bridge is a traffic roundabout and from it three lanes turn off to the right. One is Ferry Lane, actually like a bridle path and extends a long way by the side of the Colne Brook to the Thames bank, passing on the right a house which may have been a ferry cottage. At the end on the left is a shanty town before the right of way turns right to terminate at the ferry landing place where there are some fairly new concrete steps. On the other side, now in Surrey, is the much enlarged Runnymede Hotel, at Egham. This was the Egham ferry.

Copper Mill Road is a reminder of the extensive copper works set up in the former paper mill on the other side of the main road. It was another enterprise of Thomas Williams of the Temple Mills near Marlow.[32] His partner was Pascoe Grenfell (1761–1838) who bought Taplow House and followed Williams as MP for Marlow after the death of the latter. The business thrived at Wraysbury, employing a lot of men and being just beyond the jurisdiction of the City of London, evaded taxes. After the business failed the mill returned to paper making.

Wraysbury parish was enclosed in 1803 and allotments bordering the Colne Brook or Mill River were given to various landowners, including Thomas Williams, the Dean and Canons of Windsor for manorial rights and John Simon Harcourt.[33] Some

Landing stage for the Bells of Ouseley opposite Wraysbury. Postcard sent from Staines on 8 October 1933.

The Bells of Ouseley, the historic inn at Old Windsor, before modernisation. From an old postcard posted in Taunton on 14 February 1904.

villagers objected to the way the apportionment took place and petitioned the Lord of the Manor. To placate them, he had inserted into the Bill a clause awarding a strip of land eight yards in width on either side of the Colne Brook to the inhabitants of Wraysbury in perpetuity. They were given the right to cut withies from the river and also the right to dredge the river and deposit the silt on the banks. Naturally this arrangement led to abuses which prompted the parishioners in May 1962 to seek an opinion from the new Master of the Rolls, Lord Denning. He opined that no way could the parishioners lose the right, nor could any individual waive it on their behalf, nor could they 'do any corporate of waiving', except by a new Act of Parliament. Nothing was said about who were the riparian owners under this settlement. Nor was it clear who was responsible for the upkeep of the track. Half way down the lane was the site of commercial premises which were offered for sale by public auction on 5 October 2010.[34] In the schedule was included a section of the River Thames and the secluded lane by the side of the Colne Brook over which there were public rights of way. In April 2011 these matters are still in debate.

## STAINES

Major excavations in connection with the building of the M25 bridge were undertaken and the findings published in 2000.[35] It was revealed the course of the Thames had altered but there was a causeway running along the south side of the river from Staines towards Old Windsor dating from the thirteenth century and built by Thomas de Oxenford a rich wood merchant. He could have utilised an existing Roman road. The causeway was the cause of much legislation in medieval times regarding its upkeep. Evidence of a ferry was discovered on the foreshore in the form of a concrete setting, perhaps the base of a flight of steps.

The London Stone at Staines marks the beginning of the Jurisdiction of the City of London over the Thames River. In the Middle Ages it marked the end of the tidal river. At first the stone stood below Staines Bridge but was ordered to be removed to

The London Stone near Staines long before it was moved higher up the bank and forgotten. From the Halls' *The Book of the Thames* 1859.

above in 1619 when it was decayed.[36] Later it was removed again higher up the bank. In 1986 the stone was rediscovered in brambles and rescued. The ancient stone, only about 60 centimetres high, was preserved in Staines (Spelthorne) Library, and a very good replica made to stand on top of four graduated plinths. With diligent searching it may be found in the Lammas Recreation Ground on Wraysbury Road (Exp.160 027 717), B376 on the outskirts of Staines. Follow the path to the river, although the way is blocked, walk around the amenity block to a children's' play park and in the opposite corner is a small area railed off with a black gate surrounding the stone. Such a significant memorial from the golden days of our most beautiful and historic river deserves better than this ignominious resting place, from where the River Thames cannot even be seen.

> A boat, a boat haste to the ferry,
> For we'll go over to be merry
> To laugh and sing and drink old sherry.

*c.* Seventeenth-century round.[37]

# Bibliography

ALLISON, K. J. et al. *Deserted Villages of Oxfordshire*. Leicester Dept Eng. Local History, 1966.

ANDERSON, J. R. L. *The Upper Thames*. Eyre & Spottiswoode, 1970.

ARKELL, W. J. *Oxford Stone*. Faber, 1947.

ARNOLD, Matthew. 'The Scholar Gypsy' etc. from *Collected Poems*.

ASHBY-STERRY, Joseph. *Poems*. 1886 (http://thames.mo.yk/thames).

BAGSHAWE, R. W. *Roman Roads*. Shire, 1996

BANFIELD, Jennifer et al. *Picture History of Goring & Streatley*. G&S Local Hist. Soc., 1986.

BATEY, Mavis. 'Nuneham Courtenay. An Oxfordshire Eighteenth Century Deserted Village'. *Oxoniensia* XXXIII, 1968.

BELLOC, Hilaire. *The Historic Thames* (1907). Webb & Bower, 1988.

BERESFORD, Maurice. *The Lost Villages of England*. Lutterworth, 1965 (corrected edn).

BEWICK, Thomas. *History of British Birds*. Edward Walker, Newcastle, 1821 edn.

BEWICK, Thomas. *A General History of Quadrupeds*. Fifth edn. Edward Walker, Newcastle, 1807.

BIRNEY, Nan. *Bray. Today and Yesterday*. Thames Valley Press, 1973.

BLAIR, John. *Waterways and Canal Building in Medieval England*. Oxford, 2007.

BLOXHAM, Christine. *Folklore of Oxfordshire*. Tempus, 2005.

BLUNT. *August Ramble down the River Thames*. (British Library holding)

BONEHILL, John et al. ed. Paul Sandby. *Picturing Britain*. Royal Academy, 2010.

BOYDELL, John *see* COMBE

BRITTON, John. *The Beauties of England & Wales Vol. 1 (Beds, Berks, Bucks)*. 1801.

BYNG, Hon. John. *The Torrington Diaries* (ed. A. Bruyn Andrews). Eyre & Spottiswoode, 1934.

COMBE, William. *A History of the River Thames*. John Boydell, 1794–1796.

COMPTON, Hugh J. *The Oxford Canal*. David & Charles, 1976.

COOK, C. H. (BICKERDYKE, John). *Thames Rights & Thames Wrongs*. Constable, 1894.

CORDREY, Edward. *Bygone Days at Iffley*. Author, 1956.

DAVIES, Gareth Huw. *A Walk along the Thames Path*. M. Joseph, 1989.

de MARÉ, Eric. *Time on the Thames*. Architectural Press, 1952.

DE SALIS, H. R. A. *Bradshaw's Handbook of Inland Navigation*. Blacklock, 1918.

DICKENS, Charles (son). *Dickens's Dictionary of the Thames* (1887). Old House Books, 1994.

DITCHFIELD, P. H. *The Cottages & the Village Life of Rural England*. Dent, 1912.

DITMAS, Edith. *The Ditmas History of Benson* (1983). Bensington Soc., 2009.

EADE, Brian. *Forgotten Thames (in old photographs)*. Sutton, 2002.

EADE, Brian. *The Changing Thames (in old photographs)*. History Press, 2009.

EVANS, R. J. W. *St Michael's Church, Cumnor*. Eleventh edn. Church Publ., 2010.

GEDGE, Paul. *Thames Journey*. Harrap, 1949.

GELLING, Margaret. *The Early Charters of the Thames Valley*. Leicester University Press, 1979.

GIBBINGS, Robert. *Sweet Thames Run Softly*. Dent, 1940.

GIBBINGS, Robert. *Till I End My Song*. Dent, 1957.

GIBBON, Geoffrey. *Through the Saxon Door. Somerford Keynes*. Author, 1969.

GILSON, C. J. *Old Windsor. A History of the Parish Council*. 1981.

GLADWIN, D. D. *Passenger Boats on Inland Waterways*. Oakwood Press, 1979.

GOTCH, Christopher. *The Gloucester & Sharpness Canal & Robert Mylne*. British Waterways, 1993.

GRAHAM, Malcolm. *Henry Taunt of Oxford*. Oxford Illustrated Press, 1973.

GRIGSON, Geoffrey. *English Excursions*. Country Life, 1960.

HADLAND, Tony. 'Thames Valley Papists'. (http://www.users.globalnet.co.uk/~hadland)

HALL, Mr & Mrs S. C. *The Book of the Thames from its Rise to its Fall*. Virtue, 1859.

HARDMAN, J. S. *Wallingford, A History of an English Market Town* Lambourn (author), 1994.

HARPER, Charles G. *Thames Valley Villages*. Chapman & Hall, 1910.

HARRIS, J. R. *The Copper King. Thomas Williams of Llanidan*. Landmark, 2003.

HARRISON, Colin et al. *John Malchair of Oxford, Artist and Musician*. Ashmolean, 1998.

HARRISON, Ian. *The Thames from Source to Sea*. HarperCollins/getmapping, 2004.

HARTLEY, Dorothy. *Water in England*. Macdonald, 1964.

HERBERT, Nicholas. *Road Travel & Transport in Georgian Gloucestershire*. Carreg, 2009.

HERTSLET, C. et al. *The Justice of the Peace (reports) Vol. XXXVI*. Richard Shaw Bond, 1872.

HINCHCLIFFE, Tanis. *North Oxford*. Yale, 1992.

HOUSEHOLD, Humphrey. *The Thames & Severn Canal*. Sutton, 1983 (enlgd edn).

JERVOISE, E. *The Ancient Bridges of the South of England*. Architectural Press, 1930.

JOHNSON, Michael. *Holy Trinity Church, Cookham*. Church guide, 2005.

KIFT, Mary. *Life in Old Caversham*. Reading (author), 1980.

KRAUSE. *Pictorial History of the River Thames*. 1889 (British Library holdings).

LANG, Andrew. *Oxford Historical & Picturesque Notes*. Seeley, 1890 (new edn).

LESLIE, G. D. *Our River*. Agnew, 1881.

MARGARY, Ivan D. *Roman Roads in Britain*. Phoenix House, 1955.

MATTINGLY, Joanna M. 'Cookham, Bray & Isleworth 1422-1558'. *Thesis*, Univ. of London.

MAY, Brian et al. *A Village Lost & Found. 1850s stereoscopic photos*. F. Lincoln, 2009.

MORRIS, William. *News from Nowhere*. Reeves & Turner, 1891.

NEEDHAM, Stuart P. *Runnymede Bridge. Research Excavations Vol. 1*. 2000.

OPHER, Philip. *Oxford Waterways*. Heritage Tours, 2006.

PAYNE, Ernest A. *The Baptists of Berkshire Through Three Centuries*. Carey Kingsgate, 1951.

PEBERDY, R. B. 'Navigation on R Thames in Late Medieval Ages'. *Oxoniensia* LXI, 1996.

PENNELL, J. & E. *The Stream of Pleasure. A Month on the Thames.* Fisher Unwin, 1891.

PETERS, G. H. *Humphrey Gainsborough at Henley-on-Thames 1748–1776.* Author, 1948.

PEVSNER, N. & SHERWOOD, J. *Oxfordshire. Buildings of England.* Penguin, 1974.

PEVSNER, N. & TYACK et al. *Berkshire. Buildings of England.* Yale, 2010.

PEVSNER, N. & WILLIAMSON, E. *Buckinghamshire. Buildings of England.* Penguin, 1994.

PHILLIPS, Geoffrey. *Thames Crossings, Bridges, Tunnels & Ferries.* David & Charles, 1981.

PILKINGTON, Roger. *Thames Waters.* Lutterworth, 1956.

PLOT, Robert. *The Natural History of Oxfordshire.* Second edn, corrected etc. Brome, 1705.

PRIOR, Mary. *Fisher Row. Fishermen, Bargemen ... in Oxford 1500–1900.* Clarendon Press, 1982.

RIVINGTON, R. T. *Punting Its History & Techniques.* Author, 1983.

ROBERTSON, H. R. *Life on the Upper Thames.* Virtue, Spalding & Co., 1875.

RYAN, Ernest K.W. *The Thames from the Towpath.* Saint Catherine Press, 1938.

SHARP, David. *The Thames Path* (National Trail Guide). Revised edition. Aurum, 2005.

SHORTER, Clement. *Highways & Byways in Buckinghamshire.* 1910.

SHRIMPTON's *Rambles & Rides around Oxford.* Shrimpton, *c.* 1886.

SMITH, A. H. *The Place-Names of Gloucestershire. Part One. Rivers, etc.* Cambridge, 1964.

STANFORD'S *New Map of the River Thames Richmond to Lechlade. c.* 1900.

STAPLETON, John. *The Thames. A Poem.* C. Kegan Paul 1878.

SWAYNE, Diana. *The Story of North Hinksey.* Oxford, the author 1973

TAUNT, Henry W. *A New Map of the River Thames.* Fifth edn. *c.* 1889.

TAUNT, Henry W. *Fairford Church etc: Lechlade & District.* Third edn, enlgd. Thos Powell, nd.

TAYLOR, John 'The Water Poet' in *Travels,* sel. & edt John Chandler. Sutton, 1999.

THACKER, Fred S. *The Stripling Thames. The River above Oxford.* Author, 1909.

THACKER, Fred S. *The Thames Highway: Vol. 1 General History* (1914). David & Charles, 1968.

THACKER, Fred S. *The Thames Highway: Vol. II Locks and Weirs.* Author, 1920.

THOMSON, E. R. *Materials for History of Cricklade.* Cricklade Historical Soc., 1950.

TOMBLESON's *Panoramic Atlas of the Thames.* G. W. Bacon, *c.* 1890.

Victoria County Histories: volumes for Berkshire, Oxfordshire & Gloucestershire

VINCENT, J. E. *The Story of the Thames.* Smith, Elder, 1909.

WALKER, J engr. *The Copperplate Magazine.* Harrison & Co. (1792)

WESLEY, John. *The Journal of the Rev. John Wesley,* edited Rev F. W. Macdonald. Dent EML, 1906.

WILLIAMS, Adin. *Lechlade, being a history of the town etc.* 1888

WILLIAMS, Richard. *Mapledurham House* (house guide). 1977.

WOOLACOTT, Amy. *Crossing places of the Upper Thames.* Tempus, 2008.

WRIGHT, Patrick. *The River: The Thames in Our Time.* BBC, 1999.

# Notes

## Abbreviations

| | |
|---|---|
| BGAS | Bristol & Gloucestershire Archaeological Society |
| BHO | British History Online |
| BL | British Library |
| Glos Archives | Gloucestershire Archives (GRO) |
| NMR | National Monuments Record |
| OS | Ordnance Survey |
| TNA | The National Archives |
| VCH | Victoria County History |

## PREFACE

1. Farrington's Diary. Vol. II
2. Berks RO, D/EX992.
3. Oxford DNB website.
4. Malcolm Graham, *Henry Taunt of Oxford* (1973).
5. *The Thames Path. Proposed Long Distance Route from the Thames Barrier to the Source at Kemble* (Published from Cheltenham, June 1987).
6. David Sharp, *The Thames Path*, p. 15.
7. C. G. Harper, *Thames Valley Villages Vol. 1*, p. 287.
8. *Berks, Bucks and Oxon Archaeological Journal*, Vol. 6.
9. www.riversaccess.org/

## CHAPTER 1

1. G. Grigson, *English Excursions*, p. 135. Shining Fords.
2. D. Hartley, *Water in England* (1964), p. 99.
3. R. W. Bagshawe, *Roman Roads* (1996), p. 14.
4. Private communication from Iain Bain.
5. D. D. Gladwin, *Passenger Boats on Inland Waterways* (1979), p. 4.
6. M. Prior, *Fisher Row* (1982).
7. R. T. Rivington, *Punting* (1983).
8. G. Limbrick, 'Frontier Territory along the Thames' in *British Archaeology Journal* Issue 33, p. 12.

9.   *BGAS* Vol. 23, p. 130.
10.  *BGAS* Vol. 107, p. 114.
11.  M. Gelling, *Early Charters of the Thames Valley* (1979), pp. 3, 26, 32.
12.  G. H. Davies, *A Walk along the Thames Path*, p. 80.
13.  Gelling, *Early Charters*, pp. 138–145.
14.  Hartley, *Water in England*, p. 103.
15.  J. Mattingly, 'Cookham, Bray and Isleworth Hundreds' (Doctoral thesis)
16.  Oxford DNB, 'John Wyclif'.
17.  Tony Hadland, 'Thames Valley Papists' (Website, 1992).
18.  E. A. Payne, *The Baptists of Berkshire* (1951).

## CHAPTER 2

1.   Tombleson's *Panoramic Atlas* p. 5.
2.   Ex info. David & Linda Viner and Halls' Book of the Thames p 10.
3.   Amy Woolacott, *Crossing places of Upper Thames*, p. 45.
4.   Blunt, *August Ramble Down the Upper Thames*.
5.   Geoffrey Gibbon, *Through the Saxon Door*, p. 1.
6.   Ivan D. Margary, *Roman Roads in Britain Vol. II*, p. 264.
7.   Cricklade Historical Society, *St John's Priory & Hospital*, p. 1.
8.   Patrick Wright, *The River*, p. 109.
9.   Ireland, *Picturesque Views on the River Thames, Vol. 1*.
10.  Blunt, *Ramble*.
11.  Ann Cole, 'Place Name Evidence for Water Transport' in Blair, *Waterways & Canal Building in Medieval England*, p. 55.
12.  Mr & Mrs S. C. Hall, *Book of the Thames*, p. 29.
13.  *BGAS* Vol. 57, pp. 192–93 & 204.
14.  Blunt, *Ramble*.
15.  Halls idem p. 39.
16.  VCH Glos. Vol. VII, p. 97.
17.  Wilts & Swindon Archives 1337/9.
18.  Ibid. 1033/288.
19.  Ibid. 1033/289.
20.  Harper, *Thames Valley Villages Vol. 1*, p. 64.
21.  Adin Williams, *Lechlade*, p. 22.
22.  Commons Registration Act Ref. 13/U/58 pp. 272–274.
23.  A. H. Smith, *The Place-names of Gloucestershire Vol. 1: Rivers etc.*, p. 107.
24.  Nicholas Herbert, *Road Travel & Transport in Georgian Gloucestershire*, p. 21.
25.  *The Times*, 2 April 1852 p. 6 Issue 21079: Col. F.
26.  Lechlade Town website, 20 Dec. 2007.

## CHAPTER 3

1.   Fred S. Thacker, *The Thames Highway Vol. I* p. 16.
2.   Ibid. Vol. I pp. 63–66.
3.   www.british-history.ac.uk/report.aspx?compid=22808&strquery=cricklade ferry
4.   Thacker, *Thames Highway* pp. 68–69.
5.   www.british-history.ac.uk (as above).

6. Thacker, *Thames Highway* p. 89.
7. www.thechequers-burcot.co.uk/historychequers.html
8. www.thisistamworth.co.uk/news/scandal-MP/article 27823-28.
9. GRO TS/181 Act 28 Geo III c 51.
10. GRO TS/194 (1-86).
11. Humphrey Household, *The Thames & Severn Canal* p. 86.
12. Christopher Gotch, *The Gloucester & Sharpness Canal & Robert Mylne* pp. 7–8.
13. Davies, 'Thames Navigation Commission'. Thesis. Berks RO.
14. Berks RO. D/EX 1451-1500. Intro to catalogue.
15. G. H. Peters, *Humphrey Gainsborough at Henley-on-Thames 1748–1776* pp. 15–17.
16. Berks RO D/EX1457/1/132.
17. Davies, 'Thames Navigation Commission' p. 80.
18. Hadfield, *Canals of S & SE England* p. 216.
19. Thacker, *Thames Highway* p. 167.
20. GRO TS/226 letter of 19 Feb 1827.
21. Berks RO 1457/1/152/1-4.
22. Berks RO 1457/1/89.

## CHAPTER 4

1. GRO D1180/5/31.
2. GRO D1180/4/46.
3. Wright, *The River* p. 118.
4. GRO TS/200/4 41 & 42 Vict. Session 1878.
5. GRO TS/200/3.
6. GRO TS/200/5.
7. GRO TS/198/12/1 & /2.
8. GRO TS/D1180/9/36.
9. Bradshaw, *Handbook of Inland Navigation* p. 385.
10. The National Archives MT 49/111.
11. *The Globe* 4 May 1887.
12. *The Times* 28 July 1891 issue 33388 col C.
13. Berks RO D/TC 69.
14. *The Times* 4 Aug 1930 issue 45582 col B.
15. The National Archives MT 49/111.
16. *The Times* 12 Oct 1937 issue 47813 col E.
17. *The Times* 9 April 1946 Issue 50422 col F.
18. *Country Life* 19 April 1973 p 1072.
19. GRO Q/RU c/28.

## CHAPTER FIVE

1. Website, Ironbridge Gorge Museum 'Sweat & Toil'.
2. Thacker, *Thames Highway* p. 101.
3. Ibid. p. 109.
4. Prior, *Fisher Row* App IV p. 364.
5. GA Act 11 Geo III c 45.
6. GA TS/181.

7. GA Act 11 Geo III c 45.
8. Berks RO D/TC/1 Minute book, p. 85.
9. Berks RO D/EX 1457/1/1.
10. Berks RO D/TC/1 Minute book, p. 85.
11. Act 35 Geo III c 106.
12. Daniel Nash Ford's 'Royal Berkshire History' (website).
13. Berks RO D/Ex 2066 pp 81, 82–5, 97.
14. Thacker, *Thames Highway* p. 164.
15. Berks RO D/TC/21.
16. Berks RO D/EX1457/1/162.
17. Powys-Lybbe Ancestry, Chapter 5 (website).
18. GA TS 226.
19. Berks RO D/TC/27.
20. www.archive-org/searchphp? query=thames
21. Justices of the Peace Journal 18 Oct 1872 p. 646.
22. Fred S. Thacker, *Thames Highway Vol. II* p. 429.
23. TNA MT 49/111.
24. 'The Lazy Minstrel on the Thames' (website).
25. Nineteenth-century British Library Newspapers – Medmenham Ferry (website).
26. River Thames Guide – Walking & Cycling the Thames (website).
27. *The Times* 13 Aug 1955 Issue 53298 p 8 col E.
28. *The Times* 18 Aug 1955 Issue 53302 p 10 col CD.
29. Sharp, *Thames Path* p. 16.
30. *The Thames Path – Proposed long-distance route*. In Oxford City library – Local Studies.
31. 'Floating down the river' (website).
32. Bill Nichols, 'Spuduka's pill box log' (website).
33. Local information.

## CHAPTER SIX

1. Williams, *Lechlade* p. 2.
2. VCH Glos. Vol. VII p. 106.
3. Herbert, *Road Travel & Transport* p. 21.
4. Ireland, *Picturesque Views of the Thames Vol. I* p. 35.
5. Berks RO D/ELV catalogue.
6. Household, *Thames & Severn Canal* p. 161.
7. *Faringdon Folly* (newspaper) issue 248 Mar 2010.
8. Thacker, *Thames Highway Vol. II* p. 47.
9. *Brief history & guide to Eaton Hastings church* (guidebook)
10. Blair & Golding, *The Cloister & the World*.
11. Berks RO D/TC/27.
12. Berks Archaeological Society Vol. 64 1969.
13. Berks RO D/EZ/141/4/1-4.
14. Images of England (website), ref no 251550.
15. John Stapleton, *The Thames. A Poem* p. 7.
16. faringdon-online (website).
17. N. Pevsner and J. Sherwood, *Buildings of England, Oxfordshire*.
18. Thacker, *Thames Highway Vol. II* p. 60.
19. British Listed Buildings (website).

20. Thacker, *Thames Highway Vol. II* p. 63.
21. Ibid. p. 66.
22. Ibid. pp. 69/70.
23. Oxfordshire Historic Environment Record ref PRN 9016.
24. VCH Oxfords Vol. 13 pp. 80–82.
25. GA TS/182/3 p. 18.
26. Ibid. p. 75.
27. Wikipedia, Shifford Lock.
28. 'Rural Slum Clearance' in *Berks, Bucks & Oxon Archaeological Journal* no. 38.
29. Arkell, 'Place Names & Topography in Upper Thames Country' in *Oxonsiensia* Vol. 7, 1942.
30. J. R. L. Anderson, *The Upper Thames* p. 53.
31. Fred Thacker, *Stripling Thames* p. 137.
32. Ibid. p. 226.
33. Ibid. p. 158.
34. www.wetroads.co.uk
35. Wade, 'All the 214 bridges across the Thames'. Typescipt in BL.
36. VCH Oxfords Vol. 13 pp. 80–82.
37. Brian May et al., *A Village Lost & Found*.
38. Thacker, *Thames Highway Vol. II* p. 72.
39. Ibid. p. 73.
40. Sharp, *Thames Path* p. 53.
41. Thacker, *Thames Highway Vol. II* p. 74.

## CHAPTER SEVEN

1. Wikipedia, Newbridge, Oxfordshire.
2. VCH Berks Vol. 4 p. 345 note 13.
3. VCH Oxfords Vol. 13 p. 150.
4. 'Where Thames Smooth Waters Glide' – Hart's Footbridge (website).
5. *Oxoniensia* Vol. 11 p. 181.
6. Arkell, Place Names Oxfords (website).
7. Blair & Golding, *The Cloister & the World* p. 70 (website).
8. Where Thames – Bablockhythe (website).
9. VCH Glos. Vol. VIII p 34.
10. TNA C 143/128/1.
11. Cumnor & District Historical Society (website).
12. Paul Gedge, *Thames Journey* p. 115.
13. www.roundabout.co.uk (*Oxford News*).
14. Private conversation.
15. *Oxford Mail* 15 June 1964. Oxford Local Studies Library.
16. H. R. Robertson, *Life on the Upper Thames* p. 76.
17. Krause, *Pictorial History of the Thames* p. 25.
18. Berks RO QSB/87.
19. www.oxonctc.org.uk/annual.html.
20. victorianaweb
21. Cumnor & District Historical Society – Recollections (website).
22. northmoorvillage.co.uk
23. Thacker, *Thames Highway Vol. II* p. 90.
24. Information Board at Eynsham Abbey ruins.

25. 'Eynsham Cartulary no 508' in *Eynsham Record* 1987 p. 11.
26. R. J. W. Evans, *St. Michael's Church, Cumnor A Guide* p. 7.
27. Atkins, 'Beating the Bounds' in *Eynsham Record* 1993 p. 34.
28. Wesley, *Journal* Vol. 3 EML p. 160.
29. Geoffrey Phillips, *Thames Crossings, Bridges, Tunnels & Ferries* p. 38.
30. Oxford DNB. 4th Earl Abingdon.
31. Chamber, 'Eynsham under the Monks' in *Oxford's Record Society* 1936 p. 73.
32. Cumnor & District Historical Society - census 1901 (website).
33. *The Times* 13 May 1964 Issue 56010 p 7.
34. *The Times* 29 July 1981 Issue 60992 p 4.
35. www.the-river-thames.co.uk/news06.htm
36. www.eynsham.org/tollbridge.html

## CHAPTER EIGHT

1. Robert Plot, *Natural History of Oxfordshire* chap 2.
2. Thacker, *Thames Highway* Vol. II p. 100.
3. Thacker, *Stripling Thames* p. 44.
4. GA. TS/182/3 Mylne.
5. Prior, *Fisher Row* pp. 125, 280.
6. *Oxonsiensia* Vol. 71 p. 423.
7. Linford, P., 'Port Meadow, Binsey' *EH Research Report* 58, 2006.
8. artnet.com – under WM Turner of Oxford, Past auction results.
9. www.igreens.org.uk/binsey_poplars.htm
10. Shrimpton's Popular Handbooks, *Rambles & Rides Around Oxford* p. 33.
11. Hugh J. Compton, *The Oxford Canal* p. 145.
12. Oxford Oral History Archive LT 434.
13. *Oxonsiensia* Vol. 49 p. 78.
14. Information on site.
15. *Oxoniensia* Vol. 49 pp. 57–100.
16. Hon. John Byng, *Torrington Diaries* (ed. A. Bruyn Andrews) Vol. I p. 4.
17. Britton, *Topograhical & Historical Description of County of Berkshire* p. 166.
18. E. Jervoise, *The Ancient Bridges of the South of England* p. 5 (quote from Leland).
19. Oxfordshire Studies, MSS P Nort d/944.
20. Prior, *Fisher Row* p. 189.
21. Colin Harrison et al., *John Malchair of Oxford, Artist and Musician*, pp. 110, 115.
22. English Heritage – Images of England IoE number 249751 (website).
23. Diana Swayne, *Story of North Hinksey*.
24. Oxfordshire Studies, People index – under Ferry Nos 16 & 17.
25. *Rambles & Rides*, p. 103.
26. Oxfords RO QSB/86.

## CHAPTER NINE

1. Oxford DNB.
2. R. T. Rivington, *Punting, Its History and Techniques* p. 138.
3. *The Times* 20 May 1937 p 13.
4. Rivington, ibid.

5. Edward Cordrey, *Bygone Days at Iffley* p. 22.
6. www.geograph.org.uk/photo 288898.
7. Rivington, *Punting*, photo no. 17.
8. Oxfordshire streets – Boundary stones (website).
9. River & Rowing Museum. Accession 2004.57.16 (website).
10. *Charters of Abingdon Abbey*, OUP 2000–2001.
11. GA, TS/182/3 p45.
12. Thacker, *Thames Highway Vol. II* p. 134.
13. Wikipedia, Siege of Oxford.
14. Sandford-on-Thames village magazine, *The Link*, April 1993 (website).
15. Oxfords RO B5/36/D/1.
16. RHS Bibliography Trans. 84 p 64–65 1939 (website).
17. Wikipedia, Sandford-on-Thames.
18. Sharp, *Thames Path* p. 64.
19. VCH Oxfords Vol. 5 pp. 234–249.
20. K. J. Allison et al., *Deserted Villages of Oxfordshire*.
21. Oxford DNB, 1st Earl Harcourt.
22. Mavis Batey, 'Nuneham Courtenay. Oxford's Deserted Village' p. 112.
23. Bonehill & Daniels, Paul Sandby – Picturing Britain p. 202–203.
24. Website, Radley Parish Council – tree planting.
25. Thacker, *Thames Highway Vol. II* p. 147.
26. *British Archaeology Journal*, Vol. 33 April 1998 p. 12.
27. N. Pevsner, Tyack et al., *Buildings of Berkshire* p. 100.
28. Thacker, *Thames Highway Vol. II* p. 158.
29. D. D. Gladwin, *Passenger Boats on Inland Waterways* p. 5.
30. Jervoise, *Ancient Bridges of the South* p. 6.
31. *Buildings of Berkshire*, ibid.
32. Local information.
33. Article by G. R. Naylor, www.culhamvillage.org.uk.
34. Thacker, *Thames Highway Vol. II* pp. 167 & 171.
35. Local information.

## CHAPTER TEN

1. Stapleton, *The Thames* p. 14.
2. Appleford-on-Thames website.
3. *Rambles & Rides*, p. 45.
4. Chandler (ed), *Travels through Stuart Britain* p. 142.
5. VCH Berks, Vol. 4 pp. 384–390.
6. Where Thames smooth waters glide, under Clifton Hampden bridge (website).
7. Thacker, *Thames Highway Vol. II* p. 173.
8. GA, TS/182/3.
9. Phillips, *Thames Crossings* p. 64.
10. Act 27-8 Vic cxliv p 445.
11. Roger Pilkington, *Thames Waters* p. 113.
12. VCH Oxfords Vol. 7 pp. 16–27.
13. Online, *Oxford Journal* 14 Oct 1843.
14. Information on site.
15. *Berks Archaeological Journal*, Vol. 70 (1979–80) p. 21.
16. *Berks, Bucks & Oxon Archaeological Journal* Vol. 14 (1908–9).
17. Herts Archives, D/EGd/T4.

18. Wikipedia, Poohsticks.
19. Ivan D. Margary, *Roman Roads*, Vol. 1 p. 150.
20. Thacker, *Thames Highway Vol. II* p. 442.
21. Thacker, ibid. p. 180.
22. Brian Eade, *Forgotten Thames* p. 38. Website, thamesphotos.co.uk.
23. Thacker, *Thames Highway Vol. II* p. 181.
24. Berks RO, D/EX 992.
25. VCH Berks Vol. 3 p. 532.
26. Thacker, *Thames Highway Vol. II* p. 184.
27. Gladwin, *Passenger Boats* p. 5.
28. Oxford RO, QSB/40.
29. British Record Society. Index to Probate Records of Oxfords 1997 p. 83.
30. Winterbrook website.
31. Oxford RO, QSB/40.
32. The Baldons & Nuneham Courteney Newsletter. Aug 2010 (website).
33. *Berks, Bucks & Oxon Archaeological Journal* 1896.
34. Ibid. Vol. 18.
35. VCH Oxfords, Vol. 12.
36. Edith Ditmas, *The Ditmas History of Benson* p. 79.
37. G. D. Leslie, *Our River* p. 126.
38. Sims, *Thames Navigation Commission Minutes Part 2 1787 & 1788*, Berks RO.
39. Thacker, *Thames Highway Vol. II* p. 156.
40. Ditmas, *History of Benson* ibid.
41. Berks RO, Thames Conservancy Board D/TC 332.
42. Eade, *Forgotten Thames* p. 40.

## CHAPTER ELEVEN

1. Gareth Huw Davies, *A Walk Along the Thames Path* p. 65.
2. Thacker, *Thames Highway Vol. II* p. 190.
3. J. S. Hardman, *Wallingford, A History of an English Market Town* p. 129.
4. Thacker, *Thames Highway Vol. II* p. 197.
5. Berks RO, D EX/1457/23.
6. Thacker, *Thames Highway Vol. II* pp. 198–199.
7. Hardman, *Wallingford* p. 129.
8. Thacker, *Thames Highway Vol. II* p. 200.
9. Local information.
10. Maurice Beresford, *Lost Villages of England* p. 381.
11. Oxfords RO E 195/d/1.
12. Oxfords RO SL 162/1/D/5.
13. *The Times* 17 May 1894.
14. C. H. Cook, *Thames Rights & Thames Wrongs*.
15. Thomas, *Ickneild Way* p. 214.
16. VCH Berks Vol. 3 footnote 51.
17. *Buildings of Berkshire* – Cholsey.
18. English Heritage, Listed Buildings – Oxfords ref. PRN 20792.
19. Thacker, *Thames Highway Vol. II* p. 202.
20. Oxfords Photographic Archive ref HT 6027.
21. VCH Berks V p. 506.
22. English Heritage – Images of England ref 248003.

23. Goring & Streatley LHS – Picture History p. 47.
24. Cornwall RO AR/37/42 & /48 &/53.
25. BHO, Accounts of Henry VIII.
26. Goring & Streatley Picture History, p. 2.
27. Berks RO, D/EX 1453/1.
28. Powys-Lybbe Ancestry. Chapter 3 (website).
29. Thacker, *Thames Highway Vol. II* p. 211.
30. G&S Picture History p. 91.
31. Online Library of Liberty, 30. Walking Tour etc.
32. Tyne & Wear Museums – Art online. C. N. Hemy.
33. www.richard-green.com/
34. Thacker, *Thames Highway Vol. II* p. 210.
35. Beresford, *Lost Villages of England* p. 283.
36. Thacker, *Thames Highway Vol. II* p. 213.
37. Local information.
38. Farr, 'Gatehampton' unpublished.
39. Thacker, *Thames Highway Vol. II* p. 227.

## CHAPTER TWELVE

1. Thacker, *Thames Highway Vol. II* p. 221.
2. Index to probate records of Oxfords., pub British Record Society 1997, p 105.
3. Information board at site.
4. Acts L&P 32 Geo III c 97.
5. 'Crossing the Thames' – Whitchurch Bridge (website).
6. Berks RO D/TC/21. Towpaths rental book.
7. Oxfords RO St. 2/2/03 & St. 2/2/D/2.
8. Website press release Feb 2011.
9. Richard Williams, *Mapledurham House* p. 23.
10. Harper, *Thames Valley Villages Vol. I* p. 300.
11. *The Times* 28 July 1871 p. 11 issue 27127.
12. Thacker, *Thames Highway Vol. II* p. 225.
13. Ibid. p. 223.
14. Website, Francis Frith ref 43007.
15. Cook, *Thames Rights* p. 82.
16. *The Times* 10 March 1931 p. 11 issue 45767.
17. Mary Kift, *Life in Old Caversham*.
18. Thacker, *Thames Highway Vol. II* p. 228.
19. Jervoise, *Ancient Bridges of the South* p. 10.
20. Thacker, *Thames Highway Vol. II* p. 230.
21. Hampshire RO SM 50/2714.
22. Oxfords Local Studies BB/79?1634.
23. Kift, *Caversham*.
24. Thacker, *Thames Highway Vol. I* p. 167.
25. Thacker, *Thames Highway Vol. II* p. 234.
26. *The Times* 23 Mar 1911 p. 3 Issue 39540.
27. *The Times* 5 Feb 1913 p. 23 Issue 40127.
28. Wessex Archaeology, 1997 *Reading Waterfront* p. 182.
29. Thacker, *Thames Highway Vol. II* p. 238.
30. Horseshoe Bridge – Reading (website).
31. *Berks Archaeological Journal*, No. 78.

32. Thacker, *Thames Highway Vol. II* p. 250.
33. Gladwin, *Passenger Boats* p. 6.
34. Thacker, *Thames Highway Vol. II* p. 251.
35. *The Times*, 28 Aug 1902 p. 6 Issue 36858.
36. *The Times*, 11 Sept 1902 p. 6 Issue 36870.

## CHAPTER THIRTEEN

1. Images of England, ref 41328.
2. Berks Ro Ref A2A.
3. VCH Berks, Vol. 3 pp. 191–197 footnote 48.
4. Website, David Nash Ford's Royal Berks History – Wargrave.
5. Thacker, *Thames Highway Vol. II* p. 258.
6. 'Where Thames Smooth Waters Glide' – Wargrave p. 5 (website).
7. J. & E. Pennell, *The Stream of Pleasure. A Month on the Thames* p. 84.
8. Berks RO CPC 145/15/1/1-93.
9. Berks RO CPC 145/17/4/1-22.
10. *The Times* 20 Nov 1937 p. 9 Issue 47847.
11. Berks RO, D/TC 69, Expenses ledger 1909.
12. Thacker, *Thames Highway Vol. II* p. 259.
13. VCH Oxfords Vol. 4 p. 63.
14. Thacker, *Thames Highway Vol. II* p. 259.
15. Wargrave Local History Society News, Nov 2003 (website).
16. Thacker, *Thames Highway Vol. II* p. 259.
17. Ernest K. W. Ryan, *The Thames from the Towpath* p. 126.
18. Wikipedia, Marsh Lock.
19. Thacker, *Thames Highway Vol. II* p. 267.
20. Phillips, *Thames Crossings* p. 97.
21. Thacker, *Thames Highway Vol. II* p. 271.
22. Thacker, *Thames Highway Vol. II* p. 278.
23. Eade, *Forgotten Thames* p. 63.
24. *Jackson's Oxford Journal* 20 Aug 1870, Issue 6125 (website).
25. Ultimate River Swimming (website).
26. Thacker, *Thames Highway Vol. II* p. 279.
27. Records of Bucks, Vol. 4 p. 57.
28. Centre for Bucks Studies, D 30/2.
29. Ibid. D 30/10.
30. Ibid. D 30/36.
31. Ibid. D 30/42-43.
32. Images of England, ref 47001 (website).
33. Shorter, *Highways & Byways in Bucks* p. 202.
34. *Buildings of England – Bucks* p. 468.
35. Plaisted, *Parsons & Parish Registers* – Medmenham, 1932.
36. *Daily News* 23 May 1898 Issue 16273 (website).
37. *The Times*, 29 Mar 1899 issue 35789 p. 13.
38. Thames Valley Archaeological Services Ltd – Watching Brief 2004 FHM 03/121.
39. Middle Thames Antiquarian & Historical Society, News Bulletin Vol. 2 1968.
40. Berks College Agriculture website.
41. Thacker *Thames Highway Vol. II* p. 285.
42. 'The Scroll', *Maidenhead Archaeological & Historical Society* 1974.
43. Information Board on site.

# CHAPTER FOURTEEN

1.   Thacker, *Thames Highway Vol. II* p. 290.
2.   www.bridgemanart.com
3.   Thacker, *Thames Highway Vol. II* p. 293.
4.   www.britishlistedbuildings.co.uk/en-46265
5.   Shorter, *Highways & Byways in Bucks* p. 207.
6.   Eade, *Forgotten Thames* p. 68.
7.   *Buildings of England – Bucks* p. 441.
8.   Thacker, *Thames Highway Vol. II* p. 300.
9.   Berks RO D/TC 69.
10.   Interview with Ken Townsend.
11.   www.bourneendbucks.com-ken goes down
12.   Interview with Ken Townsend.
13.   Thacker, *Thames Highway Vol. II* p. 315.
14.   Joanna M. Mattingly, 'Cookham, Bray & Isleworth' (thesis) p. 14.
15.   Berks Archaeological Society, Journal 2 1891–3.
16.   Where Thames Smoothly (website).
17.   Middle Thames Antiquarian & Historical Society, Bulletin Vol. 2 p 66.
18.   Thacker, *Thames Highway Vol. II* p. 317.
19.   Centre Bucks Studies D/158/49.
20.   *The Times*, 11 April 1955 Issue 53302 p. 10.
21.   Berks RO D/TC/21.
22.   Thacker, *Thames Highway Vol. II* p. 316.
23.   Acts L & P 1-2 Vic c x.
24.   Phillips, *Thames Crossings* p. 105.
25.   Thacker, *Thames Highway Vol. II* p. 316.
26.   Ward, *Archaeology of Taplow Court*. Survey 1997.
27.   'The Scroll', *Jrnl Maidenhead & District Archaeological & Historical Society* Vol. 3 No. 3 p. 13.
28.   Oxfords RO Hey/III/IV/1 etc.
29.   'Where Thames Smoothly' – Boulter's (website).
30.   Thacker, *Thames Highway Vol. II* p. 327.
31.   David Nash Ford's Royal Berks History.
32.   Jervoise, *Ancient Bridges of the South* p. 12.
33.   Berks RO, M/AC/1/1/1.

# CHAPTER FIFTEEN

1.   Thacker, *Thames Highway Vol. II* p. 336.
2.   Ibid., p. 337.
3.   Nan Birney, *Bray Today & Yesterday* p. 142.
4.   Cooke, *Descriptions of Plates to Thames Scenery*.
5.   http://monkeyisland.co.uk/live/history.
6.   Rivington, *Punting* p. 62.
7.   Thacker, *Thames Highway Vol. II* p. 345.
8.   Jervoise, *Ancient Bridges of the South* p. 13.
9.   Phillips, *Thames Crossings* p. 119.
10.   Berks RO, D/TC/27.
11.   www.bridgemanart.com/image.aspx?key=thames ferry & filter.
12.   Phillips, *Thames Crossings* p. 124.

13. 'Timespan' *Journal of Middle Thames Archaeological & Historical Society* Vol. 28, 1985 p. 32.
14. Thacker, *Thames Highway Vol. II* p. 369.
15. Phillips, *Thames Crossings* p. 124.
16. 'Timespan', p. 32.
17. Thacker, *Thames Crossings Vol. II* p. 369.
18. 'Timespan', p. 32.
19. BHO, Hen VIII Letters (accounts 1535–6).
20. 'Timespan', p. 32.
21. Phillips, *Thames Crossings* p. 127.
22. Bucks Local Studies, Q/AB/5/25b.
23. Ibid. Q/AB/5/20.
24. Ibid. Q/AB/14.
25. Phillips, *Thames Crossings* p. 130.
26. English Heritage, Listed Buildings ref 40379.
27. Website, wraysbury.org./history/manors htm
28. C. J. Gilson, *Old Windsor. A History of the Parish Council.*
29. www.artfund.org/artwork/2115/the-bells-of-ouseley-at-runnymede
30. Gilson, *Old Windsor.*
31. BHO VCH Bucks, Vol. 3 pp. 320–5.
32. National Library of Wales (website).
33. www.wraysbury.net/environment/eight_yards.htm
34. www.rightmove.co.uk/property-for-sale/property-27756598.html
35. Stuart P. Needham, *Runnymede Bridge. Research Excavations Vol. I* p. 7.
36. Information Board, Spellthorne Museum.
37. Squyer MS, 490, 76, seventeenth-century Songs & Lyrics.

# Index

Multiple references e.g. Oxford, Thames, Thacker are listed as *passim* i.e. throughout.